A scene from the interrogation of Patsy Ramsey — June 25th, 1998

<u>DETECTIVE HANEY</u>: **What if those fingerprints belonged to one of the two of you?**

<u>PATSY RAMSEY</u>: **Well, I don't know.**

<u>DETECTIVE HANEY</u>: **Let's go back to your line of reasoning here. If they were not — now talk to me.**

<u>PATSY RAMSEY</u>: **Okay.**

<u>DETECTIVE HANEY</u>: **Look at me! If they are not yours and they are not John's, then they would be someone else's.**

<u>PATSY RAMSEY</u>: **Right.**

<u>DETECTIVE HANEY</u>: **But now I am telling you they are not somebody else's. Those prints belong to one of the two of you.**

<u>PATSY RAMSEY</u>: **They do? You are sure?**

<u>DETECTIVE HANEY</u>: **I'm telling you that it isn't somebody else's.**

From the files of the NATIONAL ENQUIRER

P9-CCO-793

JonBenet

THE
POLICE
FILES

Edited by
Don Gentile and David Wright

American Media Inc.

FROM THE FILES OF THE NATIONAL ENQUIRER:
JONBENET — THE POLICE FILES

Copyright © 2003 AMI Books, Inc.

Cover design: Phil Aron
Interior design: Debbie Duckworth
Cover photographs — JonBenet Ramsey: R. Simons/Polaris;
John and Patsy Ramsey: Getty Images

ISBN: 1-932270-03-5

First printing: January 2003

Printed in the United States of America

10 9 8 7 6 5 4 3 2 1

TABLE OF CONTENTS

INTRODUCTION

PATSY RAMSEY'S EYES suddenly flash, and for a split second you imagine she's going to leap from the sofa in the police interrogation room and grab for the throat of the case-hardened cop who's just accused her of murdering her 6-year-old daughter, JonBenet.

Scientific evidence, her pursuer repeats calmly, links her to the sensational killing.

"I don't give a damn how scientific it is!" The former Miss America contestant spits the words out defiantly, a trembling finger pointing directly at her questioner. "Go back to the damn drawing board — I didn't do it!"

One detective would say later in that instant he saw the "Southern belle vanish and a steel magnolia emerge."

And now you can eavesdrop on that compelling confrontation — and dozens more captured in more than 40 hours of secret police videotapes and transcripts as they grill Patsy and her millionaire husband, John.

The murder of "Little Miss" beauty queen JonBenet has shocked and fascinated America to an extent few killings have. And now the National Enquirer has obtained the evidence that reveals exactly what happened when police were finally able to interrogate the Ramseys.

For the authors of this book — veteran National Enquirer reporters who've covered the case for six years — and for the millions of Americans who've followed its fascinating twists and turns, the Ramsey tapes finally shed light on the Boulder Police Department's pursuit of John and Patsy Ramsey.

You will feel as if you're in the sparsely furnished interview room with Patsy as investigators play cat-and-mouse with her — letting her know that there are fingerprints on a key piece of evidence — but not divulging whether they are hers or her husband's. You will sense the shock she says she feels on learning that day for the first time that JonBenet was sexually violated prior to her death.

And you will be gripped by the tension as she leaps to the defense of her 9-year-old son Burke: "Burke Ramsey did not do this, okay?" Patsy snaps angrily at her interrogators.

"He did not do this — get off it!"

The John and Patsy Ramsey you will hear talking in the pages of this book often come across very differently from the way they've been perceived by Americans ever since JonBenet's murder.

Caught on videotape at her most vulnerable, Patsy is often charming, sometimes little-girl-like: vague in her responses one minute, the next minute transfixing her listeners with a seamless transformation to drama queen.

You will feel the pressure the day she's forced to change her story in midstream about a vital piece of evidence.

And you'll hear her compelled to discuss the most intimate aspects of her life.

You will hear John Ramsey describe himself to cops as "quiet, a nice guy, doesn't talk a lot."

And soon afterward you will feel his embarrassment as he is forced to talk a lot — about a "Fatal Attraction" mistress and his relationship with Patsy, as well as the day he became so inflamed with jealousy over Patsy's meeting with a mysterious man in a Rolls-Royce that he kicked the kitchen door!

This amazing book captures the drama of the JonBenet murder case in the only way it can properly be told: in the actual words of John and Patsy Ramsey — and the investigators who, rightly or wrongly, have had them in their sights for so long.

JONBENET RAMSEY was no ordinary little girl. In addition to her parents' affluence, the tiny blonde of tender years was already a beauty queen — a heralded winner in the pampered universe of "Little Miss" beauty pageants.

It was a nether world unknown to most Americans at that time, and many were horrified as television showed video after video of JonBenet onstage. Not only was she costumed like a Vegas showgirl in feathers and sequins — hair primped and makeup perfect — but she sang and danced for the pageant judges with a seductiveness far beyond her kindergarten years.

She was a strikingly beautiful child who had inherited the poise and good looks of her mother, Patsy, a former Miss West Virginia, who would turn 40 only three days after her daughter's body was found.

JonBenet's long fair hair framed green eyes and a smile that overwhelmed other contestants, and just six days before her death she had won her latest title — Little Miss Christmas. The trophy was already displayed in a custom-made hutch in her bedroom that held her sparkling tiaras and pageant crowns.

The last Christmas Day of JonBenet Ramsey's short life — December 25th, 1996 — began like that of millions of other children across America. She and her 9-year-old brother Burke excitedly woke their parents at the crack of dawn to open the pile of presents waiting under the Christmas tree downstairs.

By 7 a.m., JonBenet had already discovered her new bicycle, which her 53-year-old father — president of a successful sales company — had smuggled in under the Christmas tree as she slept. There was also a gold I.D. bracelet inscribed with her name and the date: 12/25/96. Her maternal grandmother had sent her a gold ring, and there was also a gold cross necklace from one of her aunts.

Later on Christmas afternoon, the Ramseys — loaded with more gaily wrapped presents — piled into Patsy's white Jaguar for the short ride to the home of their closest friends, Fleet White and his wife, Priscilla. The two families were inseparable. Fleet and John sailed together. Their sons, Burke and Fleet Jr., were the same age. The Whites' 5-year-old daughter, Daphne, was JonBenet's best friend.

Patsy had wanted JonBenet to wear a red sweater and black velvet pants that would have matched her own outfit. Instead, the independent little girl insisted on dressing in her favorite clothes — black velvet jeans, a white crew-neck shirt with a sequined star on the chest, and a black velvet vest.

The cozy party at the Whites ended around 8:30 p.m.

On the way home, John stopped the Jaguar twice to let Patsy deliver gifts to other friends. And JonBenet, weary from the day's excitement, fell fast asleep in the backseat.

According to her parents' account, she was still sleeping when they got home. John carried her upstairs to her bedroom. Patsy removed her pants and put long johns on her daughter. She tucked JonBenet under the covers still wearing the crew-neck shirt. It was about 9 p.m.

At 5:30 the next morning, Patsy awoke in the third floor master bedroom of the sprawling house they had spent $1.2 million buying and remodeling. John was already showering. They planned to fly at 7 a.m. in their private plane to their lakeside home in Charlevoix, Michigan, to spend an extended Christmas with John Andrew and Melinda Ramsey, John's grown children from a previous marriage, and Melinda's fiance, Stewart Long.

Patsy dressed hurriedly, walked downstairs to the second floor, where her children's bedrooms were located, and then down a spiral staircase leading to the first floor, intending to make coffee before waking JonBenet and Burke.

She stopped abruptly on the staircase when she saw three sheets of lined white legal paper lying across one of the stairs below her. She stepped over them, turned around and read the first few words on the first page.

Then she ran, screaming hysterically, for her husband.

What Patsy had found was a chilling ransom note, printed with a black Sharpie pen. Following is a copy of the original three-page letter, which was addressed to John:

Mr. Ramsey,

Listen carefully! We are a group of individuals that represent a small foreign faction. We do respect your bussiness but not the country that it serves. At this time we have your daughter in our posession. She is safe and unharmed and if you want her to see 1997, you must follow our instructions to the letter.

You will withdraw $118,000.00 from your account. $100,000 will be in $100 bills and the remaining $18,000 in $20 bills. Make sure that you bring an adequate size attaché to the bank. When you get home you will put the money in a brown paper bag. I will call you between 8 and 10 am tomorrow to instruct you on delivery. The delivery will be exhausting so I advise you to be rested. If we monitor you getting the money early, we might call you early to arrange an earlier delivery of the

(continued on next page)

money and hence. I earlier ~~discuss~~ pick up of your daughter. Any deviation of my instructions will result in the immediate execution of your daughter. You will also be denied her remains for proper burial. The two gentlemen watching over your daughter do not particularly like you so I advise you not to provoke them. ~~Speaking~~ to anyone about your situation, such as Police, F.B.I., etc., will result in your daughter being beheaded. If we catch you talking to a stray dog, she dies. If you alert bank authorities, she dies. If the money is in any way marked or ~~tampered~~ with, she dies. You will be scanned for electronic devices and if any are found, she dies. You can try to deceive us but be warned that we are familiar with law enforcement countermeasures and tactics. You stand a 99% chance of killing your daughter if you try to out smart us. Follow our instructions

and you stand a 100% chance
of getting her back. You and
your Family are under constant
scrutiny as well as the authorities.
Don't try to grow a brain
John. You are not the only
fat cat around so don't think
that killing will be difficult
Don't underestimate us John.
Use that good southern common
sense of yours. It is up to
you now John!

                    Victory!
                    S.B.T.C

STRANGELY, JOHN insisted that his wife dial 911, despite the fact that she was screaming and hysterical. A dispatcher took her frantic call at 5:52 a.m.

The first police officer to arrive, Rick French, found no signs of a forced entry or a struggle. He wrote in his report later that Patsy was wearing full makeup and was dressed in a red turtleneck sweater and black pants. He didn't know they were the same clothes she had worn to the Whites' party.

He noted that Patsy paced back and forth, then sat down in an overstuffed chair in the sunroom. French suddenly realized uncomfortably that her eyes were riveted on him, watching everything he did — but, oddly, he says Patsy was trying to hide it by spreading her fingers over her eyes.

Linda Arndt and Fred Patterson, the first detectives sent to the scene, were intercepted a mile from the house by another officer with an urgent message.

"Be aware," he told them. "French says to tell you something doesn't seem right."

The huge 6,866-square-foot house was far from a secure crime scene. Five friends — Fleet and Priscilla White, John and Barbara Fernie and the family's minister, the Rev. Rol Hoverstock — had arrived to comfort them and help organize the ransom money. They mingled, unchecked, with the investigators.

At 7 a.m., John and Fleet White went upstairs to wake Burke. Curiously, White later told police, Burke never once asked why the house was full of policemen, or where JonBenet was. And, oddest of all for a kid who had his own pilot-training video and had been living for the moment his dad's airplane took off, he never asked why they weren't flying to Michigan. Later, police would find proof that Burke was actually awake earlier that morning.

Following procedure, one detective asked John for samples of his and Patsy's handwriting. John handed him a lined legal pad he identified as Patsy's. As another officer leafed through the pad, he found a page with words written in the same ink and printing style as the ransom note. It began, "Mr. And Mrs."

Then came a vertical line like the first downstroke of an R. The stunned cop wondered if he'd found on Patsy's pad an abandoned first attempt at the ransom note.

Patsy, meanwhile, appeared to be doing her best to throw suspicion on her housekeeper, Linda Hoffman-Pugh. She told detectives the woman's handwriting resembled the writing in the note and that Linda had money problems.

And, far from comforting each other, John and Patsy had so little contact with each other that two members of a victims' advocacy group, called in to help, came to the conclusion that they must be either divorced or separated.

At 1 p.m., three hours past the kidnappers' stated deadline, frustrated Detective Linda Arndt suggested to John Ramsey that he and Fleet White search the house to see if they spotted anything missing or unusual.

John led the way straight downstairs to the basement, quickly pointed out to White a window that was cracked, then walked to the wine cellar and unlatched the door.

The other man heard John yell, "Oh my God, oh my God!" as he peered into the dark room. Then, as White ran to his side, John switched on the light — and they saw the body of JonBenet lying wrapped in a white blanket on the cold concrete floor.

Her father dropped to his knees beside her, ripped off a piece of black duct tape covering her mouth, pulled from one wrist the cord binding her hands together, and picked her up under her armpits.

A stunned Detective Arndt first realized that the crime had escalated from kidnapping to murder when Ramsey came running up the stairs screaming, holding JonBenet's stiff, lifeless body in front of him.

A narrow cord hung from the youngster's right wrist. A similar cord encircled her neck like a noose, and the end of the cord was tied around a broken piece of wood. The device resembled a dog leash or garrote.

JonBenet's lips were blue, and in the cold language of the police report, "she had an odor of decay to her."

John laid the body on a rug in the hall. Detective Arndt — her judgment overcome by compassion — picked JonBenet up and placed her close to the Christmas tree.

John then knelt by JonBenet and, ignoring Arndt's pleas not to touch her again, began stroking her hair before lying down beside her, one arm around her.

The detective was surprised that there were no tears when he rose to his feet. Instead he blurted out, "It has to be an inside job. Nobody knows about the wine cellar in the basement."

Suddenly Patsy appeared, lurched toward the body and threw herself on top of her dead daughter. Incredibly, she was allowed to lie there, weeping and moaning, while John and their friends formed a circle around them, held hands and followed Rev. Hoverstock's lead in saying "The Lord's Prayer."

They had barely said "Amen" when Patsy threw her arms into the air and screamed, "Jesus, you raised Lazarus from the dead — raise my baby from the dead!"

Hours earlier, Officer French had sensed that something was "not right." The police officers who followed him were just as puzzled. Why hadn't Patsy and John comforted each other? Why did it seem he had gone directly to the wine cellar? And Fleet White was already wondering if he had imagined that John had screamed BEFORE he switched on the light in the pitch-dark cellar.

What followed just 25 minutes after the discovery of the body also raised eyebrows. A horrified police officer overheard John Ramsey calling his pilot and telling him to ready the plane for a flight to Atlanta that evening.

The Ramseys have family in Atlanta, true. But would they really have left Boulder with JonBenet's body still lying beneath the Christmas tree and a murder investigation just beginning?

We'll never know. John Ramsey canceled his order to the pilot after police objected.

AT 8 A.M. ON DECEMBER 27TH, Dr. John Meyer, the Boulder County Coroner, began the autopsy on JonBenet. One of the first things he noticed was a heart, drawn in red ink, on the palm of her left hand.

The cord around the little girl's neck had left a deep red indentation. And she had been struck so hard on the right side of her head that the blow caused a skull fracture 8 inches long. One piece of skull measuring 1 inch by 1 inch had been driven into her head, causing a deep bruise that extended along the entire length of JonBenet's brain.

Dr. Meyer noted the presence of blood in her vaginal area. There was a mild abrasion, and the hymen appeared to have been torn — trauma consistent with penetration by a finger. He carefully removed dark blue cotton fibers from the skin in her pubic area and concluded that she may have been wiped down with a blue towel or piece of clothing. He told Detective Arndt he believed that JonBenet had been subjected to sexual contact.

The coroner was unable to pinpoint the time of death, but reported that he found pineapple in JonBenet's small intestine. From its condition, experts later estimated that it was swallowed roughly two to five hours before she died.

The cause of death, said Dr. Meyer, was asphyxia due to strangulation — but he indicated that the massive blow to the head could have been equally fatal. He also concluded that JonBenet was alive during both acts of terrible violence.

Internationally known forensic psychiatrist Dr. Judianne Densen-Gerber, who has investigated hundreds of sex crimes, studied the autopsy report and concluded that injuries to JonBenet's vaginal area — new and healed — raised the chilling possibility that she had been the victim of sexual abuse in the past.

"In simple terms, the killing of little JonBenet is a sex-abuse murder," said Dr. Densen-Gerber. "There is clear evidence of prior sexual abuse — done in the weeks or even months prior to the murder."

Dr. Todd Grey, Chief Medical Examiner for the state of Utah, also read the autopsy report and was struck by the numerous abrasions on JonBenet's body.

"This wasn't a gentle killing — this kid was fighting," he said.

At 9:30 a.m. on December 27th — 32 hours after the discovery of JonBenet's body — Detective Linda Arndt and Sergeant Larry Mason drove to the home of John and Barbara Fernie, where John and Patsy were staying, for what they expected would be a formal interview with the parents.

Instead they were greeted by Mike Bynum, a Boulder lawyer and close friend of John and Patsy. To Arndt's astonishment, Bynum informed her that the Ramseys had retained other attorneys — and that in the future the lawyers would have to be consulted first.

Next, the Ramseys hired Pat Korten, an expensive, high-powered public relations executive from Washington, D.C., to handle the media and further insulate them from direct questioning.

But their "lawyering up" and refusal to talk to police quickly backfired.

Within days, national television talk hosts and their guests were arguing openly about the possible guilt or innocence of John and Patsy. Journalists and television crews from across America and around the world filled Boulder's hotel rooms.

THE POLICE — hamstrung by mistakes they'd already made at the murder scene and desperate to catch up by grilling John and Patsy — chose this time to make a fateful move. Lead detective Commander John Eller threatened that if the Ramseys didn't talk to his detectives, he would not release JonBenet's body for burial.

He was forced to back down, but the damage was done.

A seemingly concerted war of nerves between the family and investigators began. On February 13th, 1997, Boulder District Attorney Alex Hunter announced that he was considering seeking the death penalty against whoever killed JonBenet.

His deputy, Bill Wise, caused an uproar when he told the county commission that costs incurred in the case might be recouped because "one of the suspects has money."

Both John and Patsy had given handwriting samples to police and investigators were becoming more and more convinced that Patsy was the author of the ransom note.

It was against this tumultuous background that the Ramsey lawyers met secretly with a deputy district attorney to negotiate terms under which John and Patsy would agree to be interviewed at the end of April 1997.

It was finally worked out: John and Patsy would be interviewed one after the other, over the course of only a single day. And they would be supplied with copies of case documents, including all their prior statements, beforehand.

At least one angry detective believed that in the final agreement the D.A. "gave away the store."

Cast of Characters

I
THE INTERROGATORS

Trip DeMuth — Boulder County Assistant District Attorney who helped question Patsy in June 1998.

Tom Haney — Former chief of patrol division in Denver and a veteran detective. He was brought in by the Boulder District Attorney to work on the case and led the questioning of Patsy Ramsey in 1998.

Michael Kane — Former assistant U.S. attorney hired by the Boulder District Attorney to prepare and present JonBenet's murder case to a grand jury. He helped to question John Ramsey in 1998.

Mary Keenan — Boulder County Deputy District Attorney who questioned the Ramseys about their suspicions concerning Bill (Santa Claus) McReynolds. Keenan was subsequently elected District Attorney.

Dan Schuler — Colorado detective who helped question the Ramseys about Bill (Santa Claus) McReynolds. He also questioned Burke Ramsey over three days in early June 1998 in Atlanta.

Lou Smit — Legendary Colorado Springs detective lured out of retirement by the Boulder District Attorney to work on the JonBenet case. He helped to question John Ramsey in 1998. He subsequently came to believe that the Ramseys were innocent and went public with his views.

Steve Thomas — Boulder police detective who led the questioning of the Ramseys in 1997. He later resigned, blasting the conduct of the District Attorney's office in a sensational resignation letter.

Tom Trujillo — Boulder police detective who helped question the Ramseys in 1997.

II
THE OTHER PLAYERS

Mike Archuleta — John Ramsey's private pilot. He was standing by to fly the family to Charlevoix, Michigan, on December 26th, 1996.

Ellis Armistead — Ramsey private investigator. He sat in on the interrogation of Patsy Ramsey in June 1998.

Linda Arndt — Boulder detective and the only police officer in the house when JonBenet's body was discovered.

Pinky Barber — A close friend of Patsy Ramsey in Boulder.

Joe and Betty Barnhill — The Ramseys' elderly neighbors. They were caring for JonBenet's pet dog, Jacques, at the time of her death. They had also stored her surprise Christmas present — a bicycle — and were among guests at the Ramseys' Christmas party on December 23rd, 1996.

Dr. Francesco Beuf — JonBenet's pediatrician.

Patrick Burke — Patsy Ramsey's attorney. He sat with her during the interviews.

Michael Bynum — Lawyer and close friend of the Ramseys who first advised them to hire attorneys.

Tom Carson — Chief Financial Officer of John Ramsey's computer software company, Access Graphics.

Paulette Davis — Patsy's youngest sister.

John Douglas — Former FBI profiler. He was hired to work for the Ramseys' own investigative team.

John and Barbara Fernie — Close friends of the Ramseys. They were called to the Boulder house by Patsy after she made the 911 call. John Fernie helped raise the $118,000 demanded in the ransom note. The Ramseys stayed at their home briefly after the murder.

Rick French — The first Boulder policeman to arrive at the Ramsey home. He warned colleagues, "Something doesn't seem right."

Linda Hoffman-Pugh — The Ramseys' housekeeper. She and her daughter, Ariana, attended the December 23rd Christmas party after helping Patsy prepare for it. Patsy told police that the ransom note writing looked like Linda's.

Rol Hoverstock — The Ramseys' pastor at St. John's Episcopal Church in Boulder. He was in the house when JonBenet's body was found and led a prayer service over her body.

Alex Hunter — Boulder county's longtime District Attorney, now retired.

Lucinda Johnson — John Ramsey's first wife.

Pat Korten — Washington, D.C., public relations expert hired by the Ramseys after the murder.

Stewart Long — Then-boyfriend, now-husband of Melinda Ramsey.

Larry Mason — Boulder detective sergeant who was an early member of the JonBenet investigation team.

Bill McReynolds — Former journalism professor who played Santa Claus at the Ramsey Christmas parties. Beloved by JonBenet, he was subsequently named as a suspect by both John and Patsy. He died in September 2002.

Janet McReynolds — Bill's wife. She had written a play about the kidnapping and torture of a child and was also the target of suspicion cast by the Ramseys.

Glenn Meyer — A tenant of Ramsey neighbors, Joe and Betty Barnhill. He was present for a while at the Ramseys' Christmas party in 1996.

Dr. John Meyer — Boulder County Coroner who performed the autopsy on JonBenet.

Bryan Morgan — John Ramsey's attorney. He was present with him during the interrogations.

Fred Patterson — Boulder police detective who arrived at the house with detective Linda Arndt, but left before the body was discovered.

Don Paugh — Patsy's father, JonBenet's grandfather. He worked for his son-in-law at Access Graphics.

Nedra Paugh — Patsy's mother, who once said, memorably, "As long as Mr. Ramsey brings the money in, we'll spend it." She died in March 2001.

Pam Paugh — Patsy's younger sister, and like her, a former Miss West Virginia and Miss America contestant.

Mervin Pugh — Husband of Ramsey housekeeper, Linda Hoffman-Pugh.

Beth Ramsey — John Ramsey's daughter from his first marriage. She was killed in a car accident in January 1992.

Burke Ramsey — JonBenet's brother. He was nine years old at the time of the murder. He lives with his parents in Atlanta.

Jeff Ramsey — John Ramsey's brother. He lives outside Atlanta.

John Andrew Ramsey — John Ramsey's son from his first marriage. He was a student at Colorado University at the time of JonBenet's death.

Melinda Ramsey — John Ramsey's daughter from his first marriage.

Randy Simons — Photographer who took many of the memorable professional pageant photos of JonBenet. He was picked up by police 10 months after the murder when he was found wandering naked down a street in Genoa, Colorado. He told cops, "I didn't kill JonBenet."

Glen and Susan Stine — Close friends of the Ramseys. Glen was Vice President of Budget and Finance at Colorado University in Boulder at the time of the murder. John, Patsy and Burke lived with them for several months after the murder.

Chet Ubowski — Handwriting expert for the Colorado Bureau of Investigation, who compared the writing of the ransom note with that of John and Patsy.

Stuart and Roxie Walker — Close friends of the Ramseys in Boulder.

Rod Westmoreland — John Ramsey's longtime close friend and stockbroker. His help was enlisted in raising the ransom money. After JonBenet's funeral, he hosted a reception for the mourners at his palatial Atlanta home.

Fleet and Priscilla White — The Ramseys' closest friends in Boulder prior to the murder. Afterward, they vehemently opposed their hiring of lawyers and their decision not to immediately speak to police. They were involved in a bitter scene in Atlanta during the gathering for JonBenet's funeral and were subsequently branded as the possible killers by John and Patsy. They were officially cleared by police.

Fleet White Jr. — Son of Fleet and Priscilla White. Burke Ramsey's good friend.

Daphne White — Daughter of Fleet and Priscilla White. JonBenet's best friend.

Bill Wise — Boulder county's former top Deputy District Attorney.

Chris Wolf — Boulder financial analyst. His girlfriend turned him in to police as a suspect. The Ramseys also named him as a suspect in the book they wrote. Wolf sued them.

Denise Wolf — John Ramsey's secretary at Access Graphics.

L. Lin Wood — The Ramseys' current attorney. He won hefty libel damages for Richard Jewell, the man wrongly accused of being the Olympic Games bomber.

The two sides finally met — four months after JonBenet's murder — in a room at the Boulder County District Attorney's office.

Patsy Ramsey was questioned by Detectives Steve Thomas (ST) and Tom Trujillo (TT). Also present were Peter Hofstrom, chief trial deputy of the Boulder County District Attorney's office, Ramsey attorneys Patrick Burke and Bryan Morgan, and Ramsey private investigator Jon Foster.

Thomas would later describe Patsy as "magna cum laude smart and Miss America pretty, cancer survivor strong and drama queen talented, tenacious and determined." To Thomas, she was no longer "distraught and disheveled, she was immaculate in a blue suit . . . a silver angel pin on her lapel and gold earrings . . . and her perfume reached across the table . . . .

"When I had a question, she would lean so close across the narrow pine table that we were almost in kissing distance."

<u>STEVE THOMAS:</u> Patsy, I want to speak specifically to you and tell you that we appreciate you coming to the table today, uh, and your involvement with this and our intention, and I can speak for myself and I think the other persons on this side of the table, is to establish some sort of ongoing dialogue . . . I appreciate your comments of wanting to work with us and, and we desire that as well . . . .

<u>TOM TRUJILLO:</u> Okay. Kind of tell me a little bit about

yourself, your background, where you were born, kind of the nuts and bolts kinds of stuff.

PATSY RAMSEY: I was born in Parkersburg, West Virginia, November 29, 1956. I attended school there ... I moved to Atlanta in the summer of 1979 and was working for McCann Erickson Advertising Agency ... and in 1980, November, I married my husband, John.

TT: Okay. What kind of clubs were you in? What kind of activities did you do in high school?

PR: I was a cheerleader in the 10th grade. I was on the drill team my senior year.

TT: Drill team?

PR: ... dancing, with the band ... I was in student government there ... I was president of the student body when I was in the 9th grade ... in junior high school. And I was very active in the speech and debate team there and, uh, participated regularly in that group.

TT: Where did you go to college at?

PR: West Virginia University.

TT: What was your degree in?

PR: Journalism.

TT: How'd you do in college with your journalism degree?

PR: I graduate magna cum laude ... my emphasis was in advertising so that's what I did for ... some short time after I graduated.

TT: Okay. And you were Miss West Virginia, Miss America, about what year did all that happen?

PR: 1977.

TT: Okay. Did any scholarships come out of that?

PR: Yes. I, uh, there was some scholarship for winning Miss West Virginia. I can't remember exactly how much, and then at the Miss America pageant I won a non-finalist talent award, and I think it was a $2,000 scholarship for that.

TT: I've got to ask which talent.

PR: (Laughter) "The Kiss of Death" dramatic dialogue
. . . actually what happened, uh, I did the Miss Jean
Brodie (a dialogue from "The Prime of Miss Jean
Brodie") . . . in high school . . . and uh, placed
nationally with it and then I had done that for Miss
West Virginia and won with that and then when you go
to Miss America you have to go through this business
of um, in the event you make the top ten and you're on
television, there are all these rights and royalties or
whatever they call it and . . . they have to give you
clearance, okay. And to make a long story short, I was
unable to get clearance for this. Uh, I can't remember
exactly the details, but uh, I ended up writing a
dialogue that I used and . . . it had a lot of the same
characterizations and that kind of thing . . . I was
definitely thrilled when I won the talent, you know,
because it was a real chore getting there.

ST: I bet.

TT: . . . Atlanta in '79 and who did you live with down
there?

PR: I lived with Dan and Claudia McCutcheon . . . who
had been friends from Parkersburg.

TT: Did you guys move down there together?

PR: Well, I went to Atlanta with Dan's sister,
Stephanie, who was my age.

TT: Okay.

PR: And we had been roommates in college for a year and
we went down to visit her brother and sister-in-law . . .

TT: Uh huh.

PR: . . . who had also gone to high school with us so we
were all friends. And um, we went, I think initially
for just a short visit and then came back a few weeks
later to, and decided to move to Atlanta. Stephanie

had gotten a job and, and I was still interviewing with advertising agencies.

TT: You get a job with Hayes Computers, you think?

PR: No, I, that was much later . . . I had worked with McCann Erickson Advertising Agency.

TT: Okay, so you worked as an advertiser to start with?

PR: Right.

TT: When you first moved to Atlanta you lived in an apartment building?

PR: Uh huh.

TT: Same place that John lived, is that right?

PR: Well, we were, we were guests at Dan and Claudia.

TT: Okay.

PR: You know, kind of sleeping on the couch there . . . in a one bedroom apartment and John lived upstairs.

TT: All righty. Um, tell me about some of the TV shows you guys watch. You specifically. Uh, say in recent history, last, the last year . . .

PR: I don't watch TV much.

TT: Okay.

PR: You guys, who guys?

TT: You, John, Burke.

PR: Burke likes Discovery.

TT: Okay. Discovery Channel?

PR: He likes the Discovery Channel.

TT: Okay.

PR: And John likes the Weather Channel.

TT: Okay.

PR: He's a pilot.

TT: Is that because he's a pilot?

PR: Yeah. And he watches that . . . and he likes old movies.

TT: Okay. Do you, do you get to the movies at all? Have you been out to see any shows at all?

The ransom note contained similar dialogue and themes taken from the movies "Dirty Harry," "Speed," and "Ransom."

PR: Oh, I have . . .

TT: I, I know it's difficult in the last couple of months . . .

PR: Right.

TT: Let's say before December, what kind of movies have you and John gone out to see?

PR: Well, actually we didn't go out to movies very much because we had a home theatre (in John and Patsy's bedroom) . . . so we would — usually we'd see everything about a year after it came out.

TT: Once it came out on video?

PR: Yeah, but we, you know, the kids liked to watch movies up there . . .

TT: Uh huh.

PR: . . . we watched "Forrest Gump" and . . .

TT: Do you and John watch movies at all up there?

PR: Uh, yeah, but I usually fall asleep. He, he usually goes, gets the movies and they're not my favorites and I usually fall asleep.

TT: Okay. What kind of, what kind of movies did he, do you guys end up starting to watch?

PR: Um, he likes Mel Brooks . . . He liked "1941." He loves "Animal House." I got him that for Christmas, and uh . . .

TT: So the kind of comedy type movies?

PR: Uh huh.

TT: Okay. Patsy, are there any concerns in the neighborhood up there or have there been any concerns in the neighborhood up there . . . door to door salesman? Any of your neighbors talk about prowlers, anything like that over the last six months?

PR: Yeah, sometimes children, you know, like a, um, black children. I mean, they don't look like they're from my neighborhood or nothing, or look, you know like they're from Denver and they have candy bars . . .

TT: Okay. How close are you to your neighbors?

PR: Do I know them very well? Well, the Barnhills (Joe and Betty) across the street . . .

TT: How often do you talk to the Barnhills or have you talked to the Barnhills in the past?

PR: Uh, I kind of keep, you know, they're elderly . . . and I would kind of, you know, every two or three days probably . . .

TT: Kind of keep in touch with them?

PR: Uh huh. They, they kept our dog a lot . . . when we went out of town or whatever. Joe was, last year about this time, around Easter time, he was quite ill with some respiratory stuff and I was taking groceries and dinners and . . .

TT: Kind of taking care them?

PR: Yeah. Kind of keeping my eye on him.

TT: . . . Can you think of any names that come up as far as people that don't like you? Don't like Patsy? Who don't like the family at all?

PR: You know. If that's the case, I'm not aware of it.

TT: Okay. Nobody's talked about the problems that they've had with you?

PR: No.

TT: Up through the years, as the companies have merged together, any bad feelings between employees maybe getting squeezed out, um, anything like that that you're aware of?

John Ramsey was president of Access Graphics in Boulder, a computer sales company formed from the merger of three firms.

<u>PR</u>: Not that I'm aware of. I think, when, when they merged, uh, to the best of my knowledge, when they merged to form Access, all the three companies that were merging all played a role somehow, you know . . . Nobody got squeezed out, I don't think.

<u>ST</u>: . . . let me jump in with one quick one on Access, uh, um, I was charged with investigating a lot of the aspects of Access employees that had been dealt with, a lot of the VPs over there and so forth . . . I was made privy to some information that there may be some sort of either IPO offering or management buyout. Uh, was anybody going to get hurt by that over, uh, in the Access corporate office? Was that going to hurt anybody that would . . . ?

<u>PR</u>: But, I don't know what IPO is?

<u>ST</u>: An Initial Public Offering if they, if they took the company public, um.

<u>PR</u>: You know, I, I really don't know anything about that.

<u>ST</u>: Okay. Fair enough.

<u>PR</u>: John didn't really discuss . . .

<u>ST</u>: Okay.

<u>TT</u>: . . . business matters with you?

<u>PR</u>: Not, no.

Patsy was asked what medications she was taking. She said she was using antidepressants — the drug Paxil each day and Ativan, a quicker acting medication, when she needed it.

<u>TT</u>: Um, I'm going to talk about the medical stuff. I know you had cancer about three years ago.

<u>PR</u>: It will be four years in July . . . I was diagnosed.

<u>TT</u>: And you went out to Washington to take care of that?

<u>PR</u>: Bethesda, Maryland (at the National Institute of Health).

<u>TT</u>: Um, everything's going okay with that?

<u>PR</u>: Yeah, I just had a checkup.

<u>TT</u>: Okay. Kind of a, who handles the finances for the family, the checkbooks, pays the bills, that kind of stuff?

<u>PR</u>: He does.

<u>TT</u>: John takes care of all that kind of stuff?

<u>PR</u>: Well, I have a checkbook that I write, you know, my kind of, the personal things, you know, like, whatever, housekeepers or household kind of stuff . . .

<u>TT</u>: Is that the checkbook you wrote the check to Linda Hoffman out of? . . . She was going to borrow $2,000, is that right?

Just before JonBenet's murder, Ramsey housekeeper Linda Hoffman-Pugh had asked to borrow $2,000 from Patsy to pay off debts.

<u>PR</u>: Right.

<u>TT</u>: On uh, the, on Friday . . . that's when she was due back in the house. Christmas was Wednesday.

<u>PR</u>: Right. Oh yeah, I think that's right, yeah.

<u>TT</u>: Okay. Do you remember if you ever wrote her a check for that $2,000, because I know she talked about it?

<u>PR</u>: Right. I don't think I did, because I think, I was thinking about that as I walked down the stairs that morning, that I, oh, I've got to remember to leave that check . . . and then everything broke loose.

<u>TT</u>: Patsy, let's um, let's kind of go back to December

23rd. I know you had a party at your house, quite a few people at the house.

PR: Uh huh.

TT: And I think I actually have a pretty good idea of who was all in the house ... at that time, but kind of walk me through the party real briefly, um, you know a couple of people that were there ... what kind of activities occurred, and who was in what parts of the house, that sort of thing if you would?

PR: Um. The 23rd we had, uh, the Whites over and she had a lot of family in so they were all guests. Fleet and Priscilla and their two children and, uh, her sister, Allison, and her boyfriend, Allison's boyfriend, and I can't remember his name, but ... Allison's daughter, uh, and I can't, Heather, is her name ... and the Stines, Glen and Susan Stine and their son, Doug ... and I think Susan's mother was there and Glen's mother ...

TT: Okay.

PR: ... my father (Don Paugh) and let's see, who else? Um, the Fernies, (John and Barbara Fernie).

TT: What did you guys do at the party?

PR: Uh, Joe and Betty Barnhill were there, too.

TT: Okay.

PR: Um, we had dinner and Santa Claus came, Mr. & Mrs. Santa Claus came, and we always had a little poem kind of thing. Give everybody a little gift from Santa ... and the kids decorated gingerbread houses.

TT: The poem you're talking about is that what, I know, one of the pictures you have, uh, Santa's reading ... out of a black book ...

PR: Right.

TT: ... And that's, who does the poem for that?

PR: Me.

TT: Okay. That's the poem in the black book?

PR: Right.

TT: Okay. About how long, what time did the party start that night?

PR: . . . Uh, kind of early because I, if I remember I, Santa Claus had two engagements that night and so he came, I can't remember whether it was like 5:30 or 4:30 or somewhere in there.

TT: So fairly early in the evening?

PR: Fairly early, yeah.

TT: Okay. About what time did it break up?

PR: Oh, probably, I don't know, nine-ish, 8:30 . . . sometime like that.

TT: All right. Um, and this is when they, they decorated the little gingerbread houses . . . ?

PR: Right.

TT: . . . And that kind of stuff. Okay. How do you, how do you decorate gingerbread houses with that many little kids?

PR: Well, I bought the gingerbread houses at Safeway . . . already stuck together . . . then I bought this huge big tub of frosting . . . and Priscilla brought these frosting bags . . . or something like you decorate a cake with, and I bought just bunches of jelly beans and M&Ms and all the, gum drops, you know, and all that stuff and the kids just . . .

TT: Squirted it out and stuck . . .

PR: . . . Squirted it out and stuck it on, you know, it was all over the place.

TT: Okay. Did, um, did Linda come, Linda Hoffman?

PR: Yes.

TT: Was she there also?

PR: Yes, and her daughter. She had helped me all day getting ready for the party and she stayed through Santa Claus.

TT: Okay. Um, did anybody else show up that night? White, Stines, Don Paugh and the Fernies, Barnhills, Mr. & Mrs. Claus, Linda and her daughter . . . anybody else that you can remember that was over there that night?

PR: Um, well, John told me that this man came to the door looking for the Barnhills . . .

TT: Okay.

The visitor was a man who rented a basement room at the Barnhill home.

PR: I don't remember seeing him, but John said he let him in . . .

TT: Okay.

PR: . . . And kind of showed him to the Barnhills. You know my dad said he remembers him, this man being there and I think my dad said he invited him to eat something and . . .

TT: Okay. So did, uh, Betty and Joe Barnhill know him?

PR: Apparently, yes.

TT: . . . Okay. Patsy, let's move over to the, uh, to the 24th. I want you to start kind of, actually let's go more towards the afternoon of the 24th. That would be . . . Christmas Eve. The kids are all excited. Kind of run me through that in the same fashion. What did you guys do?

PR: Well, we, um, uh, went to church, the family church service which was at 4 or 4:30 . . . something like that. And, uh, after that we went to Pasta Jay's for dinner . . .

PR: And then we drove around town looking at Christmas lights and we drove up to the star up on the mountain (a huge lighted star on Flagstaff Mountain that shines down on Boulder from Thanksgiving to the

New Year) . . . I remember JonBenet was miffed because we wouldn't let her get out and she wanted to walk up into the star . . . and, uh, she just had her little velvet Sunday school shoes on, you know, so she was, she said, "Well, what's the use coming up here if you can't even go up to the star?" Um, so then we came down, down from the star and we wound around by the Whites' house and, uh, I think, and we went in there for a few minutes and, uh, then we went home.

TT: Okay.

PR: And, you know, got everybody ready for bed.

TT: Okay. About what time?

PR: I don't know exactly. . .early evening.

TT: Okay. Early evening. . .where did everybody sleep that night?

PR: Well, JonBenet was in her bed in her room . . . and Burke was in his bed and we slept in our room.

TT: Okay. Do you have an idea if JonBenet moved over towards Burke's room at all that night? Slept in his room?

PR: Um, I can't remember . . .

TT: Okay. Is that something that she would normally do?

PR: No.

TT: Sleep in Burke's room? I know everybody's got, you got, they both have two beds in their rooms?

PR: Yeah, right, um, I don't think so. I just can't remember.

TT: Okay. How about December 25th, Christmas Day? How did that start out? Who got up first and that sort of thing?

PR: Uh, well, the kids came up and woke us up and John went down, he went to get everything ready, you know, get the lights on, get the music on, you know . . . uh, I think he, he said . . . Santa Claus brought me a bicycle so he had to go get that under the tree . . . and then we all went down and, into the living room. That's where we had the Christmas.

TT: Okay. Big tree in the living room. Okay. Because I know there's kind of trees all over.

PR: Right.

TT: (Where) do you normally store the Christmas presents, say before the 25th?

PR: . . . The basement. I had them all in the basement.

TT: Okay. Why don't you walk me through the rest of the 25th? What all did you guys do that day?

PR: Well, I continued to wrap some presents. I went back down to the basement on the washing machine area there and wrapped for taking the stuff to the lake . . .

The day after Christmas, the Ramseys, and their children were headed off in John's private plane to their lakeside vacation home in Charlevoix, Mich. They were going to first stop in Minneapolis to pick up John Andrew and Melinda Ramsey, John's children from his first marriage, and Melinda's fiance, Stewart Long, who were arriving there via commercial jet from Atlanta.

PR: . . . And the kids were playing with their toys . . .

TT: Okay. And then about what time did you guys go over to the Whites' house that night?

PR: Um, um, dinner-time-ish, you know, five or six or something like that.

TT: All right. What did you guys do at the Whites' house, kind of, how many people were over there?

PR: Well, that whole group of her family was still there . . .

TT: About what time did you get home from the Whites that night?

PR: Well, we stopped a couple of places on the way home to drop off Christmas gifts.

TT: Okay.

PR: By the Walkers (Stuart and Roxie Walker) and the Stines (Glen and Susan Stine) ... and I imagine it was about nine-ish, something like that.

TT: Okay. Sometime, nine, after nine, something like that?

PR: Some, yeah.

ST: Uh, quick question. Give me some more detail, Patsy, if you will, on, on the daytime and afternoon of the 25th. Um, we sort of moved quickly to that evening but, but, uh ... walk me through that day.

PR: Well, we opened our presents and, uh, try to have them do it slowly so ... it's not over with in five minutes, you know, and we all opened our things and then we had breakfast and, uh, I was packing, as well as wrapping gifts that day. We were, we were going to go to the lake on the 26th so I was putting a few things together for that trip and, um, and trying to get the presents together to take up there and then I was packing our suitcases to go, we were going to go on a Walt Disney cruise on ...

ST: Big Red Boat?

PR: Bid Red Boat, on my birthday, the 29th. So I was, had summer clothes, trying to get all that ready, so, uh, and packing and, uh, I think I colored my hair that afternoon, like with one of those quick, you know, uh ...

ST: Everybody stayed home the whole day. No trips out on the 25th prior to going to the Whites?

PR: Uh, John, I think went out to the airplane to kind of, he always kind of checks, checks it out.

ST: Prior to a flight?

PR: Yeah. So he went out there that afternoon and the

kids were just in and out playing . . . JonBenet was
making this little jewelry thing and Burke had this
car that he was playing with.

ST: So you and the kids were home the whole day . . .

PR: Yes.

ST: . . . Prior to going to the Whites and John returned
from his short outing . . .

PR: Right.

ST: . . . Uh, and that was his only trip out that day?

PR: As best I can remember. Yes.

ST: Patsy, I'm going to jump back just a little bit . . .
Patsy, one of the things certainly that we've taken a
great deal of interest in and looked at is, uh, John's
bonus . . . that a gross amount minus some FICA and
taxes and so forth, roughed out to equally the $118,000
(ransom demand). To the best of your knowledge,
anywhere in the home, was that information available
or displayed?

PR: I, I do not know.

ST: Okay. How immediate did it come to your mind or
John's mind, uh, that that, uh, amount of money asked
for in the ransom note roughly equaled John's bonus?
Were you aware of that on the morning of the 26th?

PR: Was I, was I aware of what now?

ST: The bonus amount equaling . . .

PR: I was not aware . . . I didn't know that he had
gotten a bonus.

ST: Okay.

PR: . . . He takes care of all that stuff and I didn't
know, I think at some time that morning he, I remember
him saying that that might be close to a figure that
was a bonus that he had gotten, but . . .

ST: Okay . . . do you know what John's salary was in
relation to a bonus being $118,000?

<u>PR</u>: I don't know any of that.

<u>ST</u>: Are you not privy to any of the financial information in the household?

<u>PR</u>: Well, I'm sure I'm privy. I can see it if want to, but . . .

<u>ST</u>: Okay. That's not your day-to-day affair?

<u>PR</u>: That's not my day . . . no.

<u>ST</u>: Okay. I certainly have chased leads far and wide on SBTC (the ransom note was signed off, "Victory! S.B.T.C.") and has that, and over the last four months, brought anything to mind?

<u>PR</u>: No.

<u>ST</u>: Have you had any time to think of any theories of significance of what that acronym, uh, might relate to? I've heard everything from Smyrna Bank and Trust, Southern Bell Telephone Company to, uh, everything under the sun, uh, any thoughts on that, Patsy?

<u>PR</u>: I mean, I have racked my brain, I mean, if you say . . . have I spent any time on this, I have, you know . . . I don't have a clue what that is . . .

<u>ST</u>: . . . Your mom thinks it's son-of-a-bitch Tom Carson (Access Graphics chief financial officer).

<u>PR</u>: Yeah, she told me that, too.

<u>ST</u>: Was there a problem with Tom Carson and John Ramsey?

<u>PR</u>: Not that I'm aware of. That, you know might be something you can ask him . . .

<u>ST</u>: Patsy, one of the things that, that I'm, certainly have to ask you about is we try to think of who would have had any reason or intent or motive to have done something like this. And what might have pushed them to do something . . . would be terribly strong feelings and, um, uh, have there and I need to ask you this, um, has there been any spurned or scorned lovers or infidelities in your marriage to John, uh, that we need

to look at as a, as a possible factor in this?

PR: No, absolutely not.

ST: And, and let me ask that another way. Have there been any infidelities in your marriage to John?

PR: No.

ST: . . . one person that we have not been able to run down, that I certainly want to exhaust in this thing is, uh, a woman who Lucinda (John Ramsey's first wife) revealed to us as having had an affair with John that ultimately led to the dissolution of their marriage. Um, that was some time ago, but, um, I think people have been reluctant to share that with us. Do you know who this person was?

PR: No, I'm not aware of anything like that.

ST: Are, are you aware of prior to today, because I had to ask Nedra and Pam and Paulie (Patsy's sisters, Pamela Paugh and Paulette Davis) and, uh, if they were aware of this person, while we were in Georgia so we could find her, and make sure she's not some kook that laid in wait for 20 years . . .

PR: Uh huh.

ST: . . . Um, is today the first time you've been made, made aware of this woman?

PR: I don't know of any woman with, I don't know anything about this, no.

ST: Okay. Are you aware that John had some sort of infidelity according to Lucinda?

PR: No . . .

ST: Okay. So you certainly wouldn't know this woman's name then?

PR: No.

ST: . . . Let's get off that for a minute and I'm going to let Tom take you back into the 24th and 25th.

TT: Actually, let's start back on the morning of the

25th, um, let's kind of break it down into small hours. What time did you guys get up that morning?

PR: Early.

TT: Before sunrise?

PR: Six-ish probably.

TT: Okay. Patsy, take me through, say, the first three hours of, of Christmas morning with you and John and Burke and JonBenet. Kind of, kind of in a by minute, step-by-step of what you guys did for the first couple or three hours.

PR: Well, we went down the stairs and passed out Christmas presents.

TT: About how long did it take you to pass out Christmas presents? I know you talked about you kind of did it slowly . . .

PR: Yeah.

TT: About how long did that take?

PR: I don't know. Hour, maybe . . . I mean to pass them out and opening them. I try to get everybody to take turns, you know. Of course, their piles are bigger than my pile so . . . they open two or three and then I open one . . .

TT: . . . What did you guys do after you open the presents up?

PR: Uh, I think we made pancakes.

TT: Okay. Had some breakfast? Um, about how long did it take to eat breakfast?

PR: I don't know, a half hour.

TT: After, after breakfast how did the family split? What did you guys do?

PR: Oh, the kids were just playing with their stuff, you know, and I was, I don't remember exactly . . . I was, you know, trying to get clothes ready to go two different places. I remember that . . .

And then a bunch of kids started showing up to, you

know, they want to see what each other got and, you know. Burke set up his Nintendo, Nintendo 64 and . . .

TT: During the early morning hours, the morning hours before the kids got there, did everybody go and get dressed, I take it?

PR: At some point in the day, yeah.

TT: During the day, about what time did, uh, John go down to the hangar and check on the plane?

PR: Oh, I don't know. I don't know, lunchtime, after lunch, I, I don't remember.

TT: Okay. Did you have lunch that day?

PR: I'm sure we did.

TT: Okay. Do you have any idea about, what did you have for lunch?

PR: I don't remember.

TT: About how long was John gone when he went out to check the plane?

PR: Oh, probably a couple of hours.

TT: So he left about noon, afternoon sometime. Gone till two, 3:00 in the afternoon?

PR: Um, yeah.

TT: Okay. And were . . . kids over to the house that whole time playing with John, excuse me, JonBenet and Burke?

PR: Uh, a better part of that day, I would say.

TT: Okay. Did, uh, did Burke and JonBenet play together during that time? Did the little girls and little boys mix up at all?

PR: Yeah.

TT: Play together.

PR: Yeah, they were all, yeah, a lot of them were in Burke's room playing that Nintendo and she was, I remember coming up there and checking on them and they were, the boys were mostly sitting around

playing the Nintendo and she was, had this little
jewelry making kit right there in the, in the doorway
of Burke's room . . . so I made a couple with her.

TT: Okay. During the time that John was gone, was that
when you were wrapping the gifts and trying to get all
the suitcases packed . . . ?

PR: Stuff ready, right, uh huh.

TT: . . . And stuff ready to go. Okay. And you wrapped
the gifts downstairs?

PR: Yeah.

TT: Okay. About how many gifts were you wrapping that
day to get ready to go?

PR: Oh, I don't know. A couple of shopping bags full . . .

TT: Okay. This is for John Andrew and Melinda . . .

PR: And Melinda and Stewart . . . Melinda's boyfriend
was going to be up there, too.

TT: Okay. Where were you packing the suitcases there?

PR: Um, the suitcases for the cruise I think I was
packing in John Andrew's room, which is that room up
on the same area as JonBenet's room . . . with the black
bedspread on it.

*Although John Andrew lived in Atlanta at his mother
Lucinda's home, he was attending Colorado University in
Boulder. A suitcase that belonged to John Andrew was
found in the basement of the Ramsey home near the room
where JonBenet's body was found. The suitcase had been
placed beneath a broken window that led to a grated well
outside the home. Some investigators believe an intruder
lifted the grate, got down into the window well and entered
the Ramsey house by breaking a window. In this theory of
the crime, the intruder needed to step on the suitcase to
reach the window and exit the home.*

TT: Okay. That's John Andrew's room?

PR: We refer to it as his room . . . the guest room, whatever. Um, I had two or three black suitcases in there and I think I had my suitcase up in my dressing room . . . packing.

TT: And were you packing suitcases for the trip to the lake separately or was that all together?

PR: No, it's not together.

TT: Okay.

PR: Those were two separate trips. The lake I think I was just packing a plastic bag . . . because we have clothes up at the lake . . .

I just remember I was trying to get clothes ready for four people to go in two different places . . . and the kids were playing, then I, you know, got them dressed and then we, they were in play clothes and so we changed and got cleaned up to go over there . . . and I think I colored my hair.

TT: Okay. Did John help you get packed up at all?

PR: Uh, he, I believe, put some presents in the, in the Jeep.

TT: . . . You left, left for the Whites about five, 6:00 . . . any other friends that weren't related to the Whites or your family? Any other people over there at the Whites' house that night?

PR: Uh, I don't recall.

TT: Okay. So everybody's, everybody's pretty much related to the Whites?

PR: Right.

TT: Was this kind of a spur of the moment or was it planned to go to the White's house that night?

PR: It was planned to go there.

TT: Yeah.

PR: We had gone there last year, Christmas dinner.

TT: Okay. Who all did you let know that you were going over to the Whites? Did you let the Barnhills know or anybody like that?

PR: Uh, I don't remember. I think I, seems like I did call Betty that day to see if they had anybody over there with them or, you know, if they were okay or . . . and I may have told her that we were going. I don't remember exactly.

TT: Check to see if anybody had come over to visit the Barnhills?

PR: Yeah. I just wanted to make sure they had something to eat and all that . . .

TT: About what part, what part of the day did you call Betty to make sure she's okay?

PR: Um, sometime that afternoon.

TT: Okay. What did, what did you do at the Whites' house that night?

PR: We, um, had dinner. I called Fleet's mother, Fleet called his mother and I talked to her. She was ill. She was usually there, because Christmas is her big, she likes Christmas.

TT: Okay. Where does she live at?

PR: . . . California, but they have a residence in Aspen . . . and she was in Aspen.

TT: Okay. So give me kind of a step-by-step, get to the Whites, 5:30, 6:00, 6:30, whatever, what time did you have dinner that night? What did you do before dinner, after dinner?

PR: Well, we had, um, I think we had cocktails, kind of, she had some cracked crab . . . and we sampled some of that and I remember she kind of, for some reason, made a little plate for JonBenet or I remember her making a special plate for JonBenet for some reason so she would have some crab . . . 'cause my kids like seafood and, uh, we nibble on that and, I uh, we had dinner and I can't remember what we had.

TT: Was it like a buffet, sit down, what kind of dinner was it?

PR: I just, I just, I don't know. I can't remember.

TT: Was it a formal plates around the table type . . . ?

PR: Well, we had, she usually puts up several tables in her living room. She had several tables in her living room, in her dining room . . . there were a lot of us there and, uh, we sat at the table, you know, she had a place for everybody . . . and, uh, she had little gifts for the kids. They had these little paper jewelry things that JonBenet and Daphne got and, um. Fleet and John were down on the floor helping them make those.

TT: Okay. About how long did you stay at the Whites' house?

PR: Oh, several hours, you know, I, something like 9:00 or so, eight.

TT: Okay.

PR: Eight or nine. We had to get up early so we didn't . . . stay really late.

TT: Okay. So, other than the dinner with the little gifts, any other social activities go on that night, caroling or just socializing? What else happened?

PR: Uh, I think some carolers came. Some neighbors came to the door caroling and Fleet, big Fleet and little Fleet, I think went out with them for a little bit. Um, maybe Daphne went with them.

TT: JonBenet and Burke go out with them to carol?

PR: I just can't remember.

TT: Okay. Got home about 8:30, 9:00. What's the first thing you guys do when you got home that night? Actually, let me step back. Before you got home you went over to . . .

PR: Walkers and dropped of a little gift . . . and Stines and dropped off a little gift and drove home and JonBenet was asleep. She had fallen asleep in the car.

TT: Did you have to wake her up to get her inside or . . . ?

PR: Well, she was just really zonked and John carried her up to her room . . . and, I, uh, you know, ran up behind him and, or in front of him, I can't remember. Maybe, or it might have been in front of him to turn the bed down.

And he laid her down and I got her undressed and put her, I left her shirt on her and, uh, went in the bathroom and tried to find some pajama pants and all I could find was some, like long underwear pants . . . and put those on.

TT: What color of top did she wear to bed that night? What color top was she wearing actually to the Whites' house like?

PR: Well, she wore this little outfit that I had gotten her at the Gap. We had a little, little riff over that, 'cause I wanted her to wear, I was wearing a red sweater and I wanted her to wear this red sweater with her black velvet pants, 'cause I was wearing black velvet pants and it was Christmas and all that.

And she didn't want to wear the red shirt just because I was wearing it. She wanted to wear the shirt that went with the outfit which was a Gap outfit that I had bought her when we went shopping for her and it was a little white, kind of neck like this . . .

TT: Kind of a crew neck?

PR: . . . Crew neck and it had a little, little rhinestone, little kind of sequin kind of star thing on it.

TT: Okay.

PR: So I just left that on her.

TT: Okay. And I'm sorry. What kind of pants, what color of pants . . . ?

PR: They were black velvet. Black velvet jeans, kind of like, from the Gap. Some little black velvet vest.

TT: And what were you wearing Patsy, a, a red turtleneck and black . . . ?

PR: Velvet jeans, yeah.

TT: Okay.

PR: Velvet pants. And I have a Christmas sweater I was wearing.

TT: And what color was that?

PR: Red with all kinds of . . .

TT: And that was over the turtleneck?

PR: Yeah.

TT: . . . When you say you wore black velvet jeans, were those like a, a, were they a jean material . . . ?

PR: No, they're, no, no, no. They're black velvet.

TT: So John carries JonBenet upstairs, puts her to bed. You pull up the bed sheets. You find this top for her to wear or you just . . . ?

PR: We just left her top on her.

TT: . . . You leave the top on . . .

PR: Yeah.

TT: . . . Uh, find a pair of . . .

PR: Bottoms.

TT: . . . Bottoms for her to wear. Um, did she wake up at all during this?

PR: No.

TT: Stayed pretty crashed out?

PR: Uh huh.

TT: Okay. Sound asleep the whole time then?

PR: Uh huh.

TT: Okay. What did Burke do? Did he fall asleep on the way home also?

PR: No.

TT: Okay.

PR: He didn't. I think he was, he's still wanting to play.

TT: Okay. What did Burke do when you got home then?

PR: Um, I don't remember exactly, but I think he went to go play with something. I think maybe he and John were fussing with something. A toy he wanted to put together or something.

TT: ... Burke and John go downstairs to play?

PR: No, I don't really, don't remember where they were. I was, after I got her ready for bed I just kind of ran about doing my last minute things and ...

TT: Okay. What kind of last minute things did you have to take care of?

PR: Well, just, you know, presents. I mean, I put some presents by the back door and I don't remember exactly, just things to go to the lake or, and so we're doing a couple of, you know, getting things ready cause we were leaving so early in the morning ... getting things kind of laid out ready to go and that kind of thing.

TT: About what time did you head up to bed that night?

PR: Um, probably around 9:30, 10:00 something like that.

TT: Okay. Um, did you guys try to wake up JonBenet at all or did she ... ?

PR: She was zonked.

TT: Sound asleep. Didn't wake up at all?

PR: Uh huh.

TT: Was she awake at all when you were over at the Stines' house?

PR: Uh, well, I just went to the door. We didn't all go in. I just went to the door ... and gave them a basket of something ... for a Christmas present or something. We were going, I remember, cause I had a big basket in the car to take to the Fernies, but since JonBenet had fallen asleep and it was getting kind of late ... I think we just decided not to go to the Fernies.

TT: Patsy, do you have any idea what time, uh, Burke went to bed that night then?

PR: . . . I don't know exactly.

TT: Okay. What time did John go to bed that night? Do you remember hearing him come upstairs at all?

PR: Yeah. I remember him coming to bed. I don't know what time it was. It was shortly after I came to bed.

TT: Okay. That night, were you able to sit up and read after you kind of took care of things? Get things ready in the morning. Go up to your room. Do you have any time to read at all that night?

PR: I don't, I'm sure I had time to read, but I don't know. . .whether I did or not.

TT: Okay.

PR: I think I, I think I just, you know, pretty much went to sleep. I can't, I just can't remember . . . I know I was reading a book. I was working on a book, but I don't . . . remember if I read that night or not.

TT: So you go upstairs, jump into pajamas, go into bed. Did you have to take off your makeup, take off your jewelry? What's that whole sequence?

PR: Oh, I probably washed my face, brushed my teeth.

TT: Okay. What's your normal get-ready-for-bed routine, I guess, is what I'm asking?

PR: Um, take my makeup off. Brush my teeth.

TT: Okay. Take all your jewelry off then?

PR: No, I don't take them off.

TT: Okay.

PR: Sometimes, I mean, it depends on what I have on, sometimes I take it off, sometimes I don't, but . . .

TT: Okay. JonBenet, she had some jewelry on. Does she normally sleep in her jewelry, too? She had a little necklace . . .

PR: Uh huh.

TT: . . . A bracelet and stuff . . .

PR: Uh huh.

TT: . . . And the necklace, I believe, she got from Paulette?

PR: Pam.

TT: Pam.

PR: For Christmas . . . I had given her the bracelet the night of our Christmas party.

TT: Back on the 23rd?

PR: Uh huh.

TT: Okay. She didn't over the last day . . . hadn't taken that off at all then?

PR: I'm not, I don't believe so.

TT: Okay. And what about the, the rings that she wears?

PR: She had on a little gold ring that my mother had given her . . .

TT: Did she normally wear that all the time, too?

PR: Uh huh.

TT: So, you got upstairs, take your makeup off, jump into bed. John comes in shortly after that. Um, do you hear Burke go to bed at all? Do you hear him playing Nintendo, watching TV or anything like that?

PR: I just don't remember.

TT: Okay. Anything else, before everybody goes to bed for the night that you can remember happen, hearing any noises, anything like that in the house?

PR: No, I don't remember any.

ST: . . . Just let me fill in some blanks if I can, Patsy. On the night of the 25th after you came, and to the best of your recollection, I think you said it may have been 8:00 or 9:00, is that fair? Um, when you got home . . .

PR: Well, it was, I don't know exactly what time . . . but it was, you know, it was nine-ish probably. I don't, I didn't. . .remember looking at my watch or anything.

ST: Okay.

PR: It was dark.

ST: But it was shortly thereafter, uh, at some point, that, uh, JonBenet was put to bed, um, you and John went to bed, uh, I noted that, uh, I had a question. Who put Burke to bed or did he put himself to bed that night?

PR: Um, I don't know. I did not put Burke to bed.

ST: Okay. Is it typical that, that he can go to bed on his own?

PR: Well, typically one of the two of us put, put them to bed so, I, I think John was playing something with him. One of this Christmas things and he, very likely, put him to bed.

ST: Okay.

PR: I did not, so I don't know.

ST: But John, and you to an extent, put JonBenet to bed, uh, by carrying her to bed because she was asleep or out?

PR: She was sound asleep.

ST: Okay.

PR: He carried her and put her in bed and I got her, you know, pulled off everything and put her, I left the shirt on and put the pants on.

ST: And remind me, what shirt did she go to bed in? Was that the same shirt she wore to the Whites that night?

PR: Yes.

ST: Okay. And then those little white sort of thermal bottoms?

PR: Right.

ST: And what was your goodnight routine with JonBenet in her room on the night of the 25th? John was getting her down. Did you simply peek your head in or how long were you in the room with John?

PR: Oh, he just walked in and laid her in the bed and then I, I, he left . . ..

ST: You took it from there?

PR: Right.

ST: And that consisted of simply getting her under the covers?

PR: Well, I changed her and took the black velvet pants off and found those, those long underwear pants and put on her.

ST: Okay. Turned off the light?

PR: Uh, the light in her bedroom was not on. I believe that bathroom light, we usually left the bathroom light on.

ST: Do you remember how you left the door into her room when you left the room? Did you leave that open or closed or cracked?

PR: I usually leave it cracked a little bit.

ST: Okay. And is that your recollection on that night?

PR: Uh huh.

ST: Okay. And then retrace your steps for me, then did you go up and go to bed?

PR: I don't think I immediately did. I, I, uh, you know brushed my teeth and got ready for bed and I think, I think I got . . . some presents ready to go and just kind of a couple of things. Yeah, I'm sure I was getting ready to leave early the next morning.

ST: Did you change out of the clothes or the pajamas or whatever you wear to bed during your nighttime routine, brushing your teeth . . . ?

PR: Right.

ST: . . . And washing your face?

PR: Uh huh.

ST: Um, did you ever go back and check on JonBenet again . . . ?

PR: I don't believe I did.

ST: Did John ever go back in?

PR: I don't, I don't know.

ST: Okay. Um, it was how long after you put JonBenet to bed, did you then retire into bed for the evening?

PR: I don't know exactly. Maybe half hour I think, I don't, I can't remember exactly.

ST: And it was shortly after you went to bed that John then came to bed?

PR: Right.

ST: And during that half hour, 45 minutes, after you put JonBenet to bed, and that you were still up, uh, arranging presents, brushing your teeth, you don't know, uh, whether or not John went back into JonBenet's bedroom?

PR: Um, no.

ST: Would it have been unlikely for him to have gone back in and awakened her for any reason?

PR: Oh, yeah. It would have been unlikely.

ST: Okay. Can you give me, to the best of your memory, if you got home at nine-ish, was it shortly after coming home at nine-ish that you put JonBenet into bed . . . or John carried her up and put her to bed?

PR: Yeah, it was, I mean, he carried her from the car to her bed.

ST: So, were you in bed then, and I don't want to put words in your mouth, by ten or 10:30 or what time, if you can reconstruct that, did you then go to bed?

PR: I was probably, probably in bed by then. Ten or 10:30 . . . I can't remember exactly.

ST: . . . John came to bed shortly thereafter, do you recall if that was 15 minutes or a half an hour?

PR: It was probably just a few minutes.

ST: Okay. You were still awake?

PR: I was, yeah, I could, was aware of him, you know, getting in bed, but . . . .

ST: And are you a sound sleeper?

PR: Fairly.

ST: Is John a fairly heavy sleeper?

PR: Yes, I would say, he snores . . . .

ST: When John gets up during the night on occasion
. . . to use the bathroom, for example, does that awaken
you? Are you aware of when John leaves the bed?

PR: Uh huh, usually.

ST: And is John aware when you leave the bed?

PR: I don't know if he's aware when I leave or not.

ST: Okay. So on the night of the 25th at some point,
Burke went to bed, it's possible or likely that John
checked on him and made sure that he was down . . . .

PR: Uh huh.

ST: . . . But, John had put JonBenet into her bed and she
never awakened the whole time from the car to bed that
night?

PR: Not that I . . . no.

ST: Did that concern you at all or was that common
with a, a six-year-old baby?

PR: She just, she was really zonked.

ST: When you awaken the next morning, uh, do you
recall what you or John wore the following morning
when you got up?

PR: You mean what did I put on in the morning?

ST: Uh huh.

PR: Uh, I think I put on the same black velvet pants and
the red turtleneck sweater. I don't know what John had on.

ST: And on the night before, on the night of the 25th,
the black velvet pants and the red sweater, you don't
recall what your footwear was?

PR: I think, um, no, I can't remember exactly. I
usually wear these little black kind of little boots
with it, but I don't know if wore them that, I don't

remember what I wore that night.

ST: Do you remember on the night of the 25th, when you and John came home, what the lockup procedure, the security procedure for the house that night was?

PR: No, I don't.

ST: Concerning keys to the house Patsy, uh, and access to the house, outside of John Andrew being in Boulder, were there another keys outstanding other than John Andrew's and the Barnhills'?

PR: Uh, my dad had a key . . . my cleaning lady had a key, Linda. The Barnhills, I believe, actually gave two keys, because I had given her one, and she couldn't find it. I think I gave them another one. Uh, Barbara Fernie had one at one time, I'm not sure. I think I might have gotten that back from her. Priscilla had one I believe.

ST: Does Priscilla still have that key?

PR: I don't know. I can't remember. It seems like I gave it to her before we went to the lake, because she was going to have a lot of house guests and I thought if she wanted to, you know, use the house for any reason she could have the key.

ST: What is the status of the key or keys that you gave the Barnhills?

PR: The status right now?

ST: Yeah. Have you gotten those back?

PR: I haven't, no, I don't know where they are. I don't know what the status is of those.

ST: Would it be inaccurate if the Barnhills were saying that they returned the key to you? Could that be possible?

PR: Um, it could be possible I guess. I don't remember, and I think, I think I gave it to them and the intent was if I got, anybody got locked out of the house they would have a key. So I don't, I mean, it wasn't like, you know, keep this for two days and then give it back to me or something, you know.

ST: . . . Some questions for you about when John had to break in that basement window . . .

The summer before the murder, with Patsy and the children up at the vacation home in Charlevoix, John Ramsey said he did not have his key. He had to break into the house through a window beneath a grate that led into the basement, the window under which John Andrew's suitcase was found.

PR: Right.

ST: . . . but was there any reason . . . John could not have retrieved the key from the Barnhills at that time to get in rather than breaking the window?

PR: He, he may not have known they had a key.

ST: On the night of the 25th after John put JonBenet into her bed, she's zonked out sound asleep, did not awaken, um, you got her changed, um, may have left the nightlight on, may have left the door cracked. Uh, you don't know what John did for the 30 minutes or an hour that he remained up in the house prior to coming to bed? Is that right?

PR: Well, he was, I remember he was, was with Burke playing with something. I don't know what they were playing with, but . . .

ST: But he never mentioned to you that he re-awakened JonBenet for any reason?

PR: No.

ST: Take her to the bathroom so she didn't wet or anything like that?

PR: No.

ST: Did you, John or Burke have any ill effects, uh, after eating dinner at the Whites in coming home? Any feelings of intoxication or drowsiness?

PR: I, I remember just being really tired. I don't know that I was drowsy, but you know, it had been a big day. I was tired and I was anxious to get to bed.

ST: Patsy, in some ways I, I know more about your family than I know about my own, but, uh, to the best of my knowledge and what everybody tells me neither you nor John are drinkers, you're social drinkers at best. Did you have anything to drink on the night of the 25th at the Whites? A glass of wine?

PR: We may have had a glass of wine. I know John is very cautious about, I mean, knowing that he is going to fly the next, you know, does not, uh, you know, drink a lot.

ST: So certainly neither of you . . .

PR: I mean we may have had, and I'm very, I don't drink a lot because my chemo did a number on my liver so I, I don't, we just don't drink a lot.

ST: So I'm assuming neither you nor John was intoxicated . . . by any means that night?

PR: No, no, no.

ST: Often times, according to Nedra and Pam and Paulie, uh, JonBenet falls asleep with a video in . . .

PR: Uh huh.

ST: . . . Um, and that would play until I guess it, uh, exhausted itself . . . ?

PR: Uh huh.

ST: . . . And somebody would turn it off, but on the night of the 25th, uh, was that the case.

PR: No.

ST: No video? Uh, do you normally sleep with any radio or television on upstairs . . . ?

PR: Uh, sometimes John will put on a CD or something

. . . you kind of fall asleep and then it clicks off or
something.

ST: Was that the case on the night of the 25th?

PR: I don't remember.

ST: Do you know which bed Burke normally slept in, in
his room . . . ?

PR: First one in . . . right as you go in the door.

ST: And if, on occasion, JonBenet would go sleep in
Burke's room, would she get into the other bed?

PR: She'd be in, yeah.

ST: Okay. Um, what would cause that? That she got
scared at night or . . . ?

PR: No, just, I mean, that happened very seldom and, uh, I
think, oh, I think one time when I was reading to Burke
and . . . she feel asleep in that bed so I just let her sleep
there or something, but . . . usually I'd get her back in
her bed 'cause she would, occasionally wet the bed and
her bed had a plastic wrap on it and that one didn't . . . .

ST: Was it common for her to, uh, get up during the
night at all, either to, uh, use the bathroom or to go
downstairs or, uh, was she a, a fairly good sleeper that
would sleep the night through?

PR: She, she was a fairly good sleeper. She, um, very
rarely, you know, would wake up at night. If she did,
she would, you know, sometimes she would have wet the
bed and she would get up and get in that other bed or
she, sometimes would come up to our bed, but it was not
very often.

ST: . . . You did not read any nighttime story to
JonBenet on the 25th nor did John, is that right, if she
was asleep?

PR: No.

ST: And which bed in her room did you put her into on
the night of the 25th?

PR: The, the first one as you walk in the door.

ST: The most northern or next to her little dresser, uh, um ... ?

PR: Not against the window ... the one closest to the door. I don't remember what direction that is.

TT: The one closest to the door.

ST: You're like my wife. She doesn't know. She says right or left. When you retired for bed you slept through the night without getting up, or let me say it this way. You slept through the night uninterrupted until you awakened and got out of bed the next morning. Is that right?

PR: Right.

ST: And we'll certainly ask John, but as far as you know, was that the case with him as well?

PR: Uh huh.

ST: When John came to bed did he have a light on and, I don't know if he's a bed reader like I am, but did he have a light on and read at all that night?

PR: I think he did. I, he has, um, I usually leave his light on, on his side before he comes to bed and then he turns if off when he goes to bed. I think he did read awhile that night.

ST: Patsy, let me ask you a question. Uh, and this is hypothetical, but were JonBenet to have been awakened by a stranger intruder, is it your belief as her mother that she would have been more paralyzed by fear or would she have fought and kicked and screamed and yelled?

PR: I, you know, I just, I, I can't answer that. I don't know what ....

ST: Nedra suggested to me that when she might take her to the bathroom at night to prevent a bed-wetting occurrence, that sometimes she would get an elbow or, you know, a lot of this ....

PR: Well, she didn't like to be awakened . . . .

ST: Did you hear anything out of the ordinary at all on the night of December 25th into the morning of the, December 26th?

PR: Huh uh.

ST: Was the house secured to the best of your knowledge? Were doors locked and windows locked when you guys went to bed that night and awakened the next morning?

PR: I did not check the doors or windows that night.

ST: Were you going to finish the Charlevoix packing the morning of the 26th when you got up?

PR: Uh, yeah, I mean, throw in toothbrushes and last minute kind of stuff, you know . . . stuff in the car, you know, packages.

ST: . . . And was everybody on this same page about going to Charlevoix as far as, uh, willing and wanting to go? There was no dissension in the ranks that, "I don't want to go" or "she doesn't want to go?" Everybody was looking forward to this trip?

PR: Well, I mean, we were. I wasn't real crazy about going 'cause I just thought it was cramming a lot of stuff in there, you know. I told John I didn't really want to go. I'd rather, 'cause, Christmas, going to Charlevoix, then going to, it just seemed like a lot, you know, but then we decided as a family to go and, you know, been looking forward to it. We never had Christmas up there before so I called the florist and had them put up lights and a wreath and flowers and all that 'cause Melinda and Stewart were coming up and John Andrew.

ST: How did the kids feel about, I mean, Christmas is the 25th, they just get all the presents, get everything opened up, get to playing and all of a sudden the 26th they're, they got to take off to Charlevoix . . . ?

PR: Oh, the little kids?

ST: Yeah, how did they feel about that?

PR: Oh, they, they would have loved it . . . they love it up there.

TT: . . . Patsy, let's go ahead and, um, start out on December 26th when you first woke up in the morning . . . give us a, almost a play-by-play, minute-by-minute, what did you do when you got out of bed? Where was John at? That sort of thing. All the way through the morning to the afternoon. Let's kind of take it, we'll take it in little chunks.

PR: Okay. Um, we got up at about 5:30, I think. I think John got up first and I got up just right behind him and he went to his bathroom and shower. I went to my bathroom. I did not shower that morning and I just put my clothes on and, uh, did my hair and makeup and, uh, and then I started down the stairs. John was still in the bathroom and went, uh, I stopped kind of briefly there in the laundry room area (the Ramseys had a small washer-dryer setup on the second floor near JonBenet's room, and a larger laundry area in the basement). And I remember the ironing board was up, I think, and I fussed around with this little red jumpsuit of JonBenet's 'cause it had, had some spots on it and I was going to remember to do something with that when I got back and, uh, so I had, I had the light on in there in the laundry room area and, uh, um, then I started down the spiral staircase there. I came, I had come back down, I'd come down the back bedroom stairs . . .

TT: Okay.

PR: . . . from my bathroom. Um, I started down the spiral stairs and when I got nearly to the bottom I saw these three pieces of paper, like notebook-size paper, on, on the run of the stairs and, uh, I went on down and turned around and started reading, reading it . . .

TT: Uh huh.

PR: And, uh, I, I remember reading the first couple of lines and I kind of, didn't know what it was or, uh, and . . . You know after the first couple of lines I, it dawned on me, it said something about, "We have your daughter" or something . . . and I, uh, I ran back upstairs and pushed open the door to her room and she wasn't in her bed.

TT: Okay.

PR: And I, uh, screamed for John. He was up in our bedroom still and he came running down and, uh, I told him that there was a note that said she had been kidnapped. And, uh, uh, I think he, he said, I said, "What should I do? What should I do?" or something. And he said, "Call the police." and I think somewhere, I remember I said something about, you know, "Check Burke," or something and I think he ran back and checked Burke and I ran back down the stairs and then he came downstairs. He was just in his underwear and he, uh, took the note and I remember him being down hunched on the floor . . . with all three pages out like that reading it and, uh, and he said, "Call 911" or "Call the police," or something and then I did. I called them and, uh, and then I called the Whites and the Fernies and told them that she had been kidnapped or said, "Come over quickly," or something. And they came over and the policeman came and, uh, then the Whites and the Fernies were there and, uh . . . Oh, I think the policeman was asking, you know, he kind of like, I think he kind of got us . . . in the sun room or something.

TT: Okay.

PR: That little room, patio room . . . off the living room and trying to calm us down or something and, uh,

I think, I think John, uh, by that time read and, that they wanted money or something and, and, uh, he, I think he had called, uh, Rod Westmoreland, our friend and our stock broker in Atlanta.

TT: Uh huh.

PR: To see about getting that money together and uh, and, I think two other, two ladies came that were social workers (they were members of a local victim's advocate group) or something . . . and, uh, (Detective) Linda Arndt came and some more policemen. Uh, and, oh, there, uh, something in the note about they were going to call. I think it said they were going to call sometime in the morning. And Linda Arndt and some of the policemen were, they were going to set up, uh, tape recording or something up in the TV room, phone back there. And they were, I think they were busy doing that and Father Rol (Hoverstock, pastor of the Ramseys' church) came over and, uh, praying that she would be all right and, uh, uh, I think initially right away we, we thought that, um, the cleaning lady was somehow was, you know, John mentioned that I had told him about that she had called and wanted that money and all that . . . and, uh, I think I kind of looked at the writing and thought maybe it might have looked a little like hers or some, I don't know, but I think they were rushing around and trying to find out where she lived and . . . uh, you know, there was a lot of talking about her and her, everybody, her family or something.

TT: Patsy, let me back you up just a little bit. Um, actually to the, to the very beginning of the morning. You and John woke up . . . Did you have an alarm clock set or anything?

PR: Uh, I think he had it set, but I don't think it went off. I think we woke up about, you know, I don't remember it going off or anything.

TT: You don't have an alarm that was set on your side of the bed at all?

PR: Huh uh.

TT: Okay. Got up, got dressed. Do you remember what you wore that morning?

PR: Black velvet pants and my red sweater.

TT: Okay. Now you went downstairs. When you stopped there at the laundry room . . . .

PR: The laundry room.

TT: . . . . You stopped at the ironing board and laundry area. Was JonBenet's room, do you remember if the door was opened or closed at that point in time?

PR: It was, it didn't strike me as unusual, you know, I . . . .

TT: Okay.

PR: . . . And I think it was open just a little bit like I would have left it.

TT: Okay. And that's, that's kind of normally how she sleeps with the door kind of . . . ?

PR: . . . A little bit open.

TT: Just a little bit open.

PR: Cause I usually leave a light on in that hallway area there. Either the stair sconces or the, there's a light in where the washing machine is . . . right there, you know.

TT: Do you remember with the door being open just a little ways, of there being any lights on in JonBenet's room?

PR: I don't remember.

TT: Don't remember whether there was anything that was illuminating out of that room?

PR: Now her, her main light was not on, you know her lamp was not . . . .

TT: Okay.

PR: When I opened the door I could just tell that she wasn't in her bed.

TT: Okay. Actually let me back up just a bit. Main light as in the lamp . . . .

PR: Like the lamp on, yeah.

TT: . . . Next to her bed.

PR: That lamp beside her bed.

TT: Okay, so that was not on?

PR: Huh uh.

TT: . . . Why were you heading downstairs in the, the very beginning?

PR: Oh, to make coffee and kind of get a little breakfast ready and just kind of, we were getting ready to, I mean we had to be at the airport at, you know, I think we were going to take off at seven or something like that.

TT: Okay. So you were going to get to the airport about, a little before seven so you could take off at seven?

PR: Yeah, we were going to get there about a half hour before.

TT: Okay. How strict are the takeoff times when you're taking off? I mean, do you have to be there and the plane have to leave at seven by the gates . . . .

PR: No, no.

TT: . . . Or you guys got a window there?

PR: Yeah, there's a window . . . But I think we were suppose to meet Mike out there.

TT: Mike Archuleta?

PR: Pilot, yeah.

John Ramsey sometimes flew his own plane and used Archuleta on other occasions.

TT: Okay. So, you were going to try to get out there by 6:30 to meet him by seven and take off?

PR: Yeah. Something, John made all those arrangements. I don't know exactly what time . . . we were suppose to meet him.

TT: Okay. You come to the spiral staircase. You talked about the note being on the, on the stair, um, do you have any idea which stair that note was on? How far up from the bottom or anything?

PR: I think it was like, the, about the third or somewhere around there.

TT: Okay.

PR: Cause I went down to the bottom and turned around and read it, you know, like kind of leaned over it looking at it.

TT: Okay. So, it, as it was laid out and you look, you're standing on the bottom stair or the front . . . .

PR: On the floor, yeah.

TT: . . . You're looking at it, was it laid out from left to right like you would normally . . . .

PR: Yeah.

TT: . . . Read a book or something?

PR: Yeah.

TT: Okay. Um, at that point in time, do you have to step on the note or did you step over it when you came down?

PR: I probably stepped over it.

TT: Okay.

PR: 'Cause we sometimes lay papers and stuff there to go up and . . . if you step on it you might slip . . . I don't, don't think I stepped on it.

TT: Okay. You pick up the note and start to read it, um, go back upstairs to JonBenet's room? Is that correct?

PR: Well, I don't remember if I picked it or, or just leaned over and read it. I can't remember. I don't

think I picked it up 'cause I remember just then
bounding up the stairs toward her room.

TT: Do you remember hitting any of those papers, maybe
sliding or anything as you were running back up ... ?

PR: I don't remember. I just ran as fast as I could.

TT: Okay. And again when you opened her door, no
lights on that you can remember in that room?

PR: Um, her, I know her main light was not on. Her
bathroom light might have been on. I don't remember.

TT: Okay. Now does she have any little plug-in
night lights into the wall or anything like that that
she sleeps with?

PR: Um, no . . . Well, the Christmas tree. She had a
Christmas tree in there and that, that might have been
on. I don't remember if it was or not. I just don't
remember. I just remember pushing the door open,
looking at the bed and she wasn't in there.

TT: Okay. Were the sheets pulled down, the, uh, the
comforter and everything pulled down on the bed?

PR: They were kind of ruffled up, you know.

TT: Ruffled up as pulled up towards the top or
ruffled ... ?

PR: Toward the bottom.

TT: Down towards the bottom of the bed?

PR: Well, I mean, I just looked at it for a split
second. I knew she wasn't there and I screamed.

TT: Okay. You yelled for John. John comes down. Okay,
what happened, where did John read the note at when
he read it?

PR: Downstairs . . . on the wooden floor (on the first
floor) . . . right there by the TV room.

TT: Okay, um . . .

PR: He, I remember him, while I was calling 911, he was
hunched over the note and had it laid out there on the

floor 'cause there was a light. It was still kind of darkish and there was a light, hallway light on . . . he was, you know, reading it there.

TT: Okay. Patsy, do you recall who moved the note from the bottom of the stairs down to where John could read it with the good lighting?

PR: I think he did . . . .

TT: Okay.

PR: . . . Don't remember exactly, but, I mean . . . I was just, I was just nuts . . .

TT: Okay. Where, where were you at when you called 911 'cause I know there's . . . ?

PR: Kitchen.

TT: Okay. Is that a cordless phone?

PR: No.

TT: Just a, it's a regular wall phone, right?

PR: Right.

TT: Okay. Okay. So you are in there making the 911 call. John's out in the hallway reading the note, um . . . .

PR: Well, I mean we were real (close), the phone's right here and he was right there.

TT: Right around the corner. Okay. When did you check on Burke during all this? You talked about John going to check on Burke.

PR: Yeah. I think he ran and checked on him when I was up, up there, uh, you know, it just all happened so fast. I said, "Oh, my God. What about Burke?" And I think he ran in and checked him while I was running back downstairs or something . . .

But I remember he, you know, I think he ran and checked on him and, and he told me he was okay or whatever.

TT: Okay. John talked about that with all the commotion and you guys yelling and stuff, did that wake up Burke at all?

PR: No, it didn't.

TT: Okay.

PR: He didn't get up for awhile.

TT: 'Cause we talked, John went up later on and, and woke up Burke . . . .

PR: Yeah. Brought him down.

TT: Okay. Uh . . . .

PR: Got him dressed and . . . .

Patsy was unaware that Boulder police had enhanced the tape of her 911 call. She had failed to hang up the phone properly and investigators say Burke's voice is heard on the 911 tape asking, "What did you find?"

TT: Okay. So you're on the phone call, 911. John's reading the note. What happened then?

PR: Uh, that woman on 911 or whoever I was talking to . . . it just seemed like she took forever, you know. I said, I mean, she just kept saying, "Well, what is it?" you know. And I said, "Our little girl has been kidnapped," you know, and I gave her the address and, I mean, she just, I mean, just, she, I just said, "Send somebody fast," you know. Uh, it just seemed like she was just, I'm sure she had things she had to go through . . . and John just was reading that note and, and then, uh, and he went up and got dressed sometime before the policeman got there he had gotten dressed . . . and, uh, the Whites and the Fernies came over . . . .

TT: Okay. Do, who called the, who called the Whites and Fernies?

PR: I did. I did.

TT: Okay. Do you remember which ones you called first . . . ?

PR: I, I don't exactly. I think I called the Whites

first, but I can't remember exactly.

TT: Who did you talk to at the White's house?

PR: Priscilla, I think.

TT: Okay. Do you remember what you told her about what was going on?

PR: Not, I mean, I was just hysterical. I think I, I probably told her that she had been, JonBenet had been kidnapped. And, uh, to come over and . . . .

TT: Then you called the Fernies.

PR: Fernies.

TT: And who did you talk to at the Fernie house?

PR: Uh, I think I talked to John . . . I don't remember. I think John Fernie got there first, before Barbara, but I don't remember who answered the phone really.

TT: Okay. So John runs upstairs, gets dressed. You're already dressed. Who's the first person that comes in the front door? Who's the first person that makes it over to your house?

PR: Uh, well, the policeman.

TT: Okay. The policeman arrives.

TT: Who, who all was, where was John at the time that the officer arrived?

PR: Oh, I don't, I don't know. I remember I, I don't know where he was. I walked out onto the front step there and I was just, I was just kind of out of it. I was hysterical. I said that there was a note and that our daughter had been kidnapped and we were trying to get the money and I don't, I don't remember.

TT: Okay. So you met the officer when he came into, or came up to the front door?

PR: Right.

TT: You're the one that opened the door for him?

PR: Right.

TT: Okay. Um, the officer kind of herded you into

that, the sun room area?

PR: Right.

TT: And then, the way I understand it, then the Whites and the Fernies got there?

PR: I believe that's right, yeah.

TT: Do you remember who came in first, the Whites or the Fernies?

PR: I think, I think it was the Whites, but I can't remember . . . it seemed like they got there pretty quick.

TT: Fleet and Priscilla arrived?

PR: Yeah.

TT: Okay. About what time did John go upstairs and wake up Burke to have him leave, 'cause I know that was after the Whites got there. Is that right?

PR: I don't know what time that was, but it was more, it was more daylight-ish. I mean that was after every, a lot of people were there by then.

TT: Okay.

PR: Uh, and there was some discussion about what to do about Burke, and I think Fleet said he could come over to their house and play or something.

TT: What, what kind of discussion, I mean, other than Fleet saying, "He can come over to my house and play?" What to do with Burke?

PR: Well . . . Just you know, we just thought it was best that he not be around. It was, it was just bedlam, you know, and I was a mess and, you know the police trying to do their job and all and . . . .

TT: Was it, uh, was (Linda Arndt) there by the time, uh, when Burke was leaving?

PR: I don't remember exactly. She was, she was there pretty soon, but it seemed like, I remember sitting in the sun room and it was, more daylight-ish when she got there.

TT: Okay.

PR: So I don't know, I don't know what time it was really.

TT: Okay. Who called Father Rol and let him know what was going on?

PR: I think Barbara said she did.

TT: Okay. Do you have any idea about what time Father Rol got there?

PR: I don't know what time anything happened. I was just, I was just frantic.

TT: Okay. Um, again, who, who took Burke out of the house? Did John, John and Fleet do that or did just Fleet drive him away?

PR: Uh, I don't believe John left. I think that John brought him downstairs and, uh, he came over to me and . . . he had tears in his eyes. I think, I think we just said you can go over and play at the Whites. I don't remember exactly who took him out of there.

TT: . . . So John brings Burke downstairs and then, is that, that's when you told him that . . . JonBenet was missing?

PR: Yeah, I think Burke, Burke, I think John had talked to him some upstairs. I don't know.

TT: And then you, then somebody took him over to the Whites' house?

PR: Correct.

TT: Okay. And I know through the, through the morning, and, uh, before John went downstairs, can you kind of give me an idea what, what went on in the house during that time? I know there were a lot of things going on, but, kind of what you can remember?

PR: Right, well, uh, they, uh, I just remember they were setting up back there that tape stuff or whatever so that we're, and I think Linda had instructed John about what to say when they called and, uh, uh, and she was talking to me and said, uh, that they weren't sure. I guess the note said something about like we'll call at, I forget what time, 10:00 tomorrow or something and, and she wasn't sure if that was going to be that day, you know . . . the 26th that we were in, or tomorrow the 27th and I just . . . didn't want her to be gone overnight and . . . I think the phone rang sometimes and every time it rang I would just pray that, that was, you know, that they were calling and . . . it got to be later and later and nobody called and I think somehow they got the money, you know, whatever. That $118,000 that they wanted or some, I don't know how they figured out about that, but they had that ready, I think.

TT: Do you know who did get the money? Who, who was supposed to do that?

PR: I don't know. I mean, John Fernie and Fleet and John, I don't know. They were in, I was in the, in the sun room and I think, and they were all like back in the TV room talking about all that and I . . . and then it just got so long, you know, it just, I mean it was like afternoon or something and I remember walking back, 'cause . . . the hub was kind of like back there in the TV room . . . uh, so I, I walked back there and, uh, that was where the call, they were going to take the call and everything and . . . .

TT: Okay.

PR: . . . Uh, so I walked back in there and sat down for a little bit and, uh, there were some other people back there and, um, and then I heard John scream, screaming and, uh, then he just screamed uh, I think Fleet came running and said, "Call 911 and get an ambulance," or something. And I kept saying, "What is it? What is it?" And, and, uh, I think Fleet ran up and John Fernie took the phone and said, "Send an ambulance. I don't know what it is. Just send help," or whatever he said. And, and I think Barbara had a hold of me and she wouldn't let me, she wouldn't let me go in there. And then people were coming, coming back in and I looked at her and people were just white . . . I forget who, helped, helped me walk into the living room . . . I think John said she was gone and he was crying and we kneeled over her and I felt her cheek and her cheek and she was really cold . . . and I just prayed to God to bring her back . . . and so I just . . . she wouldn't be there anymore and get out of this house and I'm never coming back . . . Sorry. I don't remember what happened after that.

ST: Patsy, when you came downstairs on the morning of the 26th and discovered the note laid out as you described on the uh, uh, one of the steps, do you recall, at that point, and can you recount for me, at what point you touched the note? Were you the one that, did you grab it and run upstairs with it or were you the one that moved it to the floor? Give me an idea of what points that morning you handled the note.

PR: That was a lot in one question.

ST: Okay. When you came down the stairs the first time did you touch the note that time?

PR: I don't recall doing that but . . . I may have.

ST: Do you recall, uh, did the note go back upstairs with you when you went up to check JonBenet's room?

PR: I don't remember exactly, but I don't think so. I think I just, you know, pounced up the stairs as fast as I could. I don't, I don't think I took it with me.

ST: Do you recall moving the note from the stairs to its eventual position where John read it on the floor?

PR: I, I don't recall moving it. No.

ST: Do you ever recall touching the note?

PR: Um, not specifically, but I may have. I mean there, later on that morning there were, the note was on the coffee table and I remember, in the TV room, and we were talking about did anybody recognize the handwriting, so I may have touched it then . . . but I just can't remember.

ST: So certainly your fingerprints may very well be on the note and, and, and explained that way?

PR: Right. I, I, mean I may have touched it, you know.

Testing for fingerprints on the note was done weeks later, after handwriting analysis was completed. There were no fingerprints found on it.

ST: Okay. When you, uh, after the note and after what I'm assuming is just sort of pandemonium, after seeing the note, uh, and you called for John, you went to the kitchen and called 911?

PR: . . . I called, um, I, ran up and opened, you know, pushed open her door and realized she wasn't there and I ran to the stairwell that goes up to our room and called for John and, and, then, you know, momentarily went downstairs to the kitchen to call.

ST: Was that when John was checking Burke and the rest of the house that you made that call?

PR: Uh, I believe so. I mean everything just happened so fast right there. I, I don't remember, I just remember at one point, you know, we were saying, "What about Burke?" And John ran into check Burke and I ran back downstairs, and then suddenly he was downstairs and I mean it was just . . . so fast, you know, everything.

ST: Um, and obviously Burke was okay and he was able to sleep through this until he was later awakened. Is that right?

PR: Right.

ST: Okay. Um, but at some point John came back and caught up with you. You don't recall if it was during the 911 call or after?

PR: Well, I remember I, I remember myself being on the phone and he was crouched down on the floor there in the hallway looking, reading at the note ... and I was on the phone so I don't know which happened first or it, simultaneously or ....

I remember as I was talking to that person looking down at him in his underwear reading the note.

ST: And it must have felt like forever, but it was a matter of minutes that the first officer then later arrived. Is that right?

PR: Right.

TT: Again, some housekeeping questions and, and I touched on some of these before, but I'm going to hit them just one more time. Um, Patsy, do you have any idea which windows in the house were locked or unlocked?

PR: No, I don't.

TT: Any idea about those?

PR: I, I just you know, I don't recall checking and I couldn't say for sure which ....

TT: Okay. What about doors? Do you have any idea which doors were locked or unlocked in the house?

PR: Um, like that morning ... ?

TT: Uh huh.

PR: ... Well, typically, the only door we would leave unlocked at night is the door from the coat room there ... into the garage.

You put the garage door down and that locks, you know, you don't typically lock that metal door there. But I don't, like I said, I didn't check them ....

TT: Do you recall any lights being on in the house

when you went downstairs the first time to, to make the coffee? Do you remember any lights on in the house?

PR: Not specifically . . . I mean typically leave some lights on, but I don't, I couldn't tell you exactly.

TT: Okay. Any, any lights specifically that you normally light, leave on? The same light all the time?

PR: Well, we usually leave a light on in the TV room. That little den.

TT: At the back of the house.

PR: And typically we leave on, you know the lamppost and maybe a lamp in the sun room or something.

TT: So you kind of leave a few lights on in the house, but nothing major.

PR: Right.

TT: And you, do you recall that morning whether those lights were on? Do you remember seeing an illumination out of the corner of your eye or anything or when you see John on the floor . . . ?

PR: . . . You know, when I'm telling you that I was on the phone with 911 and he was on the floor there reading those three pages, the hall light was on and I don't you know, any one, either of us could have turned it on by then.

TT: Right. And that, that's bright and obvious . . . .

PR: Yeah, very bright, yeah.

TT: . . . Did you ever get a chance before the officer got there to read the whole note other than just the first little bit when you talked about when you first read it? Did you ever get a chance to, to read through that . . . ?

PR: I think I glanced back at it. I looked at the, to see who had signed it.

TT: Didn't read word for word . . . okay. Later on when you kind of had a chance when the note was laid in, in the TV room there, you guys had kind of a chance to look it over. Anything, any of the wording seem significant to you? Anything jump out at you from reading that note?

PR: I just, you know, I just, I didn't really read it. I just couldn't bear to read it . . . so, I mean I just, you know, I kind of glanced at it to kind of see if I recognized the handwriting, but I just, I never, I don't know if I ever did read the whole thing.

TT: Okay. So, let me make sure I got this right. You read a little bit of it. The first part of it at the very beginning, got the flavor for what had gone on and then you remember reading the signature and that, that's about the extent of the note you read?

PR: Right. I mean I, you know, I might have glanced and seen the $118,000 . . . but I don't, I didn't read the whole thing.

TT: Okay. And . . . you run upstairs to JonBenet's room. You go to the foot of the stairs going up towards your room. Is that right?

PR: Uh huh.

TT: Um, yell at John. Scream.

PR: And just call his name, "John," you know, "John" . . . as loud as I could. I mean I remember my voice kind of cracking cause I was just . . . panicked. You know, but as loud as I could. I think he got the message something was wrong.

TT: Okay. Um, again, do you remember what you told John about JonBenet. . .and the note? Do you remember the conversation that you had?

PR: It said she's been kidnapped. I don't remember exactly. I mean I was just out of my mind. I, I think she's been kidnapped. There's a note. We've got to do something, I mean, I just can't remember what, I was just running around like crazy.

TT: Okay. From the time you made the 911 call to the police, John's on the floor reading the note, till the time the officer, the first officer gets there, other than call the Fernies and the Whites, what else did you do in that, that amount of time? Do you recall doing any other items?

PR: I just prayed. I just prayed and prayed and prayed.

TT: Okay. Do you know where John, John went through his movements throughout the house?

PR: Well, I, I mean, he went back upstairs I presume, and then he came down dressed.

TT: And, the house is kind of, it's spread out. I mean ...

PR: Uh huh.

TT: Are you guys using the back part of the house to go up and down ... ?

PR: Yeah.

TT: Okay. And the note was on, the note was on the floor and John was reading it when you called the police. Is that right?

PR: When I was calling the police. Yeah, he, it was on the floor there in that back hall.

TT: Okay. And you don't recall who laid the note down there?

PR: Right.

TT: Okay. Before the police arrived and after you guys checked Burke, did either one of you run through the house and check the house at all?

PR: John, I remember him running, going like to the doors, various doors, 'cause I kept saying, "How did they get in, how did they get in?" And he, uh, checked some of the doors I remember. The door to the garage, you know, from the coat room there.

TT: Uh huh.

PR: I don't, you know, I just remember him kind of

going around checking. I think he went down to the butler kitchen there. Checked, I don't, you know, I wasn't watching what he did.

TT: Did he ever make a comment about . . . any of the doors being unlocked to you? Did he find any doors unlocked that you recall?

PR: He didn't say that he did.

The butler kitchen door, an entrance on the north side of the house, became a controversy in the case. Ramsey friend John Fernie told cops he found the door open when he arrived at the home that morning. John Ramsey didn't make such a report. Police, however, found it shut. Was Fernie mistaken? Had an intruder exited the home through the door? Had John Ramsey ever checked it at all or had he opened it to implicate a non-existent intruder?

TT: Okay.

PR: I don't remember him saying, you know, he didn't say, "Oh I found it," or something . . . .

TT: Okay. Patsy, after the 26th, have you guys been able to do any type of inventory of the house? Have you come up with anything missing at all?

PR: No, I haven't been back.

TT: Okay. Has John done anything like that? Any type of inventories to see if anything is missing?

PR: I don't, not to my knowledge.

TT: Look at it like big jewelry items, anything like that, something that . . . .

PR: Yeah.

TT: . . . You guys might see as obvious that was missing?

PR: No.

TT: Do you know about what time John woke up Burke to get him out of the house?

PR: No.

TT: When did John break that window in the basement?

PR: He, I don't know exactly when he did it, but I think it was last summer sometime when we, the kids and I were at the lake.

TT: In Charlevoix.

PR: . . . He didn't have a key and the only way he could get in was to break the window . . . to the basement there.

TT: He had to lift the grate out of the way to, to get in there?

PR: Yeah, that's the one.

TT: Okay. Any reason why that one wasn't replaced or the pane wasn't fixed or anything?

PR: No, I don't know whether I fixed it or didn't fix it. I can't remember even trying to remember that, um, I remember when I got back, uh, in the fall, you know . . . went down there and cleaned up all the glass.

TT: Okay.

PR: I mean I cleaned that thoroughly and I asked Linda to go behind me and vacuum. I mean I picked up every chunk, I mean, because the kids played down there in that back area back there. And I mean I scoured that place when, cause they were always down there. Burke particularly and the boys would go down there and play with cars and things and uh, there was just a ton of glass everywhere.

TT: Okay.

PR: And I cleaned all that up and then she, she vacuumed a couple of times down there.

TT: To get all the glass?

PR: In the fall, yeah, 'cause it was just little, you know, pieces, big pieces, everything.

TT: Do you ever recall getting that window replaced?

PR: Yeah, uh, I can't remember. I just can't remember whether I got it replaced or not.

TT: Okay. You talk to Burke about, on this. Do you remember, has he talked about hearing anything at all on the night of the 25th or the morning hours of the 26th?

PR: Um, no. I haven't really talked to him too much about it. It's been pretty hard.

TT: ... Patsy, has anybody, that you can remember, um, spent time in the basement, um, how many people have had access to the basement know about that basement cellar?

PR: Well, my cleaning lady and her husband.

TT: Linda and Mervin?

PR: Yeah, would definitely be one couple, because I had asked them at Thanksgiving time, we were going to be in Atlanta and I had hired them to put out the Christmas trees and some of the Christmas decorations, and the big artificial Christmas trees were back in that room ....

And, uh, they also washed the windows, so they may be able to recall whether that window, and he was going to do some odd jobs.

TT: Mervin was?

PR: Uh huh.

TT: Okay.

PR: Uh, fix some shelves in the playroom and some, uh, closet doors that had come off their track and some stuff like that. And so I would, it seems to me like she and I talked about that window or did, somehow I vaguely remember that if it would have gotten fixed he very likely would be the one to fix it. And at any rate they were going to wash all the windows, so they would have known ....

TT: Whether it was fixed or not?

PR: Yeah.

TT: Okay. Um, other than Linda and Mervin, anybody else know about that cellar room down there?

PR: Um. We had people come and let's see, like plumbers and stuff, but I don't know if they would go down there. I can't think who might, who had reason to know about that.

TT: Okay. You say that the artificial Christmas trees were stored in that room?

PR: Yeah, uh huh.

TT: Okay. How do they . . . .

PR: Oh, well, you know, Christmas before last, the guys that put them down there put the trees into the closed, into the cellar room there, would have been Bob, uh, Bob Wallace.

TT: With the goatee?

PR: Yes. Right.

TT: Okay.

PR: Bob Wallace and one of his friends. I don't remember what his name was.

TT: So Bob Wallace and his friend knew about that room?

PR: About that room. Yeah.

TT: How were the Christmas trees stored down there? Did you guys cover them up? Were they covered in any fashion?

PR: Well, those big ones were just set up in there. They weren't even covered.

TT: Okay. Now, were the Christmas decorations stored down there, too?

PR: Well, they were kind of hanging out in the, the wreaths and things were kind of hanging. Bob Wallace put up nails and . . . hooks and things . . . .

TT: Okay. Um, that, that cellar door, that peg (at the top of the door), does that have to be down to keep that door closed?

PR: Uh, well, no, it will close. It, you know, it kind of, sort of sticks on the carpet a little bit. I mean, it will close, but that kind of I always kind of flipped that down just so the kids wouldn't get in there.

TT: Okay. But it doesn't, the door won't open up because of the carpet without that lock down? If you leave the lock in the up position the door doesn't just swing . . . .

PR: No.

TT: Okay. Were you ever, you were not ever in the basement that morning before the police got there?

PR: No, I was not.

ST: Patsy, when were you last in that cellar basement room prior to Christmas?

PR: Prior to Christmas?

ST: Yes, ma'am.

PR: Well, I was there, I was down there a lot on the 24th wrapping, and I was there on the 25th wrapping.

ST: Let me show you a couple of things. Patsy, does this look like duct tape that you've ever owned or used or had in the home?

A strip of black duct tape was taped across JonBenet's mouth.

PR: Um, no.

ST: Do you recall ever having any duct tape or multi-purpose tape like that in the home?

PR: No.

ST: Okay. How about cord such as this? Have you ever seen or used or owned or had such cord in the home?

PR: Um, not to my knowledge, no, I've never seen . . . .

ST: Doesn't look familiar at all?

PR: No.

ST: Okay. Patsy, when were you last in Athens, Georgia?

A cashier in a Home Depot in Athens had told police she'd sold black duct tape to a woman she identified as Patsy. But police could never prove it.

PR: Athens, Georgia? Uh, probably, my stepdaughter went to college there. I was probably there for something.

ST: But, that's Melinda, I'm assuming?

PR: Yeah.

ST: And that would have been some time ago?

PR: Yeah, it would have been, well, let's see, she's been in nursing school for two years. At least a couple of years ago.

ST: And the point of my question being if somebody was alleging that you were in Athens, Georgia, between Thanksgiving and Christmas of last year would they be mistaken in that recollection?

PR: Yeah . . . .

ST: Okay.

PR: It was Rome, Georgia. I wasn't in Athens, Georgia.

TT: Patsy . . . is JonBenet afraid of the dark, at all?

PR: Uh, not, I don't think so, not that I know.

TT: We talked earlier, didn't have the night light thing plugged into the wall, and she normally slept with the bathroom light on, is that right?

PR: Yeah.

TT: Okay. Any reason for sleeping with the bathroom light on, or just, that's her normal routine?

PR: Just in case she got up in the night, and that she wouldn't bump into something.

TT: Did she ever talk about hearing sounds at night that scared her? Or any noises that she would come talk to you guys about that scared her or anything like that?

PR: Not that I know of, no.

TT: How was JonBenet's health in general?

PR: Good, I'd say good.

TT: Okay. Any major illnesses at all?

PR: Well, when she was little she had, I think the doctor diagnosed it as pneumonia, but we had . . . stuff that we made, a humidifier kind of thing that I held under her nose and . . . .

TT: Was she hospitalized any at all?

PR: No.

TT: Just a quick trip to the office and that was it?

PR: Yeah.

TT: Okay. What about any injuries, any major injuries, any major injuries to JonBenet?

PR: Burke hit her in the face with a golf club one time, and the leg . . . .

TT: Any stitches or anything like that?

PR: No, it was just kind of a skin abrasion, she had a little scar, a little teensy little scar there, but it just kind of squashed the skin up . . . she had a black eye . . . .

TT: The 25th, during the day of the 25th, do you recall seeing any injuries on JonBenet? Any scratches, abrasions, cuts, bruises, or anything like that?

PR: I don't remember, but she was always getting bruised, you know. Kids just, I don't remember anything.

TT: Nothing major . . . ?

PR: Nothing . . . .

TT: Okay. About how often do you think you took JonBenet down to Dr. Beuf's (Dr. Francesco Beuf, JonBenet's pediatrician)?

PR: Uh, I don't know. I don't know exactly, I mean

she got a cold or sniffle or something and I'd probably run her to the doctor . . . .

TT: Okay. And during that time any major complaints, other than colds and sniffles?

PR: No, not that I know of, I mean, I just can't remember, maybe there is something . . . .

TT: No, I'm just like, anything that sticks out of your mind, other than just for the colds?

PR: They had just the cold, and Burke gets strep a lot. He was there a lot with strep . . . they both had a huge case of chicken pox . . . .

TT: Pretty much normal childhood diseases?

PR: She would tend to have more respiratory kind of stuff.

TT: And just on this, just a little bit, JonBenet wet the bed every once and awhile?

PR: Yeah.

TT: About how often would that occur?

PR: Oh, maybe once a week or something.

TT: Okay.

PR: If I just didn't take her to the potty and make her go to the potty before bedtime, she very likely would wet the bed.

TT: Okay. You have any idea about, has this been going on for how long? Any time that she . . . didn't have any bedwetting problems and then started back up or anything like that?

PR: No, no, she just, I mean I've had her in Pull-ups until very recently. I kind of thought it might be better, I mean Pull-ups and those Pampers things are so absorbent, that you can't you know, the child can't feel if they're wet or not. So I thought, well, it might just be better if she felt wet than being . . . .

But she had a lot of dry nights, but she would wet the

bed probably once a week.

TT: When she wet the bed, would she come up and tell you guys, or would she just crawl onto the other bed, crawl into Burke's spare bed, what was the routine if she actually wet the bed?

PR: Well, ah, sometimes she would get up and get into the other bed (in her room) or sometimes she really wouldn't wake up until morning when she normally would wake up, and maybe she'd change her nightgown or something, and I'd find her things and pajamas in the bathroom and . . . .

TT: So, it wasn't anything out of the ordinary.

PR: No.

TT: Okay. How did John feel about this . . . .

PR: I don't know if he even knew.

TT: Okay. This was something that you took care of?

PR: Uh huh.

TT: Okay. When JonBenet would wet the bed weekly, who took care of the sheets? Is that something Linda had to take care of? How often, I guess, who would even clean the sheets, to be more specific?

PR: Well, she normally changed the beds weekly, but typically . . . I would strip the bed, you know, put them in the washer or something . . . before she got there.

TT: Do you remember back in '94, typical doctor's visit, you fill out all those forms, making some sort of a notation, on one of Dr. Beuf's forms about bedwetting and soiling. That was kind of a concern, you remember anything?

PR: No . . . I don't remember.

TT: Do you recall filling out these so-called, "yes/no" question type forms back then?

PR: If I saw it I might remember it.

TT: Okay. Anyone that you can recall that would show

any inappropriate affection towards JonBenet?
Anybody out in the pageant circuit, friends,
neighbors, anybody like that?

PR: No.

TT: Anything bothering JonBenet? Did she talk about
anybody in general or anything that was bothering
her at all?

PR: Huh uh.

TT: JonBenet got a letter from the secret Santa. Do you
know who the secret Santa was?

*JonBenet had reportedly told a friend she was going to
get a secret visit from Santa after Christmas.*

PR: Ah, secret Santa.

TT: Where did she get the letter?

PR: I'm not sure that she got the letter . . .

TT: Any secret Santa that she talked about or anything
like that?

PR: No.

TT: Okay. JonBenet ever come into your room . . .
complaining or nightmares or anything like that?

PR: I don't remember. I don't remember her doing that.

TT: . . . Ah, JonBenet, was she able to get up in the
middle of the night, if she'd wet herself, change her
clothes? Did she have any problems changing clothes
in the middle of the night?

PR: Huh uh.

TT: . . . They got dropped on the bathroom floor
. . . jump into bed and be gone for the night?

PR: Yeah.

TT: Anybody else ever sleep in JonBenet's room?

PR: My mother slept in there. And, I think when we
were gone in the summer time, John Andrew . . . one of

his friends slept in there before. I have slept in there if she was sick or something. I have slept in there.

TT: Burke ever sleep over in her room at all? In the spare bed?

PR: A time or two.

TT: And she'd sleep in Burke's room every once and a while too?

PR: Every once and while.

TT: What kinds of things did JonBenet like to do? What kind of games did she like to play?

PR: She liked crafts mostly, like making stuff. Painting, she liked painting. Watch movies and dressed up in makeup and dancing, tap dancing, singing. She got bent on taking violin one time, and I tried to talk her out of it, but she just insisted, so we got a little violin about that big, and she took that for awhile and she decided she didn't want to do that any more.

TT: What about painting classes? Take anything like that?

PR: I took painting class this fall, and she would paint with me. Again, we kind of turned our lower kitchen into a . . . kind of studio, and she would paint.

TT: So, you took painting classes in the fall?

PR: Right.

TT: What kind of classes?

PR: Down at CU.

TT: Water color or oil . . . ?

PR: I started out with oil, but then I changed to acrylic because it got on my car . . . It smelled real bad, so I switched.

TT: Do you normally keep the painting supplies in that . . . area where the checkered board stuff is (checkered tiles on the floor of the butler's kitchen)?

PR: Yeah, we had it there for a long time, and then around

the holidays, I moved all that to the basement . . . cause we put coat racks and things in there for parties.

<u>TT</u>: What part of the basement do you recall moving the painting supplies to?

<u>PR</u>: I don't remember. I think Linda took all that down there . . . I don't remember where she put it.

<u>TT</u>: . . . How much stuff are we talking about?

<u>PR</u>: Well, I had a bunch of big canvasses . . . and a big easel, a big tall easel. And then like a white caddy kind of thing, like a plastic thing that I had a bunch of paint in. It would have been a lot of stuff to flip over.

<u>TT</u>: Did JonBenet ever sleepwalk during the night, did she ever have any problems with that?

<u>PR</u>: No.

<u>TT</u>: What about anybody in the family? Anybody in the family have any problems sleepwalking, getting up at night? You remember hearing Burke wandering around at night, John wandering around at night?

<u>PR</u>: I'd hear Burke get up and use the bathroom.

<u>TT</u>: Other than that, any sleepwalking problems with anybody?

<u>PR</u>: Huh uh.

<u>TT</u>: Nedra talked about JonBenet's pageant nightgown a little bit.

<u>PR</u>: Her what?

<u>ST</u>: May have described this as her Barbie nightgown or her traveling pageant nightgown.

A pink Barbie nightgown was found wrapped up in the blanket that was tucked up around JonBenet's body. Police were told it was her favorite nightgown. Experts believe it was a sign that someone close to her committed the murder, deliberately placing one of her special items near her body.

PR: She had a Barbie nightgown, but I don't know if we had a specific pageant nightgown.

TT: Was that special to her in any way, or just a nightgown like all the other little nightgowns?

PR: Well, she had this little kind of genie kind of . . . .

ST: Maybe that's it?

TT: Maybe that's what Nedra was talking about.

PR: It might be what she's talking about.

TT: Did she have a favorite nightgown that she took to all these pageants or anything like that or —?

PR: I don't remember that.

TT: On the pageants a little bit, about how many pageants was JonBenet in?

PR: Ah, I was trying to think of that the other night. The best I can remember, about eight or ten, total I think. I mean, we, you know, it wasn't, I mean we, it was just last year about this time that we were getting all of our clothes together.

TT: So she just started . . .

PR: It wasn't, she had done a little in Charlevoix when she was four, and she was, that would have been the summer before last. And then we did one, and we really, I don't think, oh, let's see she did one. We just started in the spring I think, because I just started learning about these in Colorado like in March of last year.

TT: Okay. In going to these eight or ten pageants, you notice anybody that was, and not only just towards JonBenet, but in general, notice anybody that was odd or out of the ordinary, anybody like that?

PR: . . . I mean I never noticed anybody, cause some of the same people sort of showed up at all of them . . . I mean they were sponsored by different people, but, you know, generally sort of the same girls went to these, and just, you know, parents. John didn't go to all of them . . . it was a Sunday afternoon kind of thing. She and I would go do that, and he and Burke would go fly or something, and maybe they'd come toward the end and watch the crowning, you know. But it really wasn't too much of a dad thing, but there were, you know, some dads there.

TT: I know JonBenet has quite a few photographs, some of them the professionally done ones. Do you have anybody that did most of her portraits?

PR: Well, just two fellows. One was this David Haskel in Denver. And I met him because I had been asked to go have a photograph made by him for the "Colorado Women's" . . . newspaper that, Debbie . . . Rosenberger is the editor, here in Boulder. So she took me down there one day, and I had my picture made and so then, you know, I like him and everybody down there. And actually the makeup artist down there told me that her little girls had done pageants. I said well, you know, where do you know about these, and she called and gave me names that day.

TT: So David was the photographer before the pageants got started, before the pageant circuits started up?

PR: Right. He was taking pictures of me for the Colorado Women's News or whatever the name of it.

TT: About how many photographs did David do, about? Did he photograph at all?

PR: Yeah, then I went down, I know at least twice, and had pictures made of her.

TT: And those were glamour shot ones? Were they, what kind of portraits were they?

PR: Well . . . he said bring a bunch of different clothes. So we bought costumes, blue jeans . . . .

TT: He did a whole portfolio.

PR: A bunch of stuff, yeah. And then he really had done most of them, but they all kind of looked alike . . . so, I got the name of this other fellow, Randy Simons, who did pageant pictures frequently. And so I called him at the last minute before we went to Michigan last year, and he had some time available. So, we went out a day with him, and he did a whole bunch of them too. He did some in the studio and then did some, we went to different places around.

TT: Were these still the glamour shot type stuff, or are they portrait studio type?

PR: Well, I don't know what you mean by glamour shot, I mean, they call them character shots, like one was Little Red Riding Hood and one was in a little sun dress, and one was barefoot, you know, those fun things. And then there was some in the studios like a model, those kinds of things . . . these were just for the pageant things because they would have, they had categories that you entered. For photogenic or whatever. So those were specifically taken for those.

TT: . . . You do like a pageant resume, is that right? Or, I don't know if that resume is the right word.

PR: Like an entry form or something?

TT: Yeah, entry form or something that kind of tell people about, who JonBenet, what her likes are?

PR: Yeah. You write down that, like what's their hobbies.

TT: Right. And one of those had something about a kitty game, that was her favorite game. You remember what that's about?

PR: Kitty?

TT: Yeah.

PR: To play kitty. Yeah, she likes to play kitty . . . she and Daphne like to, they love kittens. And we had some kittens up at the lake . . . and she and Daphne like to pretend they were kittens.

TT: And that's the game JonBenet really likes or something?

PR: She and Daphne played kitty. They'd walk around on all fours, you know.

ST: Patsy, once we were told that Burke, at times, would walk through the house whittling and that was something that apparently got on Linda Hoffman's nerves somehow, to clean up after him.

PR: Right.

ST: Was this consistent with his little pocketknife?

PR: Yeah.

ST: He'd walk through the house whittling and . . . (I'm showing Patsy a photo of a little red Swiss army knife.)

PR: Right. He had one we had gotten him in Switzerland, it had his name on it. Does this have his name on it?

ST: I don't know . . . I have spoken with Linda, and she's identified this suitcase as belonging to, well, not necessarily belonging to, but a suitcase that she has used and that John Andrew has used, and that John Andrew likely had left at your house.

PR: Right.

ST: Do you recognize that blue suitcase?

PR: Yes.

ST: Can you tell me anything about it?

PR: Well, just it's old hard Samsonite or whatever, you know.

ST: And was this something that John Andrew left at the 15th Street home while he went to school at CU?

PR: Yeah, yeah, that's to my recollection. Yeah, he moved out here with a bunch of stuff and then he left a lot of stuff at our house that he didn't want to take to the dorm.

ST: Do you know where he kept that in your home, or where you last saw that?

PR: No, I don't remember where I last saw it.

ST: Where would John Andrew store his other items and effects?

PR: Some of the things are in his room I think, in the closet, and I think he put a bunch of stuff down in the basement. A computer, he had a computer and a printer, and I think that might have been in the basement, too. It's pretty big, I think it was in the basement.

ST: Do you know what room in the basement he would have, his stuff was stored in?

PR: . . . I don't know now, there was so much stuff down there. I can, it could have been anywhere.

ST: I saw a Christmas photo and have been told that on the night of the 23rd, you gave several of those men that attended that party scarves as gifts.

PR: Right.

ST: (Shows Patsy a photo) And is this scarf from your home representative of one of the scarves that you gave as gifts?

PR: Ah, I gave some like that, but John also has one like that. And that could have been . . . his, I don't know. He usually kept his stuff back in his . . . I don't. But the ones I gave out were similar to that.

Crime scene detectives found the scarf on top of a sink-cabinet combination (the Ramseys called it the wet bar) cut into the wall on the first floor near the bottom of the spiral staircase.

Steve Thomas then questioned Patsy about flashlights. A heavy Maglite flashlight found on a kitchen counter is the suspected item used to bash JonBenet's head. Neither the flashlight nor the batteries inside had any fingerprints on it.

ST: Patsy, to the best of your memory, how many flashlights did your family own or keep in the house on the
15th Street?

PR: I don't know . . . Burke had some round ones, you
know.

ST: Did John, as a pilot or for the cars in the garage or
the house, did he, do you recall flashlights?

PR: I think we had kind of a big one, I don't know where
it was. I think John Andrew gave it to John for, I don't
know whether he gave it to him for the plane or not . . .

I think it was in that drawer that, that little, we
usually kept it, I think, in that drawer. Yeah.

*The drawer in question is in the wet bar sink-cabinet
combination near the bottom of the spiral staircase.*

ST: Maybe in this room somewhere in this vicinity?

PR: Yeah, and I think it was like a big black one, you
know.

ST: Well, is this picture, and that's not a good photo.
Would that be representative of the flashlight that
you are describing?

PR: Yeah, probably . . . .

ST: And for the purpose of the tape, I'm showing Patsy
a photograph depicting, is that the kitchen table?

TT: Kitchen counter.

ST: Kitchen counter, with several items, but
including what appears to be a flashlight on it?

PR: Yeah, it appears to be. I remember a big, he gave him
a big flashlight at one time, but I don't remember.

TT: Is it plastic material it's made out of?

PR: It seemed like it was heavy, I don't know.

ST: Patsy, before we move into the next section, we're
going to get into some hard stuff and you know we're

going to get into some hard stuff and move through this and conclude our day. But I want to ask you a question . . . as to how you perceive my role and Tom's role in this investigation?

PR: Well, I hope that you are tying to find out who killed my daughter. I mean, that is the bottom line, you know. We've got to find out who did this. I'm praying that your department is doing all they know how to do in your power to do that . . . .

ST: Well, Patsy, I can tell you this, since December 28th when I was asked to participate in this case, this has been in one aspect or another, my entire life, seven days a week, every waking thought . . . And to not speak out of school, but we are committed to finding the person who did this and . . . that is the truth, and that's entirely what we're working towards regardless of what you read in the tabloids or the newspaper.

This is the first time that we've had an opportunity to sit down with you, and I've chased leads all over this country. And I've sat down with people in jail cells, and I will continue to chase any lead with any merit. But, you know, you're in the bucket, and . . . we got to get you out of that bucket, if that's appropriate. And this was a start today to getting there, but let me move through some of these questions and regardless what you think of me personally, right now, or after today, I can tell you that I am committed, and I'll go to the ends of the earth to work this case and to solve this case. Whether the Ramseys hate me or like me or are indifferent to me . . . .

PR: I appreciate you saying that. I mean, I, music to my ears.

ST: If it's appropriate, Patsy, and you're not involved and you know we're still trying to determine whether you're in the bucket or out of the bucket . . . .

PR: What's the "in the bucket, out of the bucket" mean?

ST: Well, let me give you that analogy. There is a number of people, a list if you will, that we certainly have to include or exclude off that list. I can only appreciate what your life's been like for the last four months, but what we're working towards is the resolution that we'll reach in this thing. If this is somebody you knew, Patsy, if this offender was somebody that you knew, who would have had the best opportunity to have committed this crime by entering your home, writing the note inside your home, and I don't think it's a far reach to say that the note was written inside the house given the circumstance with the pad and the character comparison and so forth.

PR: I don't know what the . . . .

ST: The note was written from a pad inside the home.

PR: It was?

ST: Uh huh.

PR: Oh, I didn't know that.

The pad, a white legal pad with other doodles and writings from Patsy was found on top of a table in the first floor hallway near the spiral staircase and the wet bar sink-cabinet combination. On one page of the pad, police found the words "Mr. and Mrs.," plus the downstroke of what could be the beginning of an "R" which they believe is the beginning of a practice ransom note.

ST: And let me ask you this, if this was somebody who came into the home that you knew, who might this person have been? Who would have had the best opportunity, if it was somebody that you know to have done this?

PR: God, I don't know. I mean, I have asked myself that question a million times. I mean, you know, anybody that had keys and I'm trying to remember everybody. I think I, you know, the cleaning lady . . . or if somebody that could have gotten to a key, or if it was actually, I don't know how to pick locks, you know. And I don't know that the doors were locked or they could have, you know, walked right in. And you know, have you seen that little side flip door in the garage? That had been locked on the inside, one of those slide locks, you know. I mean, I don't know, if that was open, they could have gotten in.

ST: Patsy, as you've thought about this over the last four months, do you think that this incident, the death of JonBenet, started out as a premeditated act or do you think it was an event that got out hand by the offender?

PR: I don't think that, I don't know. I can't begin to guess why anybody would do this.

ST: Why do you think somebody did this, Patsy?

PR: I don't know.

ST: Do you think the person who did this, under any circumstances, would deserve a second chance?

PR: A second chance?

ST: Pity or forgiveness?

PR: Oh God, no . . . .

ST: What should happen to the person that we apprehend, Patsy?

PR: I don't know what you do to people that do this. But whatever it is, strongest punishment there is . . . .

ST: Patsy, did you write the note?

PR: No, I did not write the note.

ST: Is there any reason, Patsy, that your blatted print of your hand will be on that paper when it tests?

PR: I did not write the note and I don't, what's "blatted?"

ST: This (palm) portion of your hand.

PR: I don't know. I mean, I picked it up or touched it, it may be on there, but I did not write the note.

ST: You can appreciate, Patsy, and I watched on CNN, and I tried to follow this point closely. We know that we're not a large police department, and I'm certainly the first to ask for help when something beyond me, or to go to experts. And I'm a little concerned because we've gone to the experts, the FBI, and Secret Service and Interpol and they told us there's not an SBTC. And we're having trouble with this small foreign faction, and the FBI guys in Quantico say that there were steps taken to make this look like something that it wasn't.

PR: I'm losing you here. "We're having trouble with our small foreign faction," what's that?

ST: That was listed here in the note. That was some of the content of the note. But these guys at Quantico, Virginia, with the FBI who do this day in and day out, told me they told Tom, they said, "we're having trouble with the note." Because this is what we see in the movies, but not real life. And whoever did this, all that was done was done, and all that was made was made to . . . look as something that wasn't there. And they think that this was an accident and panic on someone's part and that there was no initial intent to harm, but that things got out of hand. And Patsy, I've got to ask you, and I'll ask you right now, did you participate in anyway in the death or the events after the death of JonBenet?

PR: No, absolutely not.

ST: Patsy, do you have any knowledge of John participating in this in any way?

PR: No.

ST: If that were the case, would you come forward and tell me?

PR: Of course, yes.

ST: Patsy, will you continue to cooperate with us in the future as it's appropriate, and certainly under the advice of your attorney, but at some point, if we could take you out of the bucket and off this list. This has been my life 100 hours a week, since December 28th, and come to the table and get on our side if we can positively and definitively eliminate you from involvement in this?

PR: Absolutely, I mean, I want to work with you. Every day and every minute if it will help.

ST: Let me ask you one other thing, Patsy. I'm no expert in handwriting, but I am concerned. And I'll share with you quite frankly that I'm concerned and I'm having trouble moving away from you as being potentially involved, because the handwriting experts say, "Steve, this means nothing to you because you're not an expert, but we're seeing some indications" that you may have authored that note. Is there any reason at all that you can think of, why these experts would say that?

PR: I, I mean, I don't, I'm not a handwriting person. I've given handwriting after handwriting after handwriting. You know, maybe it's a female that wrote the note. I mean, I don't know. I mean, I don't know how to analyze handwriting, but I'm sure they're doing the best they know how to do. But, I don't know what else to do, you know. I write like I write.

ST: Patsy, has everything that you've told us today been voluntary and truthful?

PR: Yes.

ST: Tom, that's all the questions I have.

TT: Patsy, is there anything else that you know of at this point and why it would point us towards a specific suspect?

PR: Not that I can think of right now.

TT: Anything that we haven't asked you that we need you to think of, that we need to talk about, anything at all?

PR: I don't know, but you think of anything else, call me . . . I mean really and truly, I want to, I mean you say you thought about it 100 hours a day, I've thought about it every waking, sleeping moment, you know. God, and I want to work with you, you know. John and I both. Please. You know, I can't tell you how much we want to work with you. So, anything else, ask me. What does it take to move past me?

ST: Well, let me ask you this, and I know (your attorney) Pat Burke's going to jump all over me. And I know, well, let me ask you his way. I'm not asking you to take one, but hypothetically, if you took a polygraph, how would you do?

PR: I'm telling you the truth. I would, I mean, I don't know how those things work, but if they tell the truth, I'm telling the truth. I've never ever given anybody a reason to think otherwise. I want to find out who did this, period.

ST: Does that mean, yes, you'd pass it?

PR: Yes, I would pass it. I'll take ten of them, I don't care, you know. Do whatever you want.

ST: Patsy, let me make this clear to you. As much as you feel, and certainly from the media.

PR: I don't care what the media says. I do not give one diddly-squat what the media says. Sorry, I didn't mean to interrupt you. I just want to find out who did this.

ST: I want to make it clear to you that you are not the only people that we're looking at in this thing. Despite what you may know and hear to the contrary . . . .

PR: Well, I, I mean I realize that you have to look at

us, you know. And that's fine. But . . . we're not involved in this . . . .

ST: I got to tell you what's, and let me just give you a little opinion on my part. It's been hard. Today we made great strides because we've got information direct from the source that we've never had before. I've had to fly to Atlanta and talk to your mom several times to check on everything from a blanket to a key to this and that. So I think that's why this has moved very slowly.

PR: Well, we want to get together, you know.

ST: I know, I know.

PR: And all that's water under the dam and let's start new. But I want to go together here. We got to, there's somebody out there and I don't want him to do it again, and heaven forbid, you know, if they are not found.

TT: Patsy, one of the things that I will ask, is if you would ever like to speak with us again . . . I'm available 24 hours a day. And anytime you would like to talk, get a hold of him . . . and the door is always open.

PR: I mean, I think you probably understand why we were a little gun shy, you know. And on the advice of these gentlemen, you know. We got to be a team here, all of us.

Now it was late on the afternoon of April 30th, 1997 and it was John Ramsey's (JR) turn. He also faced Detectives Steve Thomas (ST) and Tom Trujillo (TT). Since Patsy's interview had lasted so long — six hours — there was only 90 minutes left for him under terms of the interview agreement.

TOM TRUJILLO: I'm going to go right to December 25th. When was it you guys left the White's house that night?
JOHN RAMSEY: Uh, it was probably 8:30 p.m., quarter to nine when we left as I recall. So we probably got home about nine-ish, 9:15 . . . drove in the back through the alley into the garage. JonBenet had fallen fast asleep. I carried her inside and took her upstairs and put her in bed, put her on her bed. Uh, Patsy came up behind me, and then I went down to get Burke ready for bed, he was down in the living room, working on a toy he got, putting it together. I tried to get him to go to bed because we had to get up early the next morning, but he wanted to get this toy put together. So I worked with him on that for 10, 15 minutes probably, and then I took him up to bed and got his pajamas on, probably brushed his teeth, and then I went upstairs from there and got ready for bed. I read a little bit. The lights went out around ten-thirty-ish or 10:40.
TT: How did you sleep Christmas night?
JR: I took a Melatonin tablet because I wanted to get to sleep fast because we had to get up early,

and I slept through the night.

TT: Now is that Melatonin an over-the-counter or prescription drug?

JR: Over-the-counter.

TT: Are you taking any other medications right now?

JR: I have been on Paxil, and Klonopin, which are both prescription anti-depressants.

TT: Okay. Let's go back to the 25th. Get home about nine, nine-fifteen-ish, Burke's downstairs playing. Do you remember what kind of toy that was?

JR: Well, it was a plastic thing he had to assemble and he had some stickers, too, and, uh, he was intent on getting it done before he went to bed, so . . .

TT: Did you help Burke get into his pajamas that night?

JR: Yeah, like I do every night. He knew we had to get up at 5:30 a.m., so he went right to bed.

TT: Okay. You went upstairs and got ready for bed. Was Patsy already in bed by the time you went upstairs?

JR: She was in bed when I went to go to bed, I remember that.

TT: Did JonBenet ever wake up when you carried her upstairs?

JR: No, she was sound asleep.

TT: Did Burke follow you guys in, or did you have to go back down to the car to get him out of the car?

JR: No, I think he came in, I don't think he was asleep.

TT: Okay. Were you in JonBenet's room when Patsy got her bedclothes on?

JR: No, I don't think so, not that I can remember.

TT: What was JonBenet wearing when you carried her upstairs?

JR: She had on a white sweater with a silver star and black pants and black vest, and that what's she had on that night.

TT: Okay. Did Patsy put her in her bedclothes then?

JR: Uh huh.

TT: Before you fell asleep that night, did you hear Burke making any sounds, noises, or anything like that? Any odd noises or sounds coming from the house at all?

JR: No.

TT: And Burke went to bed in the bed he normally sleeps in?

JR: Yeah.

TT: What about JonBenet's door, is it normally open or closed at night?

JR: It's usually partly open.

TT: About how far is partially opened?

JR: Just enough to let some light in.

TT: Does JonBenet normally sleep with a night light or any type of lighting in her room?

JR: Well, sometimes we'll leave the night light on, the bathroom there's a little night light.

TT: Does she have one of those plug-into-the-wall type night lights in her bedroom?

JR: Uh, not that I recall.

TT: Before Burke went to bed that night, after he got his little toy together, did Burke have anything to eat at all?

JR: No, I don't think so.

TT: Okay. Did you guys get out anything to eat that night?

JR: No, I didn't, and I don't think Patsy did.

TT: You don't think Patsy did?

JR: My wife. I don't think she did, no. I didn't.

TT: Okay. Do you know if JonBenet normally sleeps with the jewelry that she has on?

JR: She had a little ring that she usually wore. If I

would put her to bed, I would normally take off her necklace. Uh, that ring was fairly permanent, she wore it at all times.

TT: Does JonBenet normally . . . go to bed with the TV on?

JR: It was always kind of a negotiating point. She liked to watch movies, and it would put her to sleep, so sometimes she would do that, but I don't think that was the case that night because usually we'd have to go down and turn it off before she went to sleep. Far as I know she stayed asleep.

TT: Never woke up as far as you know?

JR: Not that I know of.

TT: Did Patsy pull back the bedcovers or anything, or just lay her right on top of the bedspread of hers?

JR: I don't remember exactly, but I would suspect the bed was not made Christmas morning, I don't remember exactly.

TT: Do you know about JonBenet's normal bedtime routines, say other than the 25th when she's sound asleep and you had to carry her up? What's the normal routines for JonBenet to go to sleep?

JR: Uh, well, we'd usually try to get the kids in the bed by 8:30 p.m. or 9 p.m. and sometimes we'd read to them, and sometimes they'd want to watch a movie and fall asleep then. They usually go up, get their pajamas on, brush their teeth, then get in bed.

TT: You guys were heading out pretty early the next morning?

JR: Uh huh.

TT: About what time did you guys plan on leaving the house?

JR: We needed to leave by 6:30 a.m., because we were going to take off about 7:00 a.m., because we were meeting John and Melinda (his children from his first marriage) in Minneapolis. The alarm was set for 5:30 a.m. I woke up a little before that, before the alarm went off.

TT: John, about what time do you think you fell asleep on Christmas night?

JR: Well, I think it was 10:30 p.m. or 10:40 p.m. probably somewhere in that range.

TT: Okay. Again before you fell asleep, do you recall hearing any noises or sounds in the house?

JR: No.

TT: Normally, do you do a walk-through to kind of make sure the doors are locked?

JR: No, I don't normally. The normal doors that we used to go in and out of the house were the garage door, the door to the garage and the door out in the hallway, the back hallway, and I would usually look to see if that door is locked, because that was the typical one the kids went in and out of.

TT: The back one out by the study area?

JR: Right, TV room.

TT: You don't recall whether it was open or closed or anything?

JR: No, not specifically.

TT: Normally, any other doors left unlocked?

JR: The only door that is normally left unlocked intentionally is the door in the garage.

TT: Between the house and the garage?

JR: Right.

TT: Who fell asleep first, do you think — you or Patsy?

JR: Uh, I don't know for sure. I suspect Patsy did because she usually does, but I don't know. I didn't notice.

TT: Did she stay up reading that night at all?

JR: No, not that I recall.

TT: Did Patsy talk about having any problems falling

asleep or taking anything to fall asleep, anything like that?

JR: No.

TT: You guys didn't have the alarm system on at all that day?

JR: No, we didn't. We haven't used it in a long time. Uh, it got set off accidentally, and all the sirens are inside the house, and it's . . . "A," I guess we would have a false sense of security, but, "B," if that thing ever went off accidentally or you know without fault, it would give me a heart-attack, I mean this was a horrible sound. I never liked that system particularly. We left it hooked up in my mind primarily because of fire detection and monitoring. As far as I know the fire alarm part always worked . . . .

TT: How did Burke feel about going up to Charlevoix? Did he talk to you about that at all?

JR: Uh, no, actually. I think, well I don't remember. I guess it was really my idea. I wanted to spend Christmas up there and I didn't want to have to haul all the presents for the kids up, so we just had Christmas in Boulder and was going up the next day, and, uh, Patsy wasn't real excited about the idea because the winter can be kind of nasty up there. We've never spent Christmas up there and that was kind of my plan.

TT: It sounded like Patsy didn't really want to go up, and had a hassle about going up to Charlevoix . . . ?

JR: No, no, not really. She was not too crazy about the idea, but . . . .

TT: She kind of came around towards the end?

JR: Yeah, yeah, she, uh, in the end was kind of looking forward to it because we were going to have the kids up there and it was going to be fun.

TT: John, what did you wear over to the Whites' house that night, do you recall?

JR: Uh, I think I had like a black knit sweater shirt kind of thing, uh, and probably wore some khaki colored pants, but I don't remember specifically. I guess I wore some kind of pants.

STEVE THOMAS: John, let me just make sure I have this right. You arrived home from the Whites approximately what time on the night of the 25th?

JR: Uh, 8:30 p.m., quarter to nine.

ST: And you carried JonBenet up from the car that was in the garage, and she did not awaken at anytime? Then you placed her upon her bed, is that right?

JR: Uh huh.

ST: Was Patsy with you?

JR: I think Patsy came up behind me, and the normal routine is that JonBenet sat behind me in the car, so I got her out of that side, and Patsy kind of got Burke out and going into the house. Uh, then she came up. I think she came up either right behind me or shortly right behind me.

ST: Were you in the room when Patsy changed JonBenet into the clothes she wore that night to bed, her pajamas?

JR: Uh, I don't think I was, no, I don't . . . .

ST: So, you can't recall with any certainty what JonBenet went to sleep in that night?

JR: No.

ST: And then you stayed up what length of time after coming out of JonBenet's room?

JR: Well I probably got Burke to bed somewhere between 9:30 and ten to ten, probably a quarter to ten, and then I went right upstairs to bed. I think lights were out about 10:30 p.m., 10:40 p.m.

ST: And after you put JonBenet to bed, until the time you went to bed and put the lights out, did you ever return to that room again that evening?

JR: No.

ST: And did you sleep the entire night from 10:30 p.m. or 10:40 p.m. until the next morning?

JR: Uh huh.

ST: And did you ever arise, or awaken and leave the bed at any time during that night?

JR: No, not that I recall.

ST: And it was then the following morning that you and Patsy got up and first discovered that JonBenet was missing, is that correct?

JR: Well, I'd gotten up at a little before the alarm went off, 5:30 a.m., 5:25 a.m., and went and took a shower, was getting dressed and, uh, heard Patsy screaming, and I ran downstairs and I think probably intercepted her maybe in the second floor landing, I don't remember exactly, but she showed me the note and . . . .

ST: Did she show the note on the second floor landing?

JR: I don't remember, uh, it seems like I came downstairs, but I think she was running up and I was running down, I think, as best as I can remember, the note was still down on the first floor.

TT: You shaved, showered, cleaned up. You're out of the shower by the time you hear Patsy scream. (On) which set of stairs is the note, front or back?

JR: Back (the spiral staircase).

TT: Is that kind of normal, the set of stairs you guys use to go up and down?

JR: Yeah.

TT: Okay. You run downstairs and about where was Patsy at when she was running up the stairs?

JR: Well, I don't remember exactly, but I think she was

kind of either coming up the spiral staircase or was up fully. I just kind of remember, kind of meeting her.

TT: You guys meet on the landing, what happened after that?

JR: Well, I'm, it's a lot of screaming going on around that, but we saw the note and read the first part. Ah, I think I might have run upstairs to look in JonBenet's room. At one point I laid it on the floor and spread it out so I could read it real fast without having to sit and read it. At some point we checked Burke, I think I checked Burke. Patsy asked what should we do, and I said to call the police, and she called 911.

TT: Patsy called 911.

JR: Yeah. I remember she was on the phone. I think that was when I was looking at the note again, which was on the floor and I was in the back hallway.

TT: Do you recall whether JonBenet's door was opened or closed?

JR: I didn't notice.

TT: Okay. When you went to check on Burke, was his door opened or closed?

JR: I can't say, I don't know.

TT: Was Patsy screaming in a high-pitched scream, shrill scream, controlled scream, how loud did she scream?

JR: It was a scream of panic . . . like something was badly wrong.

TT: Okay. When you checked on Burke, did he, was he disturbed at all by that, did he wake up at all by that scream?

JR: No, he was asleep still.

TT: Okay. Hadn't moved at all from where he was at? And you checked on Burke before the 911 call? Is that how you did, you went to JonBenet's bedroom and then to Burke's? How'd that all play out?

JR: I don't remember, I mean it was so dramatic. I think I checked on him fairly quickly, but I don't remember exactly the sequence.

TT: Let's move back downstairs. Patsy makes the 911 call. She talks through that on the kitchen phone?

JR: Uh huh.

TT: Which is right around the corner from the floor that you talk about where you were reading the note?

JR: Right, uh huh.

TT: What happened after Patsy called the police?

JR: Well, I think she called the Fernies and the Whites and just screamed at them to come over.

TT: Okay. What happened after that?

JR: Ah, well, it wasn't very long before the uniformed officer (Boulder Police Officer Rick French) showed up. And I met him, I remember talking to him in the hallway, the front hallway. And I said our daughter's missing and I remember him saying did she run away, and I said she was only six years old. And at one point, I don't remember if I had the note in my hand or Patsy brought it, but I showed him the note. And then some people started to arrive.

JR: The first officer that was there, which I think was Rick French, asked us to stay in the sun room.

They set up a recorder on the phone and started to talk with us, you know, about what, who could have done this. We spent some time talking about what I should do when I answered the phone and there was some confusion. The note said "I'm going to call between eight and 10 tomorrow." Not sure if tomorrow was today or actually tomorrow. But I was prepped to answer the phone.

TT: You woke up Burke and got him out of the house, how did that all come about?

JR: Well, when the Whites came, Burke was still asleep. And we decided it was best for him to go away to the Whites' house. I got him up and Fleet took him over to their house. And they had guest company there, so there was somebody there to watch the kids.

TT: Did you help Burke get dressed that morning?

JR: I don't remember how Burke got dressed.

TT: And did you take him over to the Whites or did somebody else do that?

JR: I think Fleet took him over, as I recall. I didn't.

TT: What happens throughout the day after that?

JR: I remember (Detective Linda Arndt) took me aside, and she went through what I should do when we talked to the caller and I must insist that I talk to JonBenet and that we need until 5 o'clock to raise the money. I'd actually arranged for the money. Ah, and I think we had by that time started to wonder if one of the housekeepers (Linda Hoffman-Pugh) might be involved. We waited until past 11 and then Linda said, why don't you take someone and look through the house and see if there's anything you notice that's unusual? Fleet was standing there and said he'd go with me. And we went down to the basement, went into the train room, which is (where) the train set is, and that's really the only window that would let in entrance into the basement. And actually I'd gone down there earlier that morning, into that room, and the window was broken, but I didn't see any glass around, so I assumed it was broken last summer. I used that window to get into the house when I didn't have a key. But the window was open, about an eighth of an inch, and I just kind of latched it. So I went back down with Fleet, we looked around for some glass again, still didn't see any glass. And I told him that I thought that the break came from when I did that last summer. Then I went from there into the (wine) cellar. Pulled on the door, it was latched. I reached up and unlatched it, and then I saw the white blanket.

TT: When you saw the white blanket, was JonBenet completely covered up? How was she laying there?

JR: She was laying on the blanket, and the blanket was kind of folded around her legs. And her arms were tied behind her head, and there was some pieces of black tape on her lips, and her head was cocked to the side.

Detective Trujillo showed concern for Ramsey at this point. But John assured him, "I'm all right."

TT: After you found JonBenet, where was Fleet at when that happened?

JR: I don't remember. Fleet was behind me, but I don't remember him from that point to when I brought her upstairs. He might have been right behind me.

TT: Tell me step-by-step how you picked her up.

JR: I found her and I . . . the first hope, of course, is that she's okay. I took the tape off her lips, and her lips were blue. And I tried to untie her hands and her arms. She was stiff, and so I was afraid that she was gone, and so I just picked her up and screamed, and then I went upstairs and laid her down on the floor . . . (someone) said she's dead.

TT: Okay. Tell me, you talked about you picked her up.

JR: I picked her up, you know, under her arms.

TT: So, she's up and down.

JR: Uh huh.

TT: Okay. You carry her upstairs that way?

JR: Right.

ST: Let me follow up on this John. John, I'm very sensitive to how tough this is, and you'll appreciate that we need to get through this. On that trip to the basement, shortly after 1 p.m. on the 26th, Fleet showed you the window, the broken basement window.

JR: No, I, I think, was the first one to enter the room. I said, you know, "This window's broken, but I think I broke it last summer. It just hasn't been fixed." And it was opened, but I closed it earlier and we got down on the floor and looked around for some glass just to be sure that it hadn't been broken again.

ST: And Fleet had talked about earlier being down there, I think alone at one point, and discovering that window. When you say that you found it earlier that day and latched it, at what time of day was that?

JR: I don't know. I mean it would have been probably, probably before 10 o'clock.

ST: Was that prior to Fleet's first trip down?

JR: I didn't know he was in the basement. I didn't know that. I mean other than that trip with me.

ST: And on the trip that you latched the window, were you alone when you went down and latched the window?

JR: Yep.

ST: And on this, what I'm assuming is only your second trip to the basement on the 26th with Fleet, how much time did you spend in the basement before moving to the cellar room door?

JR: Not very much time. A minute maybe, or less, probably less than that.

ST: And when you moved to that cellar room door to open the door, did you move the tag on the top of the door?

JR: Yeah.

ST: And did you open the door?

JR: Yeah.

ST: And was the light on or off?

JR: I think it was off.

ST: And did you turn the light on?

JR: Probably, I don't remember specifically turning it on, but probably would have, it's a dark room.

ST: From the time you opened the door of the cellar room (to) when you discovered your daughter, was this a fraction of a second or a matter of seconds, give me an idea?

JR: Instant. I mean, as soon as I opened the door I saw the white blanket. And I knew, I just saw a blanket, and I knew that was our . . . you know.

ST: And was it then you instantaneously opened the door, saw the blanket, you may or may not have turned the light on?

JR: Uh huh.

ST: You don't know, in all fairness?

JR: In fact, I don't remember.

ST: Okay. And then you moved to your daughter. Did Fleet accompany you into that room?

JR: I don't remember him being there. But I remember later thinking I didn't hear Fleet scream out or call for help or say anything at all, and that frankly seemed odd, but I might have just been out of my mind, I don't know. I don't remember, I don't remember him, I mean once I went to that door . . . and when I took those stairs, I don't remember where Fleet was.

ST: Was it fairly immediate in which you removed the tape and the binding?

JR: I immediately moved the tape.

ST: The tape first?

JR: Yeah.

ST: And do you recall if you just simply discarded the tape on to the ground?

JR: I just, yeah, I just, I don't know what I did with it, but I just discarded it.

ST: And when you say you undid the binding, was that a knotted fashion around both wrists?

JR: Yeah. I tried to get it completely undone. So when I took her upstairs, it was still partially around her wrist.

ST: John, again, how was she positioned on the blanket, was her head to the south end of the cellar room?

JR: Ah, her head was, well, the door is on the east side, and her head was going towards the inside of the cellar. So, her feet were closest to the door. The door opens this way, her hand was here.

ST: And was the line of sight immediate from where you opened the door?

JR: Virtually, I mean. Just as soon as I opened the door I saw a white blanket.

ST: And was it almost simultaneous to removing the tape and bindings that you picked up your daughter and moved out of that room with her?

JR: Not simultaneous. I mean, I bent over and I felt her cheeks and just talked to her, and I picked her up quickly and took her upstairs.

TT: John, again I'm not sure if I got the sequence right. You talked about you screamed out also, and Patsy talked about that, too. Does that mean when you first went in through the door?

JR: No, this was when I was carrying her upstairs, as I came out of the door. I just remember him (Fleet White) screaming.

TT: Did he say anything, or was he just . . . ?

JR: No, he was just screaming for attention, I guess. As I was . . . .

ST: And at that point, and certainly I can understand this, you don't know necessarily where Fleet was positioned. Do you recall coming out of the room and seeing Fleet at all?

JR: Coming . . . I don't remember that.

ST: Okay. Do you recall when you went up the stairs, Fleet being upstairs at that point?

JR: No, I don't remember. At the point I saw the blanket until I laid her on the floor, I don't remember where Fleet was.

ST: And did you ever make a second trip, you never went back down to the basement, is that correct?

JR: That's correct.

ST: And on the morning of the 26th, you made one trip alone to the basement, and it was only on the second trip with Fleet that you shortly thereafter went to this basement room?

JR: Right.

ST: Okay. When you had previously broken that basement window to gain entry to the home when you had been locked out, can you approximate what month that was?

JR: Well, I think it was last summer because Patsy was up at the lake all summer, and it would have been July or August probably, somewhere in that time frame.

ST: Did you remove that grate and get down into the window well?

JR: Uh huh.

ST: And what did you use to break the pane?

JR: Ah, I don't remember. Might have been my foot, I don't know.

ST: Okay. You reach in, I'm assuming, unlatched it and gain entry through that small window?

JR: Yeah.

ST: Did you then replace the grate onto that window well?

JR: Oh, I probably would have done it that night.

ST: Did you remove that whole grate off the well, to jump down there and get in?

JR: Ah, probably. I don't remember.

ST: Is there any reason that window went unrepaired?

JR: No. I mean it's, Patsy usually took care of those things, and I just rarely went to the basement, so it just, I guess, got overlooked. Although she did think that she asked the cleaning lady's husband to fix it over Thanksgiving when they were doing some repair work there, but I don't know if that's ever been confirmed whether he fixed it or not.

ST: And you mentioned when you went down in the morning, the 26th, and it was unlatched, did that strike you as odd or did you bring that to anybody's attention?

JR: I, I don't know. Yeah, I think it probably struck me as a little odd, but it wasn't, I mean sometimes that window would be open because the basement got hot, or one of those windows would be opened. So it wasn't . . . .

ST: Particularly unusual?

JR: . . . Out of the ordinary, but, that is, I thought about it.

ST: Okay. Sir, I have a question regarding the security of the home on the night of the 25th, which led to the morning of the 26th, and I don't know if you've had an opportunity to review the police reports that were provided to you?

JR: I scanned them.

ST: Did those, what you read in those, are those factual?

JR: Well . . . A couple of areas where I think there was some misunderstanding or wasn't correct. I did not check every door in the house the night before. I don't think I checked any door. I think I was tired, wanted to go to bed, get up early. Ah, and I think the other part I noted in there was they said I read to both kids before I went to bed, and that did not happened. What happened was the kids went to bed and then I read to myself in bed.

ST: John, let me ask you this. Do you attribute that to simply an officer's error in recollection or might you have said that and . . . .

JR: I wouldn't have said that. I think it might have been, maybe the way I said it, that was misinterpreted, but we clearly did not read to the kids that night. JonBenet was asleep, we wanted Burke to get to sleep, so we could get them up early the next morning, so . . . .

ST: You mentioned on the morning on the 26th after the note was discovered, certainly you wanted to check on your son, and you went and he was in his room unharmed. And it was a conscious decision or did you simply want to get back to Patsy, to let him sleep through this episode?

JR: Well, I think he was asleep and that was the best place for him to be for awhile.

ST: And then later in the morning, and I'm guessing and correct me if I'm wrong, but it's 7 or 8 o'clock at some point, you went up and awakened him, and he ultimately went to the White's home. Did he stay in his room, was he undisturbed this whole time?

JR: Uh huh.

ST: Okay.

JR: I think so.

ST: What phone did Patsy use to call for help that morning?

JR: The kitchen phone.

ST: And do you recall, and you only speak for yourself, can you tell me the movement of the note? Was it lying on the floor and did you leave it undisturbed, or did you grab it in your hand and . . . ?

JR: . . . I grabbed it in my hand and then remember specifically laying it out on the floor so I could read the whole thing really fast and then at one point we gave it to the first fellow who came in. And then I think . . . I lost track after that.

ST: You said you were able to briefly read the police reports that you were provided. At one point, I think that Detective Arndt notes that you were unaccounted for that morning. Is there any time the morning of the 26th, John, that you left the house?

JR: No.

ST: Okay. It would be no reason, a neighbor or anybody else, would account for you outside the home that morning?

JR: No. I didn't leave the house until we left it for good at almost 1:30.

ST: John, do you know who this person is from Shreveport who has communicated with us and is indicating that they're a friend of yours?

JR: Huh uh.

Boulder police had received an anonymous letter dated January 27, 1997 and postmarked from Shreveport, La. The anonymous writer claimed to be the mother of a little girl involved in beauty pageants and said she knew John and Patsy Ramsey. She told police the Ramseys had to be looked at as serious suspects in the death of JonBenet.

ST: And again, just for the tape, that was a . . . .

JR: No, no I do not.

ST: Okay.

JR: I have lots of new friends I didn't know about.

ST: Certainly, and am I correct in assuming then that this woman from Tucson is in that same category?

JR: Bullshit. I have no clue who she is.

In the weeks after JonBenet's death, a woman from Tucson had come forward to say she and John Ramsey had been lovers.

John was then asked if he had any suspicions about any employees at his computers sales company, Access Graphics.

JR: Certainly one of the first persons that we mentioned I think was this (man's name deleted), who was discharged and left in a very disgruntled manner. There was somebody out of our tech support group, who was really a real strange case. Three or four really strange people that we've fired, terminated.

ST: John, can you think back and — I'll tell you I feel in some aspects I know your life better than my own family's — but as far back as (your previous companies), the mergers to (form) Access, is there anybody that's been stepped on, squeezed out . . . ?

JR: Well, the, ah, and if I go way back to the early 80's, I guess, we formed a company with a group out of Syracuse, and ran for a couple of years. Closed down and a business loss, a hundred and fifty thousand, maybe. And that was not a pleasant party because it was some hurt feelings. That could be one that goes back for 25 years.

ST: John, this $118,000 (the amount of money demanded in the ransom note), do you believe that to be tied to your 1995 bonus paid in '96?

JR: Well . . . that occurred to me later as I started to think about what that number meant, and I thought, gee, that might have been the net amount of my bonus. I didn't even know that until we went back and looked. And that was paid in February of '96, and was $118,223 or something like that. And I think that's a plausible place where that number could have come from, and it certainly showed up in every pay stub of mine from then on, through the rest of the year. It was deferred compensation, so separate out of your gross pay . . . and Father Rol also said that the 18th Psalm was a very vengeful Psalm. And those are the two logical theories I've heard for that number.

ST: Tom, I want to keep going here for a minute, if you're okay with that. John, as our time is short you are certainly aware that we're going to put some hard questions to you today. There is no doubt about that, and we got through it with Patsy and her attorney and we'll do the same here. But one of the things we ask ourselves is, if this was an outside intruder who came into the home and did this, who would bear such a hatred or a grudge? Certainly along those lines, as you know, and my preference would have been to ask you and have done it discreetly. But we were made aware of an infidelity of your marriage to Lucinda, and Lucinda shared that. And that (other woman) has been a person that we have not been able to find. Is that somebody that you would share with us?

JR: Yeah. Her name was (woman's name deleted). This was in the late 70's. She worked for us, for me, for three or four years I guess . . . . The company . . . was called Southern Peripherals Instruments. And she worked for that company. We had her as a secretary. And that company, I don't remember exactly when we closed it down, but it would have been, well, let's see, kind of would been '79 or '80, 'cause I think it was before Patsy and I got married.

ST: Do you have any idea if she is still in the Atlanta area?

JR: I don't know . . . it's really one of those things your regret in life . . . you heard of the movie Fatal Attraction? I didn't go see it because I think I could have written it.

ST: With that said, John, is she somebody that bears further inquiry in this case?

JR: It seems like a stretch since it's been so long. But if I think back in my past and there was people that I've angered, certainly I angered her.

ST: If we continue to have some sort of working relationship, is that something that, certainly through your attorney, you might assist us with?

JR: I'd be happy to.

ST: John, let me ask you, quite frankly. Have there been any infidelities on Patsy's part in your marriage that would have led to bitter feelings or . . . ?

JR: No.

ST: How about on your part?

JR: No.

ST: Is that a definitive no?

JR: Absolutely.

ST: John, I've noticed you made a comment on the 26th about this being an inside job. But if this was someone that you know who did this, who would have had the best opportunity to have come into your home and move throughout your home and write a note on a pad in your home, to have done this?

JR: Well, that morning we had certainly focused on the cleaning lady. I mean she had free reign of our house, she had a key, she had . . . worked there on Thanksgiving weekend when we were out of town. There had been some very bizarre behavior. Shortly before we left town, she called and asked Patsy if she could borrow some money, and Patsy said yes. And then she called, I think it was

Saturday, and was crying and had had a fight with her sister, and Patsy said her sister was really mean and she hadn't paid her rent and she threw her out of the house. And, ah, that was my first suspicion. And based on the room was just such an out-of-the-way place that, I just don't think anybody could have walked in off the street and . . . normally it's full of Christmas stuff. I mean, it's just packed — you couldn't get in because we store all our Christmas stuff so, you know, it's . . . ah. I mean, based on what I understand there was a practice note and all of that. Somebody obviously spent some time there, and I guess found their way around the house the same time, but my, I mean, my theory is that someone came in through the basement window. Because (there) was a new Samsonite suitcase sitting right under the window, and you could have gotten into the house without that, but you couldn't have gotten out that window without something to step on. And to even have known those windows were there, wouldn't have been obvious to somebody who just was walking by.

ST: You talking about the window in the back was not obvious?

JR: Yeah. No, I mean, yeah, it's not obvious, but that is to me because that is the way to get into the house and we know that the grate could be pulled off and the windows were not painted shut and, you know, it's just I guess that's why we never gave much thought about . . . .

When I went down and looked around the house that morning, and I think I'd made a statement . . . that all the doors were locked and I had checked, I believe, every door on the first floor. And they were — appeared to be locked.

ST: So the morning of the 26th do you recall checking all the doors, and they were locked?

JR: I believe I checked all the first-floor doors, yeah. I did go out once. I went out to the door that leads into the garage to see if it was locked because there's a bunch of boxes piled in front of it and you couldn't get to it from the inside of the garage. So I did, in fact, go out of the house once, which would have been for, you know, half a minute.

ST: And that was from where to where?

JR: I went out the side door around to the back of the garage to see if that garage door into the garage was locked.

ST: And then immediately back into the house?

JR: Yeah.

ST: And that wasn't an excursion that exceeded 30 seconds?

JR: No, at max.

ST: John, one of the things, as you know better than anybody, at some point if you're not involved in this, we've got to take you out of the bucket. And you've been in it for four months and you certainly know (the reason) why you're in that bucket is you're in the house, and I don't need to say anything more than that. But — and I asked this question of Patsy and ... I'm not asking you to take one, but if you were to take a polygraph, how would you do?

JR: Well, what I've been told is that I felt tremendous guilt after we lost JonBenet, because I hadn't protected her, like I failed as a parent. And I was told that with that kind of emotion you shouldn't take a lie detector test because you did have that guilt feeling. So I don't know about the test, but I did not kill my daughter if that's what you want to ask me. She was the most precious thing to me in the world. So if the lie detector test is correct and it was done correct, I'd pass it 100 percent.

ST: John, let me tell you this. I feel like an encyclopedia salesman sometimes because I've gone to a number of people in this thing and it's hard to convince someone to take a polygraph test. But I've been successful on occasion with some people that I've been concerned about, and used what I've been told is one of the ten best FBI calligraphers to do that. And I'll ask you point blank, at some point in this, would you take a polygraph?

JR: I would be insulted if you ask me to take a polygraph test, frankly. I mean if you haven't talked to enough people who are telling you what kind of people we are. You guys, I mean, I will do whatever these guys (the attorneys) recommend me to do. We are not the kind of people you're trying to make us out to be. It's a tragic misdirection I think that you're on. And the sooner we get off of that, the sooner we'll find who killed JonBenet.

ST: And John, let me tell you my simple heartfelt response to that . . . decisions are made at pay grades above ours —

JR: I understand.

ST: — what is sometimes done and not done. But we're dedicated to pursuing the right path and the truth in this thing. And you're absolutely right, John, in that I have talked, and you know I've talked to friends and neighbors and family and associates.

JR: You're extremely thorough.

ST: Well, I take that as a compliment. But if you didn't do this, I'll go to bat as I did with John Andrew (Ramsey's college-age son by his previous marriage). I exhausted (inquiries into) John Andrew and made sure there was no way that he could have got a flight between Atlanta (and Boulder) in the middle of the night, and to the point where I checked flight schedules and passenger lists. I'll do the same for you, so I'm not taking it personally, because I don't think it's directed at me as to —

JR: It's directed into the direction that the effort has been made, from my visibility. And all I see is a lot of effort and time and money being spent to try and categorize Patsy and I as child abusers and that can't be further from the truth.

ST: Well, John, I'll tell you this. I've sat in a North Carolina jail cell with a suspected child serial killer — hoping that I could put him in Boulder on December 26th. So there's two sides to that.

JR: I know that.

ST: John, certainly I'm not pointing a finger at you. But the FBI, these guys who do it everyday, say, "Steve, there were clearly steps taken in this case to make this look like something it wasn't." This is how it happens in the movies, it is not how it happens in real life. And they said all that was done . . . was made to look like something that wasn't there. And one theory, at least, is that something happened in the house that may have been accidental that turned to panic that turned to cover-up. And . . . .

JR: That's a false theory.

ST: Okay.

JR: That's baloney . . . anyone that knows Patsy and I can tell you that that is total bullshit. Pardon my French.

ST: John, are you involved in any way in the death of your daughter?

JR: No.

ST: Are you involved in any way with the preparation of that note?

JR: No.

ST: I'm not making this adversarial because I have a great deal of affinity for you personally. Whether you hate me or like me or are indifferent to me, I will make the commitment to you as I have from the start that I will go to the ends of the earth to find the truth about your daughter. And I don't care if it was you, or whoever it was, that is what I'm committed to do.

JR: And I'm delighted to hear that. I mean, I want the killer of my daughter found. And I will do the same thing. I will spend every dime I have, I will spend every minute of time I have if that's what it takes to find who killed her.

ST: Well, let's work on getting you out of the bucket, if that's the right thing to do, and go the right direction.

TT: We're not just focused on you and Patsy — there's a whole list of people. We've got to get people off the list, is solely what we're doing.

JR: Okay.

ST: Everything as far as we're concerned today John — has it been freely, voluntarily offered and truthful?

JR: Yeah.

ST: Well, you know my commitment. And, John, I can tell you this, seven days a week . . . since this thing started and that's a hundred-hour work week we're putting in.

TT: John, we're going to have back up here for just a second. Did Patsy get up and shower and dress that morning?

JR: Well, she got up, I mean she was downstairs. I don't remember if she took a shower or not. She was, I think she was dressed when I saw her first.

TT: Do you recall whether she had make-up on, hair

brushed out and everything, when she came up and was yelling at you?

JR: I don't remember . . . .

TT: Okay. And let's hop back to the grate for just a second, 'cause I picked the grate up, it's really heavy, I mean fairly heavy. Picked it up, moved it out of the way, kind of hopped down, I mean first peeked into that window, hopped down into that window well, you ended up, have to kick the window, break the window somehow, reach in and unlatch it. How far of a drop is it (to the basement floor), or is it difficult I should say to drop from the window well . . . .

JR: It's probably, I don't know, four feet maybe, five feet.

TT: Okay. But on the outside you've got that kind of skinny narrow window well. Did you have any difficulty sliding into that or sliding down the wall?

JR: Yeah, well, as I recall, I did it at night and I had a suit on, and I took my suit off and did it in my underwear. But, it's not easy, I mean, you can get in that way, you get dirty, but.

TT: It's not a graceful way to get in?

JR: No, no.

TT: It's difficult because of the angles?

JR: Right.

ST: Tom, let me just ask John this. Do you sit down and slide through, buttocks first if you will, through a window like that or, do you recall how you went through the actual window, John?

JR: I don't . . . remember. Seems like, I mean, I don't remember, but I think I would probably have gone in feet first.

ST: Feet first, backwards?

JR: Yeah.

ST: And when you went through in your underwear, were you wearing shoes ... ?

JR: I still had my shoes on, yeah.

ST: And were those with a suit, were they business shoes?

JR: They were probably, probably those shoes.

ST: Okay. And what are those shoes?

JR: Business shoes ... shoes that I wear with a suit, just a pair of business shoes, dress shoes.

TT: John, when you went down in the basement the first time and found the broken window, it was unlocked, you latched it. Did you notice if the room was overly cold or anything like that?

JR: No, it wasn't. I didn't notice that it was.

TT: Okay. And you were fully dressed when you went through the house?

JR: Yeah, I'm sure I was, yeah.

TT: You remember any lights on in the basement when you went down the first time?

JR: Ah, no, not specifically I don't. I mean, I don't remember if any were on the first time.

TT: Do you remember turning on lights?

JR: Well, I would have had to see my way around. I'm sure I did.

TT: John, would you be willing to come back at a later date, time, to help us with this, go over anything else we need to go over?

JR: I think, hopefully, we've given you every piece of information that we have, and will certainly continue to do so.

Despite offers of cooperation, it was some 14 months before John and Patsy Ramsey sat down once again with investigators on June 23, 24 and 25, 1998, at the Broomfield, Colorado, Police Department.

The Ramseys had refused in the interim to be interviewed by any of the Boulder police, claiming they were biased against them.

Patsy Ramsey (PR) was questioned by Tom Haney (TH), an investigator with the Denver District Attorney's office and Trip DeMuth (TD), an assistant district attorney in Boulder. Her lawyer, Patrick Burke, and Ramsey private investigator Ellis Armistead were also present.

Tom Haney began the questioning of Patsy by once again taking her through the events of December 25 and 26, 1996.

<u>TOM HANEY</u>: I want you to know that some of the questions that we ask today may be very personal, and we are not trying to antagonize you or upset you, but these are questions that have arisen in the course of the investigation. They are based on facts, rumors, stories, and we feel that we have to ask all of them. Okay?
<u>PATSY RAMSEY</u>: Okay.
<u>TH</u>: Mrs. Ramsey, let's just start off by you telling us what you can about the death of JonBenet?
<u>PR</u>: Well, all I know is that her father and I put her to bed. The night of Christmas Day, 25th. And that was the

last time I saw her until the afternoon of the 26th, when John discovered her body in the basement and we had — I had found the note which said that it was a kidnapping.

So that morning we were all operating under the presumption of the facts of a kidnapping. Fact that it was a kidnapping. The police were there and they were setting up telephones and all that. They were trying to obtain the ransom money and all that kind of stuff. And then we found out otherwise.

TH: What I would like to do then is just have you walk us through and maybe first of all, just in your own words again, if you could tell us from the time that you got up on the 26th of December . . . .

PR: Okay. I awakened that morning, probably somewhere between 5:30 and six. We are going to take off for the airport just at seven, we were going to the lake house.

I got up and walked over . . . to my bathroom . . . and I did not take a shower that morning, so I don't know, you know, what exactly I did . . . other than just get dressed, brush my teeth, put on my make-up, and get ready to go.

And then I walked down downstairs . . . came to the landing . . . and there was an ironing board . . . I had a plastic bag . . . that I had just things to throw, throw in, to take for my trip. And I think I was here for a couple of minutes, just getting some clothes, things.

And then I started down the stairs, this (spiral) staircase, to go to the kitchen. And the note was on the landing, on the stairs, the bottom of the stairs . . . there was some lighting on, but it wasn't bright lights and (I) started reading the letter.

And after the first couple of sentences realized, you know, what was happening, and I ran back up these

stairs, okay, and pushed her door to her room . . . and
she was not in her bed. So I went over to these stairs
and yelled out for John, called to him and he came
down. And I said, "She's been kidnapped, here's a
note," whatever And I was panicking, you know. I
think — I can't remember exactly what I did then,
whether — I think I ran downstairs again.

I said, you know, "What do we do, what do we do?" He
said, "Call 911, call the police."

I ran upstairs, and I think — I think — I — I can't
remember if — I think asked him to check on Burke,
one of us checked on Burke, and I remember just seeing
him at the phone, trying to — and then I looked down
and John came down . . . and he kind of crouched on the
floor, he was in his underwear, and read thepapers on
the floor right there, and you know, I was trying to
get this 911 person to — it just seemed like it took
forever, to drag through, you know, crazy by that time.

Anyway, got the message across, she said she would
send somebody out, and oh, God in heaven. Oh, then I
phone — called our friends, Mr. and Mrs. Fleet White
and Mr. and Mrs. John Fernie, they live in Boulder.
I think John went back up to get dressed.

And I called them and told them that she's been
kidnapped, she is missing. And then I walked out . . . and
opened the door, and started waiting for — front door
— started waiting for the police to show up . . . and
pretty soon a squad car came — you know, officer came up.
And I remember thinking because it said somewhere in the
note, if you do that, if you call somebody, that's not
good. Blah, blah, blah. And I just remembered thinking
oh, my God, I hope they are not watching me. I mean, what
if they are watching, if the policeman comes, I mean all
this was just rushing through my head.

Anyway, he came in and — and I was just rattled. I think John came in, and I think he kind of walked us over to this sun room . . . tried to calm us down and, you know, tried to explain what happened. And then they kind of took over.

TH: . . . You said you woke up between 5:30 and six, is that correct?

PR: I would —

TH: Had you set the alarm, did you intend —

PR: I didn't set the alarm. John, it's on his side of the bed and he always sets that. I was just thinking he wanted to take off at seven, so it means we had to leave the house about 6:30, and I usually get up about 45 minutes, half an hour, 45 minutes to an hour earlier to kind of pull things together. And we just throw our clothes on and go when it's that early.

We had to leave at seven because we had to meet Melinda and John Andrew. Normally it doesn't matter whether you're five or ten minutes late, you're not meeting anything, you are not on a schedule, but we were rendezvousing with them. They were flying commercially from Atlanta to Minneapolis, so we had to take off at seven to meet their flight in Minneapolis.

TH: So you wake up and you're not sure of the time. Did you happen to look at the clock?

PR: Not — I mean, not to the minute, no. I mean — no. Sometime between 5:30 and six.

TH: Okay. And when you woke up, where was John?

PR: He was up already . . . I think he was in the bathroom.

TH: And his bathroom — okay. Did you see him or hear him at that time?

PR: I don't think I saw him. I think I heard his shower on.

TH: Let's back up a little bit. That night, did you get a good night's sleep?

PR: Yeah. Uh huh.
TH: Approximately what time did you get to sleep on the 25th?
PR: Oh, I don't know what time . . . I mean it was 10 o'clock-ish. Probably something like that.
TH: When you actually went to sleep?
PR: Well, it was pretty soon after I hit the bed, yeah, I was pretty tired.
TH: So about —
PR: About ten-thirty-ish, I think.
TH: Okay, and did — you get up between 5:30 and six. Had you gotten up at all during the night?
PR: No.
TH: Had you slept fairly well?
PR: Yes.
TH: Well rested?
PR: Uh huh.
TH: Do you normally sleep through the night?
PR: Yeah, pretty much.
TH: How about John?
PR: Through the night.
TH: To the best of your knowledge?
PR: Yes.
TH: And he normally is a pretty sound sleeper?
PR: Yes.
TH: How about Burke?
PR: Sound sleeper . . . I mean sometimes I will hear him get up and go to the bathroom, but I didn't hear anything . . . that night.
TH: And how about JonBenet?
PR: She was really a sound sleeper. She was very sound asleep that night.
TH: And you didn't wake up at all during the night?
PR: No.

TH: You didn't hear a scream, nothing startled you?

PR: (Shaking head.)

TH: And now a neighbor did hear reportedly a scream, somewhere between midnight and 2 a.m.?

PR: (Shaking head.)

TH: When you got up, were there any lights on?

PR: I am sure there were. We — we — the house was big, and twisty-turny, you know, so we nearly always left a light on in case somebody did get up or something. Because there are a lot of little steps and what not. And we are not very good about turning lights off.

TH: Is there — there particular ones that you normally leave on?

PR: No.

TH: Okay. When you got up, was it pitch black?

PR: John — John, I remember his bathroom . . . had a light.

TH: Okay. So it's shining somewhat . . . but we are talking quite a distance?

PR: Well, there is a hall light . . . that was on. Because I remember, you know, when you first look up it's like bright, you know, but I think that he was up already, he had gone . . . to his bathroom area.

TH: . . . Can you just indicate . . . the first stop you made, the first thing you did along that route?

PR: My clothes were probably thrown on the bathtub.

TH: Let me stop you there . . . those were clothes you had worn the night before?

PR: Right.

TH: Okay. Seems odd to me.

PR: I do this a lot.

Police who suspected Patsy was involved in the murder, believed she had been up all night and was still dressed in

the same clothes she'd worn to the Whites' dinner party on
Christmas Eve.

TH: Now did you intend to wear those the rest of the day
though or —
PR: Probably what I thought I would do, you know, my
thinking was I have my underwear and all that is in
these drawers here, so I put my underwear on, but I put
the black velvet pants on . . . and the red (turtleneck)
sweater . . . and then we have clothes up at the lake,
and I took a few things with me. You know, it was just
so early, I was just going to throw on whatever I had up
there. Just get in, tumble into bed and when we awake
early, you know, kind of almost get ready up there . . .
I put make up on and brushed my hair but —
TH: So this would have not been your normal
routine, though, to put the same clothes on?
PR: Yeah, I do whatever I want. I told you that. I mean
if I had a pair, you know, of black shorts on, you
can wear them two, three days, before I send them to
the dry cleaners. I might have changed the top or
something but . . . I don't like to do laundry so I —
TH: And you're getting ready for this trip anyway?
PR: Right.
TH: And there is really not a whole lot of time —
PR: No.
TH: — if you're going to leave at seven?
PR: Right.
TH: So you say you put your make-up on?
PR: (Nodding.)
TH: What brands of make-up do you wear?
PR: Different kinds.
TH: Do you know what it would have been at that time?
PR: Probably the foundation was probably either

Clinique or Chanel, my sister sells Chanel and she has samples of everything. So keeps us in samples . . . . Just guessing, I don't know.

TH: Foundation. Okay. Are there other things that you put on —

PR: Blush, lipstick. I probably didn't really do a terrific job. I mean just putting, get a little bit on and go, you know.

TH: Okay. And how long do you think all that in the bathroom took?

PR: Oh, 20, 30 minutes.

TH: And what —

TRIP DEMUTH: Is that a different brand of blush that you put on? Is that the same Clinique?

PR: I don't know. I have a drawer full of stuff. I don't necessarily use the same, you know, Chanel, Chanel, Chanel, Clinique, Clinique. Just kind of whatever jar is there.

TH: So now we are on the second floor, because you're coming down the stairs?

PR: Right, I am coming down . . . I had the ironing board somewhere here. And I had — I think I had a couple of plastic bags here somewhere . . . to take to the lake.

TH: . . . And you stopped there?

PR: Just momentary. I remember — remember laying the little red jumpsuit of JonBenet's over the ironing board, because it had a few spots on it, so I was thinking when I came back from the lake I was going to take that to the dry cleaners, and decided to lay that under there somewhere.

TH: Was that — it wasn't something you were going to take to the lake?

PR: No, no, it was something she had worn for a Christmas performance. It was a little Christmas thing.

TH: When had she worn that?

PR: She had worn it — well, she wore it, some of her pageant girls performed together in a group, some Christmas songs and things, down in a mall in Denver, she wore it for that.

TD: Is that Amerikids?

PR: Yes, that's what, who it was, yes ... I had laid that out or done something and the light was on here.

TH: The laundry room light was on here?

PR: The light here.
Yes. I was working there.

TH: Okay, did you turn it on?

PR: I don't remember.
That could have been one that was left on, I don't know. Sometimes we leave that one on.

TH: Sometimes you do?

PR: (Nodding.)

TH: But you don't recall that morning coming down into the dark or —

PR: No.

TH: So to the best of your recollection, it was on, you think?

PR: I would say either that light was on or there were also some sconces right here on the stairwell, which were dimmed and oftentimes we would leave that on, because it was dimly lit as a nightlight sort of lighting area . . . so something I am sure was on, because it wasn't pitch black walking down.

TH: How about JonBenet's room, what was the condition of the room?

PR: Well, I remember racing over and her door was just kind of slightly ajar ... three, four inches, you know.

TH: Okay. Is that the way you left it the night before?

PR: Yes, that's usually the way I left it.

TH: And is there a particular reason?

PR: Well, I closed it because if I did leave a light on out here, it would shine pretty brightly into her room so I close to make it a little darker in there. But I want to leave it so if she needed me or called out or something I could hear her, you know.

TH: So that was the normal thing?

PR: That was the normal thing to do.

TH: Did you happen to look in?

PR: No. At that time, I did not.

TH: Did you happen to notice if there was any light coming from inside?

PR: I didn't notice. Just nothing seemed unusual.

TH: Okay. So we are still at the ironing board and this little red outfit. What do you do with that, how long does that take?

PR: Just, I don't know, just a few minutes. And I don't know, I can't remember what I was doing. I just remember I was trying to get this bag ready to go to the lake, I had two suitcases . . . of the children's things, I was trying to get ready, because when we came back from the lake we were going on to Disney and the Big Red Boat.

TH: You're going to go to Charlevoix, am I saying that right?

PR: Charlevoix.

TH: You're going there the 26th at seven in the morning. How long are you going to stay there?

PR: Just a couple of days, I think, because we were due back, I think we were supposed to leave on the Big Red Boat on my birthday, which is the 29th. So would that — was that a Saturday?

TH: I think Christmas was — 25th was a Wednesday, and so Sunday would have been the 29th approximately.

PR: Well, somewhere around there. I just didn't have very much time when we got back. So I was prepacking stuff here.

TH: Let me just keep you on this. The Big Red Boat thing on the 29th, what time were you going to leave for that, do you recall?

PR: We had airline flights out of Denver . . . we didn't go from Charlevoix, we had to fly back from Charlevoix to Denver to take a commercial flight to Orlando.

TH: And do you know when you would have come back from Charlevoix?

PR: Just like the day before.

TH: Okay. The 28th approximately?

PR: Right. Or it could have, you — yeah, I think that's right. I just, I don't remember exactly whether we were leaving on Saturday or Sunday, and we were going to be on the Big Red Boat for my birthday.

TH: So you're in the laundry, you say you spent a couple of minutes there, two, five?

PR: Probably five or ten. You know.

TH: So you come — you're coming down the stairs. Are there any lights on in that spiral staircase?

PR: Um, just you know, can't remember exactly. But I mean there was enough light — it wasn't pitch black, in other words. But there was either a light coming from . . . the sconce or something. You know, interior stairwell.

TH: Okay. And I don't recall, and I was in the house but I didn't notice, the sconces, are they high up, all the way up and down?

PR: No, they are just kind of wall sort of sconces. Those you could dim, you know, raise or dim the light. So those you know, that typically would be left on at night.

<u>TD</u>: Are they on the first or second floor, the sconces?

<u>PR</u>: They go inbetween, they are in the stairway. Okay, I come down . . . some of the rooms are light here where these three pieces of paper were.

<u>TH</u>: Which running of the stairs were they on?

<u>PR</u>: Well, it wasn't the bottom one. I would say it was like — I mean, I had to bend over, you know, to look at it, you know.

<u>TH</u>: And when you first see it, what's your first reaction?

<u>PR</u>: Well, my initial reaction was that — I mean, I probably would stack things going upstairs, you know, shoes or toys or whatever . . . so there was typically always something there, going one way or the other. But this was laid out across the tread, you know. This was laid out across the treads, so I mean I just thought, well, papers, you know, John would have taken up to see or something, I don't know. And then when I came down and looked at it, glanced at it, my first reaction was that it was a note from my cleaning lady.

<u>TH</u>: Let me just stop you there. You are kind of bounding down the stairs, I would imagine?

<u>PR</u>: Right.

<u>TH</u>: Kind of get going?

<u>PR</u>: Yeah.

<u>TH</u>: You come to it, you stop and you look and see — you kind of bend over from higher up?

<u>PR</u>: No, I passed it, then turned back around to turn to look and see what it was.

<u>TH</u>: Did you step over that rung or —

<u>PR</u>: I don't think I stepped on it, because you know, you step on paper, it kind of does that. So I somehow got around it.

<u>TH</u>: Okay. And the note, and let me just hand you

— here is a copy of the note. If you just lay it out for us here on the table the way it was laid out ... now, was there sufficient light from those sconces for you to read it?

<u>PR</u>: Yeah.

<u>TH</u>: Do you wear glasses, contacts?

<u>PR</u>: No. I didn't then. I do now, a little bit. For reading.

<u>TH</u>: Okay. Can you — do you have your contacts in now?

<u>PR</u>: I don't have contacts, no.

<u>TH</u>: Can you read this?

<u>PR</u>: Yeah. You want me to read it to you?

<u>TH</u>: No, no, that's fine. But could you read it then without any problem?

<u>PR</u>: Uh huh.

<u>TH</u>: So you see it. What do you do?

<u>PR</u>: I read — I read down to about, it says, "At this time we have your daughter in our possession." For some reason, I don't — don't ask me why but ... my first flash that was in my head was I thought it was Beth . . . .

Beth Ramsey, John Ramsey's oldest daughter from his first marriage, was killed in a car accident in 1992.

<u>PR</u>: I don't know why I thought — and then "daughter in our possession, she is safe from harm, your daughter in 1997," then when I realized this was now, this was new material, this was not something — you know, papers from, that had to do with Beth. And just, I stopped and just went up the stairs.

<u>TH</u>: When you bent down to read it, did you pick it up or did you leave it on the stair?

<u>PR</u>: I just can't remember exactly ... I think I left it —

<u>TH</u>: — approximate location like it's laid out now?

PR: Yeah.

TH: Okay. So as far as getting to the bottom of the stairs, that's as far as you got?

PR: Well, I got — I was to the floor ... I got down to the floor ... and turned around and looked at it.

TD: Tom, if that's not clear ... it's laid out pages 1, 2 and 3, left to right as you were looking from the floor towards the stairs, correct?

TH: And you said that you just read that first paragraph?

PR: Uh huh.

TH: And that's when you stopped?

PR: Uh huh.

TH: Had you since or did you that day read the rest of the note?

PR: Well, I read — I came back down and John had it, you know, on the floor, and what not, and I was glancing at it, and somewhere I thought in there, because I didn't read it line by line, I looked over to see who it was from, and I didn't know who that was. And somewhere I caught in there where it said, "If you call some" — "Don't call the police," or — wherever it said that. Oh, here, "police, FBI," et cetera, "your daughter being held." And I read that and I mean, my blood just went cold. You know, I couldn't —

TH: That was some time later?

PR: Well, it was kind of all during, I mean after John came down and he had the note and I was "God, what are we going to do, what are we going to do?" And he said, "Call the police, call 911" and I was looking around reading but it said don't do that ...

TH: Have you ever since that day read the entire note?

PR: Oh, yes.

TH: Okay. Probably on more than one occasion?

PR: Uh huh.

TH: . . . And looking at it today, do you notice anything about it, anything that you recognize, anything that looks familiar, similar to anything you have seen before?

PR: This "M" kind of looks like an "M" that I have seen somebody make. I don't know — I have racked my brain over this a million times.

TH: Do you notice any similarities to, say, your style of indentation and signing off and the use of exclamation points, anything like that?

PR: Well, I mean, as you know, I have had umpteen handwriting samples and they all want to say that, you know, my "A's" look like this or —

TH: I am not talking so much about the handwriting itself. I am talking about the style of the "Mr. Ramsey?" Introduction, the indentation, the signing off at the end?

PR: No.

TH: No? Similar to your style?

PR: No. I usually sign "Regards" or something like that. "Love."

TH: So you see the note, you read that portion, you're at the bottom of the stairs, then you start back up?

PR: I ran up.

TH: Before that, that's right. But before — what was the first thing you do? Do you say something, do you do something?

PR: I went bounding upthe stairs to her room and pushed the door open. I mean pushing the door, I did not go through it, I just pushed it open and saw she wasn't in her bed.

TH: Let me just stop you there. When you pushed the door open, was there a light on in the room?

PR: There was — her lamp light was not on. You know, there was enough light that I could tell she wasn't in her bed. Now, whether that was coming from the laundry area, whether daylight was breaking or whether there was — you know, sometime we left a little nightlight here on in her bathroom, so you know, I — all I know is I was able to see that there is no one lying in that bed and the covers are ruffled.

TH: Did you go past that door?

PR: No.

TH: You didn't enter that room at all?

PR: No.

TH: Did you — did you think that possibly she had gotten out of the bed, was somewhere else in the room you didn't —

PR: It just happened so fast, and I, you know, read that letter and said "We have your daughter," your mind goes berserk. I mean I was — and then I went up there and my child is not in the bed. You know, I didn't, nothing against your questioning, but no, I didn't stand around and say I wonder if she is in here, I wonder if she is in there. I screamed for John . . . I mean my knees were like, you know, buckling. And oh, God, and he came down and I said, "She's gone, she's gone, there is a note, she's been kidnapped."

TH: Do you remember exactly what words you used, was it more than just John or —

PR: I remember my voice was just cracking. I mean it was like "JOHN," like that. I mean like, I can't even, you know, I hear my scream and I hear his scream when he came up from the basement, I mean it was just a horrible thing . . . he comes down those stairs there and . . . I am pacing. I said, "Oh, my God, you know there is a note, she's been kidnapped. She is not in her bed, you know." You know, then everything gets really, you know, who's on first kind of thing.

TH: What is John's — how is he dressed?

PR: He is in his underwear.

TH: Just shorts or, —

PR: Uh huh.

TH: Okay. And what conversation, what does he say to you?

PR: God, I can't remember.

TH: Okay. He still hasn't felt the impact of this, right?

PR: No. He said, "You know, slowdown," or "What is it, what is it?", and I said, you know, "I went downstairs, there is a letter, says she's been kidnapped." And he said, "Where is the letter?" I said — I think I said, "Oh, my God, Burke," or something. And I think he ran in to start to check on Burke . . . And I said, "There is a letter downstairs" . . . and I think I went down and got it. I just can't remember everything.

TH: . . . He goes to check on Burke?

PR: I think he went to check on Burke.

TH: Did he say he was going to go check on Burke or did you tell him to, or do you recall?

PR: I just don't recall . . . I went back downstairs.

TH: You come down the spiral stairs. The note is —

PR: The note is —

TH: — same place, different place?

PR: . . . Maybe still on the floor or something, you know. I don't know what happened to it exactly when I bounded upstairs.

TH: The second time you don't recall exactly where it was?

PR: I think it was laying around on the floor . . . It was there somewhere. I know I came down here, and I either handed it to John or he went in and picked it up. Anyway, I came over to the phone.

TH: Let's stop there. He came down the stairs. He has already gone to presumably to check on her . . . And you come down here?

PR: Right.

TH: So you get down there, he is not there. I assume, John?

PR: Right.

TH: Okay. What do you do between the time you get down there and the time that he does show up?

PR: Just kind of standing around . . . you know. I was screaming and crying and —

TH: Okay, and what — okay, what were you screaming, what were you saying?

PR: I said, "Oh, my God, how did they get in, why don't we hear anything?", you know. "Where were they, how could this happen?" I mean I was just —

TH: So you're not reading the note then?

PR: No.

TH: You're just wandering around . . . and that's the area just south of the spiral stairs?

PR: Right.

TH: And where do you see John, when did you see him next?

PR: Well, I don't know how — I mean the next thing I remember, I was — he was saying, "Call the police, call the police," he had the note and he was kneeling right here.

TH: Okay, let's stop you again . . . understandably you're pacing around?

PR: Right.

TH: And screaming. When and where do you see John?

PR: In this area.

TH: And what is he doing there?

PR: He said — you know, I said, "There is the note." I think I handed him the note here, somehow in this space he got the note.

TH: So you don't know if he went to check on Burke, came down the front stairs and then came down through the kitchen?

PR: Right.

TH: But he appears there?

PR: Right.

TH: . . . What discussion do you two have there?

PR: I mean I was just saying, "How did they get in, how did this happen, who would do this?" You know, screaming, screaming. "What's the note say?"

John is saying "Call 911, call 911.". . . he was crouched on his knees here in his underwear. He laid the papers out right there, one, two, three and was reading it . . .

TH: Let me back you up again. You said a minute ago something to the effect that maybe you went and got him the note. Do you know how he —

PR: I don't know exactly. Maybe he will remember. But I mean I left the note somewhere here, whether I picked it up and threw it down, just took off. And then came back down the stairs, and whether I picked it up, and then he came down, I gave it to him. And said, "Here's the note," or whatever.

TH: Now are you just guessing or do you know —

PR: I can't remember exactly.

TH: Okay.

PR: But I know I left the note . . . and then when he came I was walking around . . . he picked up the note or had the note somehow, was down on the floor reading it.

TH: Okay, he is there, he was in his underwear on his hands and knees. I think that's a wood floor there?
PR: Uh huh.
TH: Okay. Is there a light on there then?
PR: Yes, just this hall light . . . .
TH: Do you recall did you or he turn it on?
PR: I don't know.
TH: Where are you while he is doing that?
PR: I am on the phone right here. Phone right here.
TH: And you're standing right there. You already said that John told you to call 911?
PR: Uh huh.
TH: And then you walk over to the phone?
PR: Uh huh.
TH: And he is doing what?
PR: He's on his hands . . . like crouched on his knees, reading it.
TH: And what is he saying?
PR: Nothing much. He said, "Call the police, we have got to call the police."
TH: And how does he say it, is it like that?
PR: Just like that.
TH: Cool?
PR: Pretty —
TH: He is pretty cool and calm?
PR: I was nuts, he was — I mean, shaking, but he was trying to —
TH: You say you were nuts?
PR: Yeah.
TH: Are you still screaming, yelling, crying?
PR: Yeah, I mean I was just in shock. You know, you know, just how did they get in, who did this, my God, what are we going to do?
TH: Now, the phone that's there, that's a fixed phone?

PR: (Nodding.)

TH: Now, I have to stop you here because at my house if there is an emergency, if there is a problem and my wife is screaming and yelling and panicked, I wouldn't have her call anybody. Because they would never figure out what she is saying. And it sounds like you're in kind of an emotional state, and John, he is the CEO, he is cool, he is calm, he is down there, he is processing this note and he tells you to call 911?

PR: Uh huh.

TH: It just seems kind of odd to me. What —

PR: I don't know whether it's odd or not, but that's what happened.

TH: Okay.

PR: I mean, you know, I had it together enough to call. And I said, "This is Patsy Ramsey at 755 15th Street" or whatever . . . I think she was trying to make sure I got it out, you know.

TH: In fact, you got it out pretty good, you got the address which a lot of callers who call the police, who call 911 —

PR: — can't remember their names.

TH: Well, they don't give the address. You seemed to give the address pretty quick. When you called, did you practice this, did you rehearse, did you think about what you were going to say?

PR: No, no, just instantaneously, you know.

TH: Okay, and it just came out like that. So John is down there reading it and you call 911. You have this conversation with them. What happens at the end of that?

PR: When I hung up, they said they would send somebody out, and I don't know, I think John went to get dressed. I was you know, was just pacing around here praying.

TD: You say he was in his underwear?

PR: Right.

TD: What does underwear consist of?

PR: His briefs.

TD: Anything else?

PR: Huh uh.

TD: So he was otherwise naked except for his briefs?

PR: Correct.

TH: You said John leaves your sight?

PR: Uh huh.

TH: Do you know where he goes then?

PR: Well, not exactly. I just presume he went up to get dressed, because he came back downstairs dressed.

TH: How long was he gone?

PR: I don't know. Oh, I don't know. Ten minutes. I am just guessing. I mean, I wasn't watching my clock or anything.

TH: Absolutely. So do you know, does he go back up the back stairs?

PR: I don't know for sure. But very likely.

TH: Do you know, did he take the note with him?

PR: I don't know.

TH: So you're just pacing . . . between the front door and the telephone area on the west side of the kitchen?

PR: (Nodding.)

TH: And John leaves your sight?

PR: Uh huh.

TH: Is there any discussion with him before he goes about what he's going to do or what you're going to do?

PR: Not that I remember.

TH: Then he's gone for, you say, five or ten minutes. Where do you next see him?

PR: Oh, probably . . . when the officer came we kind of both met him there.

TH: So you didn't, between the time that you hung up

the phone and he left, you don't see John again until about the time the officer shows?

PR: Well, that's the first time I remember seeing him.

TH: Let's take a minute and think about it. Because it seems like from the prior statement that he had done some things or that you had guys had had some discussions about him checking doors?

PR: Yeah, well, you know, he did that when I was pacing back here, "How did he get in, how did he get in?" I remember John checking this door and that was usually always unlocked because that goes to the garage.

TH: Was this prior to the phone call to 911?

PR: This probably was. You know, we were just right in there. You know, I just don't — this all happened so fast.

TH: Okay . . . the garage door . . . the walk-in door. What did he do to check that?

PR: He opened the door and kind of jiggled the handle, you know, to see whether it was locked or not.

TH: Is it normally locked?

PR: It's normally unlocked, because this is the garage door and that's where you come in.

TH: So checking that and moving the handle —

PR: It sometimes accidentally gets locked, and we get locked out, but typically it's left open, left unlocked.

TH: Is it just a little button to —

PR: Yeah.

TH: When you turn that to go out and it will lock itself?

PR: Yes.

TH: But he checks that?

PR: Right.

TH: And then after that you said he . . . that door on the south side between the study and the kitchen?

PR: Yes, I think he did that.

TH: Did you see him go down there or was your feeling or you remember him going down that way?

PR: I just kind of — I mean, I was just out of my mind, I am crying, I am crying, I am stammering, and he is like walking around everywhere, like checking — sort of checking around . . . that's just, this house has so darn many doors, you know, just to see if that was left unlocked or something or maybe I don't —

TD: You do have a memory of him going down the stairs towards the butler kitchen?

PR: I think so. I can't say for sure, but I think so.

TH: Did you yourself check any doors?

PR: No.

TH: Did he ever tell you that he checked that butler door?

PR: No.

TH: So he is checking those doors and that would have been the, to put this in sequence, prior to your 911 call?

PR: Well, I don't know if it was prior or not. No, no. I think I called the 911 pretty quick, because he was still in his underwear. And I think when he was checking those doors he was dressed . . . I mean this happened, you know, within minutes of all of this going upstairs here.

TH: Almost immediately?

PR: Almost immediately.

TH: That you're on that phone?

PR: Right.

TH: And then he is reading the note and then is that when he is checking the doors or are you saying that he was dressed when he was checking them?

PR: Gosh, I don't know, I don't remember exactly. It's been a long time. These are the kinds of questions I wish we could have done way the hell a long time ago. Maybe he can remember. I just remember by this time I am hysterical.

TH: So we have made the phone call, we have checked some doors and the exact sequence of the door checking we are not sure of, but you're again standing in this area between the front door and there. Can you say how long before the officer arrived?

PR: God, it seemed like forever, though I am sure it was fairly quickly. I mean seconds are hours, you know.

TH: Sure. Do you ever again leave this floor after you made that 911 call? Do you go anywhere else, do you go down the stairs to the basement?

PR: No.

TH: You called the Whites and the Fernies. Do you recall who first or —

PR: I think I called the Whites first.

TH: Were they closer to you?

PR: Well, we had just gone there the night before, you know, and — and I just dialed them up. They and the Fernies were like our best friends, you know.

TH: Let's take the call to the Whites first. I think that was the sequence?

PR: I think so.

TH: And you called them. Who answered, what is said?

PR: I think Priscilla answered. And I mean, I don't know what I said exactly. But somehow communicated to her that JonBenet was gone and had been kidnapped and could they come over. I don't know. I was just hysterical. Then I hung up the phone and called the Fernies. And I believe John Fernie answered.

TH: Do you recall exactly what you told him?

PR: I said — I said — I am not sure if I told him — I just can't remember what I told. "Oh, please, you got to come, please can you bring someone over?" or something. I don't remember.

TH: And understanding that they are close friends, but did you ... give any thought to having all this traffic coming over?

PR: No.

TH: You had gotten through that portion of the note that talked about don't call the police, the FBI?

PR: Right.

TH: "We are watching you," or something like that?

PR: I know.

TH: How long does it take for them to get over there?

PR: Well, it would have been just pretty quick.

TH: How much after the arrival of the first officer?

PR: Not much. Just, I don't know, 15 minutes, you know.

TH: Okay. And between the time that you folks had returned from the Whites on Christmas night, and this call to the Boulder police in the morning, on the 26th, had you made or received any phone calls ... ?

PR: Not that I recall, no.

TH: Of course anything that would have disturbed your sleep you would have recalled that?

PR: Oh, yeah.

TH: Anything major in that time frame?

PR: No.

TH: Okay. Do you ever go up and check on Burke, you yourself?

PR: Oh, yeah. I mean, you mean, like that or —

TH: This morning, the 26th. Let's get you back there. We are still pacing around?

PR: Right. I don't think I did. I think John said he was

fine and — I can't — I just can't recall that I did.

TH: Okay. So do you recall at what point you and John had this discussion about Burke, you said he said Burke was fine?

PR: Somewhere in this bedlam, you know, that was —

TH: Okay, and again, prior to or after the arrival of the officers?

PR: Probably prior to.

TH: Okay. So he goes quiet then when you see him down there again, that's in fact what he had done?

PR: That's right.

TH: When he was upstairs. All right, you lost sight of him on the second floor. So Burke is fine, you don't go up there. The officer comes and then you say he takes you into the solarium . . . and you said that the Whites and the Fernies joined you shortly after that. Do they also come in here in this solarium (sunroom) area?

PR: . . . I don't remember where we were at any one point. A lot of people started coming in . . . .

The Ramseys' pastor, Father Rol Hoverstock also joined them at the home that morning, as did two women from a local victims' advocacy group. Boulder police were later criticized for not clearing the house of people who may have contaminated crucial evidence.

PR: And I was just in here, this is like my little area.

TD: The solarium.

PR: I just hover. When I was sick, I recouped a lot in there and I was just in there praying and praying and praying. And then Linda Arndt came, she introduced herself to me and said they were going to set up the wiretap, so then John was with her and kind of taking care of business, they were all back in here.

TD: This study?

PR: Yeah.

TH: Anything else?

PR: Father Rol came, he was standing right here praying.

TD: The living room?

PR: The living room.

TH: . . .Would the children normally go downstairs if they woke up or would they stay on their floor or —

PR: They would typically stay on their floor. They had a TV, play room, stay on that floor.

TD: So in the middle of the night did they ever go downstairs, if they woke up in the night, would they go down into the kitchen, let's say?

PR: I don't know.

TD: And could you hear them go to the bathroom?

PR: I could hear Burke go to the bathroom, because his bathroom is sort of more toward the end of our bedroom.

TD: How about JonBenet?

PR: I wouldn't hear her go.

TD: Could you hear her toilet flush or anything, the plumbing?

PR: Probably.

TD: Okay. Could you hear the garage door from your bedroom go up and down?

PR: No.

TH: In the earlier interview, and I think it was the one on April 30th last year, the Whites' name came up . . . because they were formerly very good friends that you called that morning, but people that you were now suspicious of or something about their behavior. Could you tell us what about them has changed and what you have noticed . . . be candid.

PR: Well, everything that — you know, I mean,

everything. Our relationship was perfectly normal
and fine, and like I said, they're our close friends who
I called first thing that morning. And it was a very
traumatic morning, obviously, for everyone there. And
people handled things differently, and I know that
— but, suffice to say that Fleet and Priscilla, Fleet
probably more so, just on a number of different
occasions started reacting very strangely.

TH: Okay. How did he react?

PR: Well, I guess the first — let's see. The first time
— I mean, you know, after we found JonBenet, I mean I
was just in shock and really was — was not paying too
much attention to things. But the first time I really
realized that something was amiss was when we were
going to go to Atlanta for the funeral . . . and there
was some like scuttle, confusion or something, why
Fleet was not going on that plane. I mean our close
friends that had been basically — you know, I don't
know what they were doing. John and my girlfriends
were bathing me and feeding me and taking me to the
bathroom. I mean I was just immobile for all intents
and purposes. And — and I just remember hearing
something that John Fernie was going to detain Fleet
because he was in no condition to be put on that plane.

TH: No condition due to?

PR: He was — and, like I say, I am kind of like just
catching, you know, wafts of these conversations. But
that was my first recollection. I picked up on
something that Fleet was not acting right. And they
were going to keep him from going on the private plane
back to Atlanta. So anyway, I didn't want to think too
much about it, and then when we were in Atlanta, I just
sort of remember Priscilla standing in my mother's
living room, family room, you know, just kind of like

this and saying, "Well, I know what's going on," and she
said, "If you would give me a few minutes of your time, I
could let you in on some things." And I turned to her and
I said, "Priscilla, how can you know so much?" And I said,
"I am the mother of this child. And I know nothing."

TH: What was she referring to?

PR: I don't have a clue. I really, I mean, you know, so
many times I wish I would have taken her up on it to
see what the hell she was talking about. There was just
her — you know, it was just this kind of, 'I know what's
going on here and you don't. And if you give me a few
minutes of your time, I could clue you in.'

TH: But she didn't give you a clue or —

PR: Didn't say, didn't say. So that was like the second
little thing. So then, let's see. We were at — we were at
my parents, and we had different friends who had come
in from Colorado and my friends in Atlanta were
putting them up in homes and what not, and my
understanding is that Fleet and Priscilla had been
invited by my brother and sister-in-law, Jeff Ramsey,
to stay in their home. So I was in bed, and somebody,
either my sister, or another friend who was staying
there or something, said that Jeff had just called to
my parents' home, and said that Fleet was totally off
the deep end, had like gotten my brother-in-law, and
my brother-in-law is — you think my husband is
docile, my brother-in-law is, you know, very docile.
Non- confrontational. So Fleet got hold of Jeff's
collar, you know, like this, in his face, you know,
being very confrontational.

TH: Is Fleet a pretty good size?

PR: Yes, he's a large man. And anyway, Jeff had called
and said to my dad, "They are on their way to your
house. Do you have a gun?" And I mean for Jeff Ramsey

to say something like this is pretty wild. So I just remember, you know, somebody scooping me up and Burke up and my mom and all this, and we went downstairs to our basement where my mother had set up some temporary beds and then like, you know, like thrown on the beds, like "Don't anybody say anything," and you know, John and my dad were going to try to calm them down or something.

TH: Okay. What do you mean again, what did —

PR: I don't know, Jeff was saying that, "Fleet is just crazy. He is crazy, he is coming over there, I don't know what's happened. You know, he's off his rocker."

TH: Did he give you a clue though? I mean here your good friends —

PR: See, I don't know, because . . . I am like hearing this third hand.

TH: Okay.

PR: All I know is there was like some big hubbub here about Fleet and Priscilla were going nutso and they were coming over and somebody just crazy, "He is crazy, he is coming over there, I don't know what's happened. You know, he's off his rocker . . . and everybody is afraid of them," and da-de-da-de-da.

TH: So do they come over?

PR: They came over. I do not see them . . . Jeff Ramsey said he did not want them staying with them. I think John Ramsey and my dad somehow got them to stay in a hotel or something.

Then my dad said, you know, I don't know what day this was, all these days were running together. But then my father said that Priscilla called, I guess they were on their way back to Colorado, she called . . . said that she didn't like what she saw in Atlanta one bit. She thought that everything — that all our friends were, you know, hoity-toity, rich snobs and blah, blah, blah. I mean, just like crazy things.

I mean, you know, here we are mourning the death of this child, for crying out loud, and she goes off on this cultural ventilation or something. You know, it just didn't, it didn't make sense.

But I think some other things happened that I wasn't really privy to. I think John may be more aware of.

But then the other time that was really frightening to me is, we had come back to Colorado, and John and I were in Father Rol's office, in the church, and my dad was sitting out in the little waiting area. And Father Rol and John and I were praying, and Fleet White burst into the door, burst into the office.

And he is just, his eyes are just wild. And you know, I kind of did this number, and he got down on his knees, and looked like — and had a business card in his hand, and he was leaning over to my husband saying, "You know what this is, John, you know what this means, John, you know what I am going to have to do with this, John, I am going to have to handle this my way, John."

I mean he was just on and on and on. And I said, "Fleet, Fleet, what is it?" And he handed me this business card and it was a business card from some journalist or something, and it had a note on the back. And it said, I don't know exactly word for word, but something to the effect of, you know, "Mr. White, there has been some question as to whether it was you or John Ramsey who removed the tape from JonBenet's mouth." You know. And about the sequence of the basement discovery.

Well, he said, "They are after me and my family now, John, I am going to have to handle" — and he was just like a maniac. And Father Rol said to calm down. And you know, he said, "I am going to handle it my way,

John, my way, John." And you know, Father Rol was just trying to get them to calm down. "It's okay, Fleet," you know. "What do you mean by your way?" You know, "Calm down. You know, it will be okay."

So that was just, that just shook me, you know, and then there are . . . subsequent things, like . . . they went to the governor of Colorado and asked that (Boulder District Attorney Alex) Hunter be taken off the case or that he was doing a bad job or something, and I mean this is like a year later, you know, and I mean they are still just — so, I mean, you know, I am trying to say, okay, everybody was traumatized, you know. Try to put my shoe on the other foot . . . and they are going to the governor and trying to, you know, I mean, just kind of weird to me.

Maybe I am reading things into it. I don't know. I can't imagine, you know, that anybody that has children — you know, when you have children, you know what a precious life that is, and you know what a — you know, I can't imagine that you can do that to another child. I can't — I can't bring myself to think that they would have actually done this. But somebody did it. You know.

And we have been told that it's a lady that knew us, knew we were leaving, knew . . . the dog wasn't there, knew we didn't use the alarm, you know, so —

TH: And these were all things that the Whites would have known?

PR: Yeah.

TH: So do you suspect Fleet?

PR: Oh, God, you know, I just — you know, I — I guess in a way I look at everybody as a suspect. And with this erratic behavior it sounds pretty freaky to me. Last night we were reading through some paperwork or something, and I don't remember whether somebody interviewed Fleet and . . . then had written up a report about their findings and that he seemed to know almost word for word the ransom letter and he commented about how the structure of it was so well tied together. I mean, I have read the ransom letter, I couldn't tell you what the structure was, you know. He seemed like really interested or something. It seemed unusual to me.

So I mean, it would be a horrible blow if I do find out that it was somebody that was that close to us.

TH: What is your current relationship with the Whites?

PR: We have not — we have not spoken.

TH: When is the last time?

PR: Well, I — when we left town . . . I remember we were staying with the Stines. Glen and Susan Stine. Fleet White went in to Glen Stine's office at the university, and leaned across the table, demanding to let the Stines see us. And Glen Stine said, "Fleet," you know, "Settle down." He was just saying that the Stines were keeping us away from them, which wasn't the case. But he was going there, he went into the vice president of the university . . . irrational behavior.

TH: This behavior that you have talked about with Fleet, pounded on the desk and things, is that out of character for him or is he kind of like that?

PR: I mean as far as I ever saw, because he was, he didn't — I don't know exactly what he did for a living. He was not working a nine-to-five job. You know, I think he was in California, had been in the oil kind of business, so he said, but so he was around the house a lot. He took the kids to school. He dressed them. He — we called him affectionately Mr. Mom and he just said he was taking a couple of years kind of hiatus to figure it out and get something else going. So he was always just very loving and he was kind of like a lovable giant kind of, you know, big guy, but just very tender and very — sweet guy, you know. So this, you know, especially that time when he was in Father Rol's office and his eyes were just crazed.

TH: Prior to the death, what was Fleet's behavior like, especially regarding JonBenet?

PR: He, I mean, adored our children. You know. They played together a lot. They were at our house, you know, a lot. My children were at their house playing. They had been up to the lake with us, a number of times, for two, three weeks at a time.

TH: Was there anything in this prior behavior that looking back now seems unusual?

PR: Well, Priscilla was never crazy about me doing this whole pageant with JonBenet, she thought that was just totally unnecessary, because she said you know, "It's just not the thing to do." Well, you know, I had grown up doing it, I enjoyed it, I had a lot of friends who had done it. I had very good experience with it. So that's what I brought to the table. My daughter was a performer, she was beautiful, she was outgoing, and flourished in that type of an environment. (The Whites' daughter) Daphne was not.

So Priscilla would oftentimes say to me, "You know, you just, you shouldn't do that, you know, that's not a good thing to happen."

I thought you know, well, you raise your children the way you do and we don't all raise our children the same. So you know, kind of looking back at that . . . did that really get to her or something? I don't know.

TH: Was there anything else in either of — either's

behavior prior to the death that you, like you said looking back now, outside of the pageant thing?

PR: No, I mean John and Fleet sailed together and Fleet has been sailing for years ... sailed big yachts in the Pacific Ocean and da-de-da-de-da ....

TH: Anything else about the Whites?

PR: Just, I mean, we just, their children were virtually the same age. I just thought we will be life-long friends, because, you know, I enjoyed her, John enjoyed him, the kids had each other ... had discretionary income to be able to go places. Although in that respect John pointed out that all the yacht races and all that stuff was always on our tab. I didn't really pay attention to who was paying for what, but we would pay for the crew and everybody. I always got the impression that Fleet and Priscilla had either family money or something like that. You know. But John said when it came down to actually, you know, splitting it or splitting the hotel or something, that never really happened.

TD: How long did you know them?

PR: We met the summer I came back from the lake the first time, so that would have been like September-ish of '94.

TD: You called Fleet "Mr. Mom." Why do you do that?

PR: Just because he was at home all the time. He took the kids to school and he went to the classroom and he, I mean — she called him ... their live-in nanny.

TD: Did Priscilla work?

PR: Huh uh.

TD: So was she home most of the time also?

PR: Yes.

TD: Who would supervise JonBenet and Burke when they would go over to the Whites' house?

PR: Both of them.

TD: Were there any excursions or outings that Fleet White took your children on as well as his children?

PR: I am sure there probably were.

TD: Any that you recall?

PR: Not right off the top of my head. I mean we went biking, out on the bike trails once all together, all of us.

TD: Would Fleet ever baby-sit the children?

PR: Well, I knew one time in particular . . . we were all up at the lake. . .and John had to fly to New York to do some business, New York City, and Melinda was up there and the Whites. And Priscilla said — she said, "John is going to New York, let's go shopping for the day." And I said, "Who would keep the kids?"

She said, "Oh, Fleet can take care of the kids." . . . When I got home, the house was a disaster.

TD: How many times, how often would Fleet be the baby-sitter for the kids, that you can remember? Can you give me any idea about that? Seldom, never, often?

PR: Well, I would say when if my kids were over there, it would not be unusual that he would be the baby-sitter, because she might go running around or whatever and he would sit or vice versa.

TD: And how often were your kids over at his home?

PR: Maybe once a week. We hadn't seen them a whole lot that fall, because our children were going to different schools. And that was a little sticking point with Priscilla.

TD: How did JonBenet feel about Fleet? Did she ever indicate anything?

PR: No.

TD: Seemed fine?

PR: Uh huh.

TD: One more question. If JonBenet was bothered by

someone, do you think she would communicate that to you, or was she a little more stoic about it, would keep it to herself?

PR: I think she would have told because we had talked about all the areas covered by your swimsuit belong to JonBenet. Not to anybody else. Mom can touch those areas because, you know, and different things, and Dr. Beuf with mommy in the room, those were the ground rules. Not daddy, not Burke, not grampa, not anybody else . . . .

TD: Did she have any difficulty approaching you and talking to you about maybe other children at school she was having difficulty with, would she share those kind of points?

PR: She did not have difficulty. She will tell me everything.

TH: While we are on the subject, tell us . . . what you told JonBenet and when and how did this start, about what belongs to her and what's off limits and what she would do?

PR: . . . Pinky Barber, a friend of mine, had been to some kind of seminar on child safety or something. And she wanted me to go along, and for some reason I couldn't attend with her, so I discussed with her what — you know, she said, well, that they spent some time talking about how to talk with your children about strangers and all that kind of stuff. And she said, "I talked to my girls about it."

. . . That's when this bathing suit thing came up. She said, "I just tell them that nobody touches you where the bathing suit touches."

And I thought that was a really great way to approach that . . . so JonBenet and I, I don't know, maybe at bathtime, maybe when I was putting on her bathing suit or something. You know, "These are JonBenet's private

parts here, you know, where the bathing suit touches
and nobody ever touches your private parts except
mommy and Dr. Beuf with mommy in the room."
TH: About when would you have started conveying this
idea to her?
PR: Probably when she was four.

*Several weeks before the Ramseys' interview, Burke
Ramsey had been questioned for six hours over three days
in Atlanta by Broomfield, Colorado, Detective Dan Schuler,
an expert in the interrogation of children. In that interview,
Burke admitted he had awakened the morning of December
26th and heard his parents talking loudly. He said his
parents might have thought he was asleep but he was
faking. He said he never got out of his bed, although the
enhancement of Patsy's 911 call indicated differently.
Although Patsy could not remember if she'd gone to check
on Burke, he revealed his mother had come into his room,
saying, "Oh, my gosh, oh my gosh."*

TH: Did you discuss anything with him afterwards
(the Schuler interview) about what went on?
PR: I said, "How was your day, Burke?" He said, "Fine."
That's it. "Anything you want to say?" "Nope." . . . I
said, "We are all done, you know, I am really proud of
you for going through that." He said, "Yeah, that was
the most boring thing I have ever done in my life."
TH: Prior to the diagnosis of your ovarian cancer,
what was your relationship like with John?
PR: Great.
TH: Okay.
PR: Good, happy, healthy marital relationship.
TH: How about following your treatment, was there
a change?

PR: Well, for obvious reasons, there was — this was — big change . . . because I was undergoing chemotherapy for nine months, and had a complete hysterectomy, which took several months to recover from. There were very loving, touching . . . through that whole thing. He was my savior, "We will get through this, you know, five steps, chin up, you know" — because I unfortunately saw a lot of cases of women in treatment where husbands or live-ins (said), "See ya."

TH: Would you say he is a pretty caring touchy, feely, huggy?

PR: Uh huh.

TH: How about since JonBenet's death?

PR: Well, there for a number of months, I mean, it was, you know . . . you have to be in a pretty good mood and pretty kind of happy frame of mind to go into all that, and I was pretty much in a fetal position crying every day all day. We were at the lake house and we both started weeping, you know, just all kinds of feelings, you know, very emotional time.

TH: Since the death I am sure you have been grieving a lot and how have you found, you know, support and comfort? Is it mainly through religion or family or —

PR: All of that . . . we are all Christians and know that JonBenet is in a better place, and we are going to be there some day.

TH: Have you and John had any periods of separation between the time of JonBenet's death and now?

PR: You mean like separation as, in like, to get a divorce separating?

TH: Well, that is one context. If you want to address that first?

PR: No, no.

TH: Okay. I suppose he's been away on business trips for extended periods of time?

PR: Not too extended. I mean he really has been curtailing that. And if and when he is away, I still can't stay by myself, so my sister will stay with me or we will stay at my mother's or my girlfriends. I can't stay by myself. We have a security system, we have a dog, we have gates, we have fences. It's just when somebody has invaded your home in the middle of the night and killed your child, you have a hard time going to bed at night.

TH: You mentioned earlier about getting counseling. How about counseling for you and John?

PR: Oh, yeah, yeah.

TH: You still going or —

PR: Uh huh.

TH: Both of you?

PR: Not as frequently now. I mean when I first started going, when I came back to Colorado after burying JonBenet, I mean I never had any experience with psychotherapy, because I never really needed it. Even when I had cancer, I didn't feel like I needed it, because I had support of my husband, my family and my faith and, you know, God healed me . . . but this was just, you know, way beyond anything.

And I realized, I mean, it was after several weeks of just being in that fetal position, crying, and just not wanting to live basically, and you think, I can't go on like this. I need help. And I wasn't real sure what was out there, because I never had any experience to know what was out there.

So actually, Barbara Fernie picked me up one day from where we were staying and I started having a panic attack, hyperventilating and all that stuff.

And she was taking me to the doctor at that time, I had a bronchial infection. By the time I got to the doctor's office I was in a full-blown panic attack, this was in January or so.

TH: In '97?

PR:Uh huh. So the physician in Boulder made a call to Rebecca Barnes — Barnhill — Barnhill, Burkhardt, Barnhill, Burkhardt . . . Barkhorn, Rebecca Barkhorn, there are so many Burkes and Barkes in my life, Barkhorn, and I saw her that day. And she put me on Paxil, an antidepressant, and Ativan . . . and she explained to me basically what was happening. That I had been through this traumatic thing, it was perfectly normal, and, yes, this can be managed by medication. So I saw her quite regularly. Like every day for many days.

TH: These panic attacks that you mentioned, was that the first time that you had suffered through one of those or had you had those prior?

PR: I had had one one other time, when I was in Boulder Community Hospital in the cancer clinic. And it was about midway through my chemo session, my nine-month session, and I guess all of sudden it just kind of came crashing in as to what was really happening. And I started trembling and shaking. The numbness in my lips.

TH: Those were your normal symptoms?

PR: Yeah. It was gone in a little bit, you know.

TH: What do you guys do for fun now? How do you and John try to put this behind you, try to forget, try to —

PR: Well, I don't know that you can forget. I mean every morning I open my eyes and it's right there. You know, a lot of time when I am dreaming and thinking, I am trying to figure out who did it, I am chasing somebody down the corridor.

But you know, Burke's in school, and — and we have
. . . homework and his activities, he's on the baseball
team in the spring and I was the team mother. And you
know, went to all his games. And we made some new
friends, we have certainly a lot of old friends that we
have known for years, but we have particularly found a
couple who has an only son. Our two boys have hit it off,
and the mom and I and the two dads enjoy each other, so
we go to dinner with them probably once a week . . . .

TH: . . . What have you done to prepare for this
interview today, what have you reviewed or looked at
or talked to?

PR: Well, the main thing I have done is prayed for this
day for a year and a half. I don't know what started off
on the wrong foot somewhere, but I have prayed and
prayed and meditated and prayed some more that we could
be here working hand-in-hand to get to the bottom of
this. So that's probably the biggest thing I have done to
prepare. We met with our attorney, and . . . I think he
gave me the document of my previous interview.

TH: From last April 30th?

PR: I think it was. I thumbed through that. There
wasn't much to it.

TH: . . . How about John with JonBenet, did they do any
special things together? Is there anything that she
liked dad to take her to do?

PR: Well, she loved her dad to be around all the time.
You know, she liked John to carry her up on his
shoulders. And they liked to bike ride. And he went to
the pageants. She was always real proud that he was in
hardware as she called it, her — trophy winnings,
medals, what not.

TH: So he managed to get to quite a few of those or
most or all?

PR: Uh huh.

TH: Because from what little I understand, it's kind of off-limits for guys, but not — not a lot of guys there?

PR: There are a lot of fathers there, brothers.

TH: Really?

PR: Yeah, brothers, sisters.

TH: You and John, what did you guys disagree about? And this is before December 25th, 1996?

PR: Oh, gosh. You know, we really don't disagree much.

TH: Never had a fight?

PR: Not that I can remember.

TH: You never got on him about, "You're a workaholic, you're out all the time, you travel all the time, spend more time here?"

PR: No. I mean he was commuting from Atlanta to Colorado for the first couple of years of this company that was building, and then when he became president of the company, you know, we moved here. Even though he would be traveling a lot or whatever, the children would see — you know, we all see each other in the morning and the evenings and — you know.

TH: Okay, but no knock-down, drag-outs over it?

PR: No.

TH: And you said that John did approve of the pageants since he attended them?

PR: Uh huh.

TH: Tell me about John. On a good day.

PR: Like what?

TH: Well, that's about as open-ended as you can get. What kind of a guy is he?

PR: He is — a great father, and great husband. You know, hard worker. Disciplined. Runs a big business, he is an entrepreneur, entrepreneurial spirit. You know, makes friends. What else —

TD: Tom, could I ask a question here. After the memorial service, I think you're being walked out with Barbara Fernie, I think it's Barbara Fernie that's walking you out on television, and you had mentioned how Roxie Walker had sort of helped you to the airplane and all that type of stuff. Where was John during these — can you talk about that?

PR: Um, I think you might be confusing the memorial service with that picture of Barbara and I that was ... played and played and played ... That was not the memorial service ... that was just a church service a couple of weeks after we came back to Boulder.

TD: Maybe I was confusing that. Anyway it struck me that John was not the one next to you, it was Barbara ...

PR: I remember Barbara, I mean John and I were kind of walking together and Barbara came on and kind of scooped me forward, you know. And then just kind of, I think she was trying to hurry me through this entourage of people that were there. Not that there wasn't anything planned or anything. I think John fell in with Father Rol or something like that.

TH: ... How about John on a bad day? Bad day at the office.

PR: Bad day at the office?

TH: And I know he's had those.

PR: Oh, yeah.

TH: Okay.

PR: Um, he really pretty much leaves it at the office. Because I will — usually when we sit down and have dinner, with the children, you know, I really like to do that every night, whether it was at home or a restaurant or whatever. But that we were all together for dinner at night and, you know, what did you do today, "What did you do today?"

And — and the kids will ramble on what about they did. I went to the furniture store and the dry cleaners, you know, those fun things. And John just, you know, would say he worked and I mean he never elaborated on anything much about what happened.

TH: Even if there was a problem?

PR: Not too much.

TH: Really?

PR: No. He pretty much kept that at the office.

TH: Because I would imagine that starting up the company and going through all that, it's got to be a bit of a strain?

PR: Yeah, uh huh.

TH: And I know some days I am able to leave it at the office and some days not.

PR: Uh huh. I don't know how much time you spent with John. He's pretty quiet, and pretty — you know, self-disciplined, and, you know, when he's home he doesn't like to take phone calls because he's on the phone all the time at the office. So, many times if the phone rings, they ask for him, I would say, you know, "He's not here, can I take a message?"

TH: Okay. How about you. How about you on a good day?

PR: Now?

TH: Yeah.

PR: Um, I get up, get Burke ready for school. Go meet my girlfriends for coffee. Come back, clean up the house a little bit. Probably run errands or go to my sister's . . . and then we have lunch with a friend and pick up Burke after school and get homework and dinner and that's it.

TH: Pretty routine stuff?

PR: (Nodding.)

TH: Okay, how about you on a bad day . . . things don't

go right, Burke's had a bad day, Mom, whatever, so you're upset?

PR: Well, the thing that makes me have a bad day these days is just, you know, if I am really unable to control my emotional distraught during the day. You know, and I have those days, I would be in bed most of the day. So, you know, I will cry, whatever.

TH: Okay, how about what sets you off on a bad day?

PR: Not too much really. I mean, I am pretty laid back. I don't likepeople hurting other people for their own self-interests. That bothers me.

You know, I mean, prior to this, I hadn't run into it at all. But since then I have run into a lot of evil people. It's just hurtful, you know. I, about three weeks ago, I was going through a shopping line at the market, and one of the tabloids had Burke's picture on it.

TH: That recent?

PR: Uh huh. And I called the manager, very politely, and I said — told him who I was, and I said — and I said, "I am Burke's mother and my friends, Burke's friends shop in the grocery story and his picture is on that magazine, and I would greatly appreciate if you remove it." No problem. He said, "I am very sorry." He said he'd take care of that.

TH: So you handled that pretty well?

PR: Uh huh . . . I try not to let myself get too tired because then I fall to pieces, would cry a lot, and get all depressed. I really try to manage my — my health, sort of, you know. I try to get a lot of rest and eat well, and don't — we have taken our TV out, we don't get a newspaper. And just not — you just can't see it, because the few times that I inadvertently have seen something, one time there was a thing on TV and I can't remember, but I sat down and, boom, there was that (forensic pathologist) Cyril (Wecht) or whatever his name is, is on. I don't know what the title is, but he was — he was saying, you know, "Call the police, or take them," and da, da, da. And — and I saw somebody held up an applause sign or what because people in the audience were going, "Yeah, yeah, yeah."

And it was just like oh, my God, I can't believe. It was just like they are talking about me. I mean I was in bed for two days, literally in bed. And John took the TV out . . .

TH: What did this Cyril Wecht say that the Boulder police should do?

PR: I can't remember. But he was just, you know, "Come on, come on," you know, riling them up like this. It was like, I mean, all you could think of was like, it was like 'crucify 'em, crucify them.'

That's what it seemed to me like, got the crowd all frenzied, you know. I am looking at these people with this hatred in their eyes and going, you know, what — you know, what is this about, why are you doing this . . . ?

TH: What changes have you seen in yourself since the death, outside of taking away the TV and the newspaper?

PR: I think the biggest change that I have had personally, um, when I had cancer, I was afraid to die because I had two children and a husband and I didn't want to leave them. And now, I am not afraid, because JonBenet had to go there. If I get cancer again, and, you know, I can see her on that side. And then, God willing, if I stay healthy, I have my son to enjoy here. So I am not — I am just not afraid anymore.

TH: How about changes in John since this happened?

PR: I think we both regret not being as security conscious as we should have. I think when you live in

a major metropolitan place like Atlanta we always
used to have an alarm, we always locked our doors. We
moved to Boulder and it just seemed so safe and small
town, you know, next door kids, and I think we just
let down our guard.

And I think we will forever be regretting that, you
know, I mean we have since gotten a dog. I am not real
crazy about dogs . . .

We have lights that come on, motion lights. We have
cameras. We have a security alarm, of course, that we
use. I know exactly who has every key, you know, and we
just — you know, were too lax.

TH: The alarm that you had at the Boulder house here,
when was the last time that you had used it?

PR: When JonBenet was probably about two years old,
we were still doing a lot of construction, and I mean
there were people in and out of that house all the
time, fixing things and I didn't know what they were
working on. I knew they were working on the alarm
system. But I didn't really think that it worked
yet. Because we had had a lot of doors and windows
taken out and put back in, so I thought it was kind of
in the works.

Well, one evening, John and I just sat down with a
glass of wine and, you know, boom, boom, boom, you
know, all things. And we went running back to the key
pad, which was back there by the garage door, and
JonBenet had pulled her little chair over next to the
door and I think she was trying to reach the garage
door button, garage door OPEN button, which was
just above it. And she pushed you know, two, three,
four buttons on that alarm keypad, and it all
— everything broke loose. I mean it was deafening.
And here came the squad cars and the ambulance and

the fire truck, you know, the whole thing. Whole nine yards.

And — and so we never really used it. They were asking me, "What's your code?" I said I didn't know I had a code because I didn't know the thing was working yet.

TH: So you never —

PR: We never had used it. But we had it, it was in the house when we bought it and we — we did whatever you do to activate the fire alarm, you know, tied into that. Smoke detectors and all. If it went off, it can call the fire people like that, but we never, you know, set it. Because it was always going, it seemed like it went off erratically, more than it was worth . . . .

TH: You say you got a dog. You had a dog up here, right?

PR: We (had) a dog in Boulder that we bought.

TH: And what — what happened, I guess the dog was somewhere else?

PR: . . . A Bichon Frise.

TH: I am sorry?

PR: A little Bichon thing, white-haired, puffy, fluffy dog. Not a hound dog. It's a little — I mean, JonBenet — we went to the puppy shop one day and she said, "Oh, that one." And, you know, they put this little white fluffy thing in her arms and, you know, I said, "Wrap it up. Yes, we will take one of everything that goes with it." I mean, it's just putty. It was a darling little dog.

We had had him running across the street to the Barnhills, that was the couple that lived across the street. And they had had a couple of small dogs that they had to put to sleep, so they became very found of Jacques. So when we would go out of town for any length of time, they would dog-sit for us. And we were getting ready to leave early, early the next morning, so Jacques went over to Joe's. God, I wish he had —

TD: Went to Joe's?

PR: He was over there.

TD: Where was he usually?

PR: He was usually at our house. I mean it was 50-50, you know.

TD: Now explain that 50-50 to me. I mean is that kind of — would he stay overnight at Barnhills or was it just 50 percent of the day?

PR: No. Some nights he would spend the night over there. And, you know, if I was going to be gone all day, maybe two — rather than leave him in the house alone, they liked to have him over there and they played with him all the time. So I would say, "Betty Ann, I am going to Denver, I won't be back until 5 o'clock or something, do you want Jacques?" "Oh, yes." And then the kids usually went over and get him . . . so it was kind of —

TD: 50 percent of the time he was not spending the night in your house?

PR: Right. Maybe not quite 50 percent, maybe 40 percent.

TD: And would he bark when strangers came around?

PR: He didn't bark a lot, but he would, yeah. Uh huh. He could bark, yeah. I think, I think when — you know, he just was so good with the kids and the kids were romping all over, you know, playing with him. I think when he sensed danger, probably would have.

TD: Where did he stay when he was in the house at night?

PR: He used JonBenet's room or we were having trouble training him, potty training him, so I had to let — had somebody teach me to have him next to my bed like on a leash, because they wouldn't soil the area where they sleep. So I started doing that, and I had to take him down in the morning, let him out. He pretty much had the run of the house.

TH: Just a couple of minutes ago we were talking about like you leaving the church and that. There has been a lot of information, I guess, that on the day of the 26th, before the police were there, you're in the solarium, John's in the study, that you guys never got together. That he wasn't near you.

And a few minutes ago you also talked that he's a touchy, huggy, close. These two just seem to be in complete contrast to one another. Some of the perception that is out there that you didn't — or that he wasn't there, or wasn't supportive, at least that day or maybe coming out of the church, maybe the days following.

PR: He is a complete support. We were completely — I mean, he was back there doing his business with Linda Arndt and they were setting up the telephone taps.She was schooling him as to what he was supposed to say when this call came in, supposed to say, "We will call you in the morning," or something like. They were getting all that set up. I was in there with — those two women were there and Barbara and Priscilla and whomever else, and he would come in — I mean I was just sitting there, you know, praying and I kept — Linda Arndt said — she said that many times they would — something like if something happened, the kidnappers would get scared and pretty likely drop her off someplace, you know, just drop her out of the car in the grocery store or something like that.

So I was just in there, I just thought at any moment I would see her coming running down the street, you know. And John would come in and he would say, you know, "Don't worry, we will get her back, it will be okay, it will be okay, they have got it under control."

You know, I mean, he came to me several times and reassured me that, you know, they are doing everything. You know, I didn't feel like he was away or something.

TH: And we are talking 5:52 a.m. until, say, 1 o'clock in the afternoon, and Detective Arndt spent 10, 20, 30 minutes maybe going over that. But again, there seems to be this distance between you two.

PR: I don't know who is saying ... this or seeming that. Now he, as far as I was concerned, there was no distance, you know ... we were both racked out of our minds because our child was missing, you know. I am sitting there in deep prayer, trying to look at all these people walking around the house, going "Am I dreaming this? Is this really happening?" you know. And he is trying his best to figure out — I mean he was trying to get the ransom money, I understand. He was, you know.

I don't know who is perceiving that there was problems with us, but there was no problem, there has been no problem and continues to be no problem.

TH: Before we totally get away from that, since that day have you given any thought, even for a minute, considered that John may have been involved in some way in JonBenet's death?

PR: Absolutely no.

TH: Not a second?

PR: Not a moment.

TH: The thought never crossed your mind?

PR: Never crossed my mind.

TH: Why?

PR: That man loved his children. Period, end of statement. I have observed him before I had children, with his three children who were not my children, and he divorced their mother, but not those children. Wherever we were in the world, that man called his children. He was there for . . . you know — I mean she never had to go back to court to ask for more money. She asked John and he sent it, he was there. I mean, there are very few fathers like that man.

TH: And I am not saying that he thought about this, planned or conspired or something for months to carry this out. I am saying did you ever for a second think —

PR: Not a second.

TH: — maybe there was an accident?

PR: No, never.

TH: Could there have been an accident?

PR: (Shaking head.)

TH: Could John have accidentally bumped, pushed, struck JonBenet?

PR: No. No. Not as far as I know.

TH: Not within the realm of possibility?

PR: Not even in the worst . . . .

TD: . . . Who would you think, if it was somebody who was — played the role of a Secret Santa for JonBenet, who comes to mind as somebody who might do that with JonBenet?

PR: I am not sure how to even — how they would — what Secret Santa? I don't understand.

TD: Bring a present to her, "I am your Secret Santa, I am going to have a special present for you after Christmas"-type of thing, or some such thing like that. Is there anybody that you can think of that comes to mind who might have that type of relationship with JonBenet?

Patsy brings up the name of Bill McReynolds. He was a retired journalism professor who played Santa Claus at

Christmas parties and outdoor events in Boulder. With his full white beard, he looked the part. For several years, the Ramseys had hired him to play Santa at their Christmas parties.

PR: Well, I mean Bill McReynolds, who played our Santa Claus, you know, was very fond of JonBenet. He was, you know, from our house, he'd take them by the hand and take them to get something to eat, you know, and he just adored her. I mean, that would be the only one I would think.

I mean the year prior he came after — to our house after Christmas, not in Santa Claus regalia, just in his street clothes, you know, and he had a gingerbread house, and he — and I looked at him and I am going, "What are you doing here, you're going to spoil the surprise."

And he said, you know, "I have this gingerbread house, and I think — thought since you all were into Christmas, I would bring it to you all." And so he told JonBenet and Burke that he was Santa Claus's brother, and that he looked like Santa Claus, except in his jeans and whatever. He said "I am Santa Claus' brother and I herd his reindeer for him during the summers." You know. And —

TD: That was the Christmas before?

PR: Before, yes.

TD: And how long after Christmas did he show up as Santa Claus' brother?

PR: A couple of days later.

TD: Okay. Did JonBenet have expectations that Bill McReynolds would go by again after Christmas 1996?

PR: No, I don't think so.

TD: Okay.

TH: Was she ever alone with McReynolds?

PR: I wouldn't say alone, no. I mean we had a Christmas party going on with other people all over the house, kids, you know, and — alone, no.

TH: On the 25th, Christmas, when you put JonBenet to bed, did she have any marks on her?

PR: Not that I noticed.

TH: Any scratches, cuts, bruises?

PR: Not that I noticed.

TH: How about, did she have any marks from markers or anything like that?

PR: I didn't notice anything that night when she went to bed. And, you know, I know there was a red heart on her hand or her forehead. I don't know when that — I mean, you know, I didn't — I didn't inspect her when I put her to bed.

TH: . . . Would she have washed her hands at a particular time?

PR: Well, at dinner, she rarely washed her hands.

TH: Would she, or perhaps she had been eating crab and you have that slimy stuff all over?

PR: Yeah, I think she is going to wash her hands. But I didn't see her. I don't know.

TH: Getting her ready that early afternoon, four or five o'clock, did you give her a bath, did she take a bath?

PR: I don't think so.

TH: You don't think you gave her one?

PR: Huh uh.

TH: Do you think she took one?

PR: No, she didn't take one . . . .

TH: Showers?

PR: Huh uh.

TH: Would she have washed her hands before getting ready to go?

PR: I'd like to think so, but I just don't know for sure.
TD: At the Whites, did somebody say, "Oh, here, get ready for dinner?" Did somebody tell her to go wash her hands at the Whites, do you remember anything about that?
PR: I don't know.
TD: How was she about washing her hands?
PR: Just typical kid, you know, if she can get by with it, she wouldn't do it.
TD: How do you know there was a heart on her hand?

At this point, Patsy made a statement that seemed incredibly incriminating. She claimed to have seen the red heart found drawn in ink on the left hand of her slain daughter. She said she saw it on the morning of December 26th but JonBenet's body wasn't found until the afternoon. Later she would change her story.

PR: Because it was on there in the morning, that's why.
TD: And you remember it from the next morning?
PR: Uh huh.
TD: You saw it the next morning?
PR: Uh huh.
TD: When you say the next morning, did you remember it from the previous evening?
PR: (Shaking head.)
TD: Did she — I mean did it get there, was that something she would do or —
PR: Well, she and Daphne, you know, a lot of times drew on themselves.
TD: Did you ever see a heart on her hand before?
PR: Not specifically a heart.
TD: What might you have seen before?
PR: Just markings, you know, just erratic marks maybe,

she had been coloring, pen or ink marks . . . .

TD: Did you ever draw anything on the palm of her hands?

PR: (Shaking head.)

TD: Was there ever an occasion when you would draw a smiley face on the palm of her hand or on her hand somewhere?

PR: As a matter of fact, I discouraged her doing that because we always did what we called the pageant scrub the night before we have a pageant. We would wash her hair real good, and scrub her fingernails, and, you know, and oftentimes she would have, you know, marker all over herself or something, on her leg or something. Say, "Honey, now don't do that, wipe it off." We had to use nail polish remover, sort of try to dilute it and get it off. So I kind of discouraged that as much as possible.

TD: There was something regarding that you would draw a smiley face when she was feeling down to perk her up. What would your reaction be to that?

PR: That I would do it?

TD: Yes.

PR: I don't remember doing that.

TD: What was your reaction when you saw that heart on her hand?

PR: Well, I just thought Daphne must have done it or something, you know, they were playing the night before. You know — you know, my mind ran things out. But Santa Claus made a point the night that he was at our house at the party and was, you know, reading this dialogue that I had written up, and then he told this story about, you know, how Christmas should be Christmas all the time, all year long. And he said, "And where is Christmas when it's not really

JonBenet, hair professionally coiffed, lipstick and eyeliner making her look much older than her tender years, as she prepares to take part in a "Little Miss" pageant in the summer of 1996.

Clockwise from top: Mom Patsy and little JonBenet; JonBenet the playful toddler; JonBenet with her brother Burke.

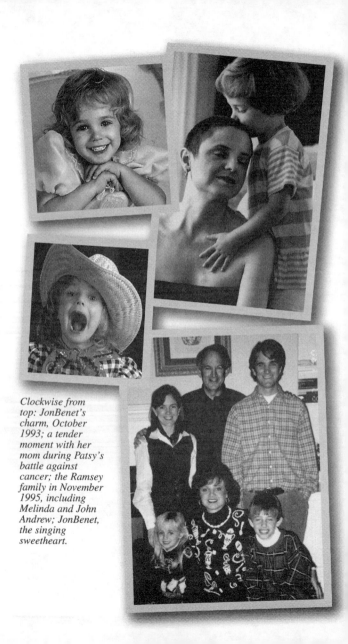

Clockwise from top: JonBenet's charm, October 1993; a tender moment with her mom during Patsy's battle against cancer; the Ramsey family in November 1995, including Melinda and John Andrew; JonBenet, the singing sweetheart.

Clockwise from top left: JonBenet struts her stuff in sailor suit pageant costume, 1995; JonBenet and Burke pose for a charming portrait, Easter 1996; JonBenet performing in a pageant; posing with Burke and pet rabbits for a formal studio portrait in 1996.

Young beauty: JonBenet at her most winsome in these professional photographs taken for her modeling portfolio in summer 1996. Top left photo was taken during her last professional shoot in November 1996.

Just a regular little girl: JonBenet at play during a modeling shoot, 1996.

Kidding around in their Easter finery: (clockwise from top) Grandmother Nedra Paugh, JonBenet, Burke and Patsy; Patsy and her children; JonBenet and Burke; JonBenet and her grandmother.

All dressed up and the world ahead of her — JonBenet in her spectacular pageant outfits in 1996.

Sweet smiles as JonBenet establishes herself as a winner on the "Little Miss" circuit. The bottom picture was taken less than four weeks before she died. The photo top left is particularly poignant: It's the last picture of JonBenet, taken at a shopping mall event two weeks before her death.

Patsy's triumph: (above) She walks the runway in the Miss America swimsuit contest in 1977. Left from top: Patsy poses at a party in April 1996; Patsy clowns at a national "Little Miss" pageant in July 1996; JonBenet crowned a winner.

Happier days: John and Patsy on their wedding day in 1980.

Clockwise from top left: Patsy, her hair growing back after chemotherapy during her cancer ordeal in 1994; JonBenet sharing a special moment with her mother; JonBenet's stepbrother John Andrew; Patsy in 1994; Burke in 1993.

In their grief: A distraught Patsy at JonBenet's funeral in Atlanta in January 1997 (right). Below, the family mourns again at the memorial service in Boulder that followed.

Clockwise from top: JonBenet's flower-covered casket is carried from the church in Atlanta after her funeral service; John Andrew and Burke reflect in the cemetery where she was buried; Patsy's face speaks her devastation at memorial service.

Grandmother Nedra Paugh, left, and JonBenet's Aunt Pam console each other at her grave in May 1998.

After the murder: (from the top) The Ramseys offer $100,000 reward after their first police grilling in April 1997; the couple face the microphones after police interviews in Atlanta in August 2000; John and Patsy try to escape the media.

Seven months after JonBenet's death, John and Patsy relax with friends Glen and Susan Stine at their lakeside home in Charlevoix. They flew there on John's plane.

Party time: (clockwise from right) The Ramseys chill out in Charlevoix, 1999; old friends Barbara Fernie (left) and Susan Stine with Patsy in Boulder, May 1997; Patsy and Susan Stine the same day.

Remembering JonBenet: August 1997: Patsy with a portrait of her daughter; and in JonBenet's bedroom in their Charlevoix home (shown left).

A happy family photograph taken on the steps of the Charlevoix house; Patsy is comforted by a friend after JonBenet's death.

Clockwise from top: JonBenet's favorite Santa, Bill McReynolds and his wife Janet; police detective Dan Schuler, who questioned Burke Ramsey; Linda Hoffman-Pugh, the Ramsey housekeeper, with picture of JonBenet; and with her husband and daughter; Joe Barnhill, the Ramseys' friend and neighbor, with JonBenet's dog Jacques.

Ramsey pals: (from left) Susan Stine, Fleet White, who was with John when he found the body, Glen Stine with John.

Pageant photographer Randy Simons (left) after his arrest for running naked in the street; John Ramsey's first wife Lucinda.

ARAPAHOE CO.
SHERIFF DEPT.

The Ramseys' home in Boulder, where JonBenet died. Below, crime scene pictures taken in JonBenet's bedroom.

CRIME SCENE

The crime scene: (clockwise from top) Investigators search for clues outside; looking down into window in basement; front door of Ramsey home; window to bathroom in basement; technician dusts for fingerprints.

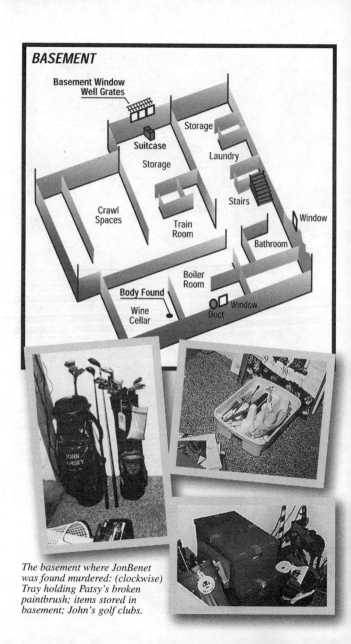

BASEMENT

Basement Window
Well Grates

Suitcase

Storage

Storage

Laundry

Crawl
Spaces

Stairs

Train
Room

Window

Bathroom

Boiler
Room

Body Found

Wine
Cellar

Window

Duct

The basement where JonBenet was found murdered: (clockwise) Tray holding Patsy's broken paintbrush; items stored in basement; John's golf clubs.

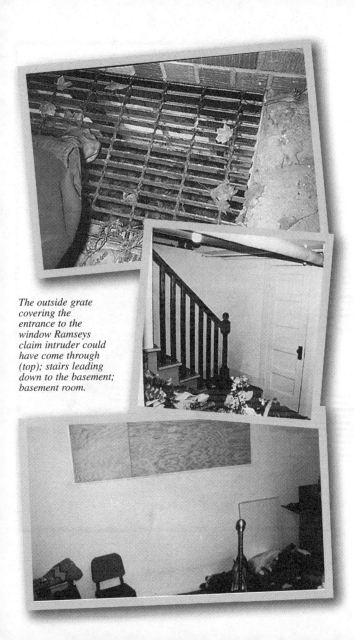

The outside grate covering the entrance to the window Ramseys claim intruder could have come through (top); stairs leading down to the basement; basement room.

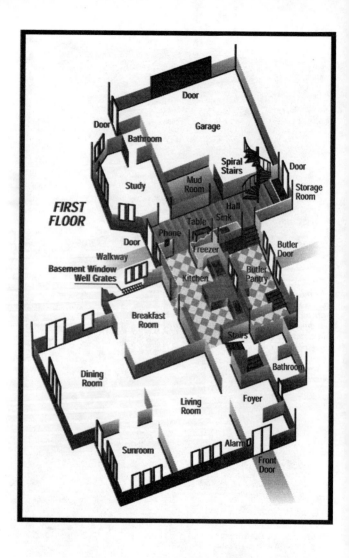

FIRST FLOOR

Door

Garage

Door

Bathroom

Study

Spiral Stairs

Door

Mud Room

Storage Room

Hall

Table

Sink

Phone

Butler Door

Door

Freezer

Walkway

Butler Pantry

Basement Window Well Grates

Kitchen

Breakfast Room

Stairs

Bathroom

Dining Room

Living Room

Foyer

Sunroom

Alarm

Front Door

Sad Christmas: Interior of the house, with the Christmas tree area where JonBenet's body was laid. Ransom note was found on the spiral staircase, close to the bottom; (right) the hallway floor where John knelt to read ransom note.

House of death: Crime scene pictures taken inside the house after the murder. From top, door to butler kitchen; butler kitchen hallway; the wall phone from which Patsy called 911.

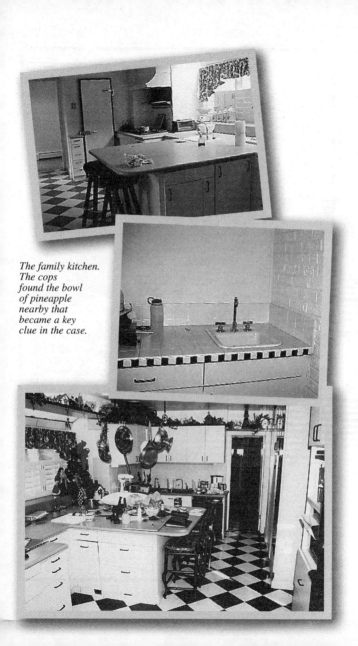

The family kitchen. The cops found the bowl of pineapple nearby that became a key clue in the case.

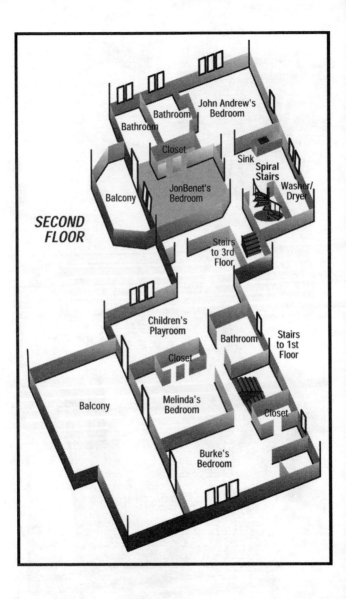

SECOND FLOOR

Bathroom

Bathroom

John Andrew's Bedroom

Closet

Sink

Spiral Stairs

Balcony

JonBenet's Bedroom

Washer/Dryer

Stairs to 3rd Floor

Children's Playroom

Bathroom

Stairs to 1st Floor

Closet

Balcony

Melinda's Bedroom

Closet

Burke's Bedroom

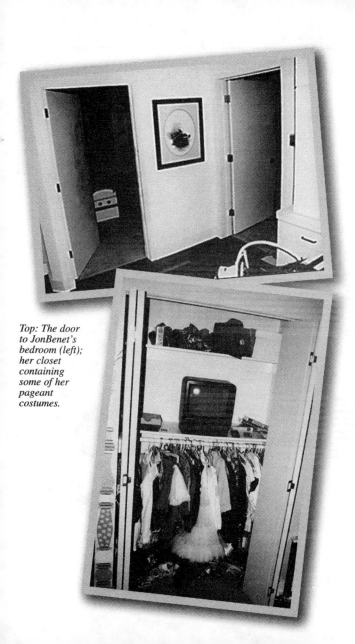

Top: The door to JonBenet's bedroom (left); her closet containing some of her pageant costumes.

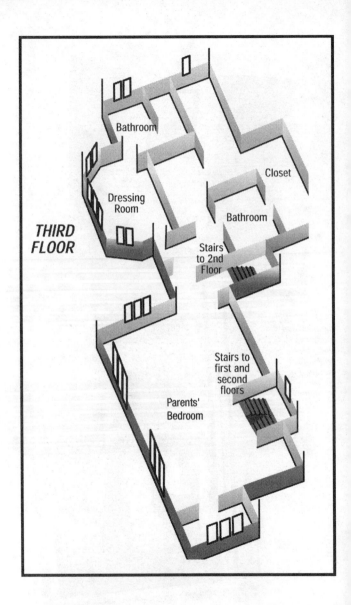

THIRD FLOOR

Bathroom

Dressing Room

Closet

Bathroom

Stairs to 2nd Floor

Stairs to first and second floors

Parents' Bedroom

Patsy and John's huge third floor bedroom in picture taken after the murder.

Murder most foul: Cops guard the house after the Ramseys leave. At right: Detectives Steve Thomas (center) and Tom Trujillo (right) leave a home in Atlanta during the investigation.

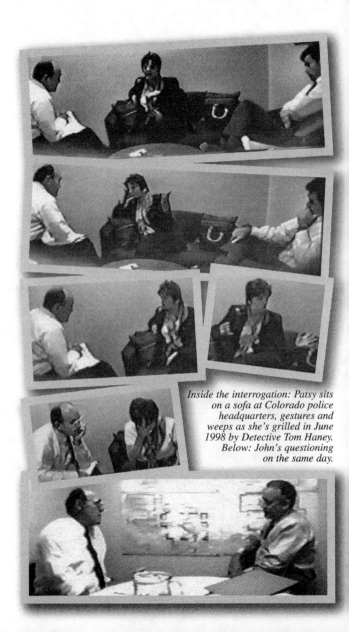

Inside the interrogation: Patsy sits on a sofa at Colorado police headquarters, gestures and weeps as she's grilled in June 1998 by Detective Tom Haney. Below: John's questioning on the same day.

The hunters: clockwise from top left: Detective Tom Trujillo; Detective Linda Arndt with her attorney; Michael Kane, who helped question Patsy; Lou Smit, legendary detective who led questioning of John; Trip DeMuth, (2nd left) Boulder assistant DA, who helped question Patsy; Mary Keenan, the new Boulder DA, is on the right; Boulder police chief Tom Koby and District Attorney Alex Hunter; Steve Thomas, a lead detective on the case.

JonBenét Patricia
Ramsey
AUGUST 6, 1990
DECEMBER 25, 1996

...RITY AND JOY

*A GIFT TO HER FAMILY
AND THE WORLD.*

HOME IN THE PEACE OF GOD.

*The place where an angel rests.
JonBenet's grave in Atlanta. The
Ramseys raised eyebrows when
they put her date of death as
December 25th.*

Christmas?", something like that . . . and he pointed
to JonBenet. And she said in her heart. Pointing. That
was a pretty good little heart, you know, I mean
— pretty well drawn.
TD: Okay.

TOM HANEY: Today is Wednesday, June 24, 1998, and the time is approximately 9:03 a.m. Again we are present in the Broomfield Police Department. Present is Patricia Ramsey . . . and how did you spend yesterday, how did you feel?
PATSY RAMSEY: Fine, great.

Patsy now changes her story about seeing the heart drawn on JonBenet's hand.

PR: . . . I think that I read somewhere talking about the heart on her hand. And truthfully, I can't — I am having trouble distinguishing whether I have read about that or whether I actually saw that. I just recently read parts of the autopsy report, and I believe that was on there. And I just, you know, now I have a picture of a heart on her hand and I can't remember whether I actually saw it or —
TRIP DEMUTH: Let me ask you this. Do you remember what color it was? Is there a color that you recall?
PR: No, I just see a red heart in my mind.
TD: But you don't know if you read it?
PR: No . . . just to be perfectly fair, to say that I saw it on her.
TH: . . . Okay. Have you and John over the last year and a half discussed the intruder theory?
PR: Yes.

__TH:__ What can you tell me, what are your — what are your feelings, insights?

__PR:__ Well, I mean, he and I both know there was someone else in the house that night. Beyond that, we don't know.

__TH:__ Have you given thought to how this person gained access?

__PR:__ Yes. I mean, we have gone to test doors, unfortunately, I am sorry to say, and there were a number of little access ways through the garage, those little doors. That was accessible. The basement window, we had a basement window that faced the front of the house, faced the Barnhills' house, where I would run my Christmas lights, so that window was unlocked. And then this window in the rear of the house ... under the grate kind of thing, that was open. If someone wanted in, they could get in.

__TD:__ The window in front, does it have bars on it?

__PR:__ It does have bars on it.

__TH:__ Did John ever explain to you the position and the way JonBenet's body was wrapped in the blanket, covered?

__PR:__ No. I believe — no, he didn't. When he found her, you mean?

__TH:__ Correct.

__PR:__ No.

__TH:__ Did you ever inquire about that?

__PR:__ No. Just too hard.

__TH:__ We touched briefly yesterday on the pageant that JonBenet was in, we talked about the possibility of some parent. Could you talk to us a little bit about how these pageants were set up, how — what kind of security, if any? You know, how much — start with how were they publicized? I mean, is it a preset group of people that's involved?

<u>PR</u>: Very small. It's open to anyone, but they don't have a tremendous number of recipients. The first way I learned about it was seeing it listed in Colorado, was through a make-up artist in Denver where I was having my make-up done for a Boulder publication and we were talking about our children. She had two girls and they did the pageants. I said, "Oh, you know, where are they, do you know where they are?"

And so she told me about her experiences with them. She said she would call or give me the name of someone who did a couple of them. So I subsequently called — I think the first one I called was — I can't remember the name. Anyway, there were two different ones. And they had events coming up in the next month or so. So I kind of inquired about it, and went down and entered.

<u>TH</u>: And when would that have been, the first one?

<u>PR</u>: Like spring or — spring of — spring, spring of '95 or '97? I don't remember.

<u>TH</u>: So, you have been involved for about a year and a half then?

<u>PR</u>: Right.

<u>TH</u>: That's great. So help me, did they have like a national organization that has like an umbrella over everything?

<u>PR</u>: Right, right, this was — they have a national group, and they would have these local events.

<u>TH</u>: Qualifying or something?

<u>PR</u>: In a hotel, you know, in a hotel and they would have staging, you know, dressing rooms and all that kind of stuff. And they had different categories, where you could choose to enter whichever categories you would like. You know — mostly modeling and the reason we did it was because we did the ones that would have talent, like singing, that kind of thing.

So then for these, like they have a western category
and all the girls would wear like a cute western
outfit. And they have sportswear and that would be
kind of a dress — you know, so they had these little
categories. And they were by age group. JonBenet was
in the 4-to-6-year-old age group. And 10-to-12. So
they weren't competing with anybody much older than
they. And you kind of just do that all afternoon, and
at the conclusion of the day, they would announce
winners in various categories. One of the categories
was photography, you know, the portfolios. You know . . .

TH: Did they, when one of these pageants was held, was
there a program that was made up with photos?

PR: Yeah.

TH: Vital information, name, address?

PR: No, I don't think it had the address. It would just
have their names. You know like here are the 4-to-6
contestants, JonBenet, Susie, blah, blah, blah, blah.

TH: And that was distributed just at the —

PR: At the day of the event.

TH: You had said these were open to anybody. Was it
like a paid admission or —

PR: Yeah, I think they charged a little something to
get in. Yeah. But mostly just parents and relatives.
Yeah.

TH: You had only been involved in it a short period of
time?

PR: Right.

TH: So, I don't know, did you have a feel for the
people who were there, were they the usual folks,
I mean it's a — I am guessing, kind of a small group —

PR: Uh huh.

TH: — that regularly competes?

PR: Yeah, yeah, you know, the kind of same ones would

be in a lot of these events.

TH: But how about some unusual face in the crowd?

PR: You kind of get to know each other. You know, like, "Oh, yeah, hi, saw you last time or," you know. Sort of get to know people. It's not that we knew each other very well . . . .

TD: I am particularly interested in the Amerikids performance, and that was only a few days before Christmas, right?

PR: (Nodding.)

TD: A short period before Christmas?

PR: This was which one, at the mall?

TD: That's the Southwest Plaza Mall?

PR: Right.

TD: Is that out in the open? Are there walkways at the mall?

PR: It was an atrium sort of area, in the mall. Where they apparently had activities going on.

TD: Right. So people that are shopping in the mall can walk by and see the show?

PR: Correct.

TD: So that was offered to anybody just walking by?

PR: Right.

TD: So there wasn't any sense of — there wasn't any security and control of who was observing this particular performance?

PR: Uh-uh.

TD: In other words, if one was walking by and they saw JonBenet, could they find out who she was and where she lived?

PR: I don't think so, no.

TD: . . . Did JonBenet ever complain of anyone at the pageant, did she ever tell you somebody bothered her?

PR: No.

TD: Anybody act peculiar around her show?

PR: No.

TD: She was also in the Christmas Parade, right?

PR: Uh-hum.

TD: She was on a float with a couple of other girls?

PR: Yes, it was a car.

TD: Okay. Oh, she was sitting in a car?

PR: Yeah.

TD: Was her name displayed anywhere?

PR: Yes.

TD: And who was she in the car with?

PR: My car with the driver, it was a BMW, and JonBenet — and I wasn't there, I was in New York at the time, John and I were out of town, but my parents took her, and there were these little girls from the Amerikids.

TD: So there were maybe four or five girls?

PR: Yes.

TD: Sitting up on the back of the Beemer?

PR: Yeah, right. I can't remember their names. I would if I saw a picture somewhere.

TD: Okay, now were all of their names displayed on the side of the car?

PR: I believe so.

TD: Okay.

TH: How about birthday, Christmas, any time of the year had JonBenet been sick, had she gotten any get well cards, birthday cards, Christmas cards? I mean not a family, not a regular, somebody that you would expect to have her get a card from? I know that's covering lot of territory, but —

PR: Well, the only one that kind of comes to mind is a letter that she — after we had come home from the lake, there was, you know, some mail there and there was a letter from Bill McReynolds.

TH: Was that in '96?

PR: Uh huh, in '96.

TH: At the end of the summer then?

PR: Right.

TH: Okay. And of course I opened it and it said that he was — I believe it said that he was about to go into the hospital for open heart surgery, some kind of a pretty major surgery, and he was going to take along with him the bottle of sprinkle dust, prayer dust that she had given him when he was at our house at Christmastime, and —

TH: Christmas '95?

PR: The previous year, right. And just that meant a lot to him, and I guess he just wanted us to know he was going to surgery. I mean I thought — I mean I was surprised that he was going into surgery, and I thought it sweet that he sent us a card.

TH: Announcing his surgery or —

PR: Yeah. I kind of got the feeling like if I don't make it through surgery and I don't see you again, I always enjoyed being with you all, you know, something like that.

TH: But it was addressed to —

PR: JonBenet.

TH: — JonBenet?

PR: Well, I don't remember exactly whether it was — was written to me or to her or —

TH: There has been some confusion over the times of the return home from the Whites . . . on the time you went to bed. I think you said 10, 10:30 . . . do you recall the time you would have left the Whites, as close as possible?

PR: No, I just don't know. I had had no reason to really look and see what time it was. I can't really say for sure.

TH: Were you looking for an excuse or, you know, "We got to get up early?"

PR: No. I don't remember that.

TH: What's your best guess, though, on the time you would have left?

PR: I don't know. Probably nine-ish or so. I don't remember.

TH: And how many stops did you make along the way?

PR: Two.

TH: And those were at?

PR: The Walkers and the Stines.

TH: And you took some presents up to both of them?

PR: Right.

TH: Did anybody take presents up with you?

PR: Best as I remember, we went to the Walkers first and I took this bottle of perfume to Roxie. And then we went to the Stines and I had a basket of things to give to them. And I think I went by myself. Burke may have jumped out of the car, because it's his friends.

TH: The Stines?

PR: The Stines. So it was either — it was either just myself or maybe Burke and myself.

TH: How long did you stay at the Walkers?

PR: Oh, around 10, 15 minutes.

TH: And then drive time from there to the Stines?

PR: A couple of minutes.

TH: And how long did you stay there?

PR: Same. Ten — maybe 10 minutes.

TH: I want to go back briefly to the time, when was it, Elizabeth, Beth Ramsey?

PR: Uh-hum.

TH: Could you tell me about that, where were you guys living, how did you find out (that she had been killed in a car accident)?

PR: We were living in Colorado, and I found out about it when John and my father came to the house, down on 15th Street and told me about it.

TH: And how — how did John react to that, how did he take that? Is this his oldest daughter?

PR: His oldest daughter. He was incredibly distraught. Devastated.

TH: Did he react in a similar fashion to JonBenet's death?

PR: Yes.

Patsy at this point was asked to begin a review of dozens of crime scene photos taken inside the Boulder home. She was asked if she saw anything unusual or out of place. For the most part she didn't.

A dust ruffle on the bed in John Andrew's bedroom — the guest room next to JonBenet's room — caught her eye. A section of it seemed tucked under the bed as if someone had crawled under there to hide, she said.

She didn't recognize a stuffed bear in Santa clothing that is on a second bed in JonBenet's room. Police later learned the bear was a gift given to JonBenet and other children at the Amerikids pageant event in Boulder, days before the murder.

Other items caught her eye in the pictures — JonBenet's hair ties on the floor of her bedroom, a red turtleneck JonBenet didn't want to wear to the Whites party, and JonBenet's backpack.

As she viewed a photo showing one of JonBenet's pageant crowns on the floor of her bedroom, Patsy broke down in tears.

Investigators questioned Patsy about furs and fur-lined boots she owned. A beaver hair was found on the duct tape that covered JonBenet's mouth. She was also asked about other footwear the family owned. An imprint of the words Hi-Tec, the symbol of the Hi-Tec footwear company, was found in cement dust near JonBenet's body.

TH: Do you own any Hi-Tec footwear?

PR: No.

TH: How about John?

PR: No.

TH: Anybody in the family that you know of has it?

PR: No.

TH: How about a fur coat, did you have fur coats?

PR: Yes, I had fur coats.

TH: Was it at the house or in storage or —

PR: It was at the house, black mink.

TH: Mink, okay. How about boots, gloves, jackets, other things that would have had fur on it?

PR: There is a leather jacket that has a fur lining, men's leather jacket. It was John's. It was reversible.

TH: Do you know what type of fur that would have been?

PR: Well, it was like real low cut, black shiny pile.

TH: Was it real fur?

PR: Yeah . . . I had a black mink like muffler kind of hat, like a ring kind of thing you wear, two balls hanging down, earmuffs kind of thing. Two balls hanging down.

TH: That was mink also?

PR: Uh huh. I had a pair of after-ski boots, black, I don't know what kind of fur it was . . . . It was kind of, I don't know, leopard fur kind of thing.

TH: Was it artificial?

PR: No, I think it's real, but it was probably mink or something.

TH: Okay. Any others?

PR: Let's see. What kind of —

TH: These after-ski boots, did you ski?

PR: Not very much.

TH: Why not?

PR: Dangerous.

TH: Do you recall purchasing some Hi-Tec boots . . . in Vail in the summer of '96?

PR: (Shaking head.)

TH: Do you recall being in Vail in the summer of '96?

TD: Or even in the fall?

TH: Or the last time you were there?

PR: No.

TD: Let me ask a question. Did you have some hiking, I don't know what you call them exactly, these hiking boot-type things . . . sort of a cross between a tennis shoe and a hiking boot sort of? Did you have anything like that?

PR: No.

TD: Any sort of hiking boots at all?

PR: No.

TD: These are sort of fashionable. People used to use for hiking and all that.

PR: No.

TD: Anybody in the family have footwear like that?

PR: John Andrew, you know, hiked. Melinda probably did.

TD: How about John or Burke or JonBenet?

PR: JonBenet had some little, little sort of suede — actually, they were Burke's. They were Stride-Rite . . . with a little kind of red tie. You know. Burke had, you know, kind of boots, kind of shoes, like kind of — they might be suede or something, kind of thing.

TD: Have you ever heard of the Hi-Tec brand footwear before?

PR: I have heard that, this name is, you know, has come up. But I —

TD: Since JonBenet's death?

PR: Yes, I read it.

TD: How about prior to JonBenet's death?

PR: No. Never heard of it.

TH: (Photo No.) 52 shows the spiral stairs coming down?

PR: Uh-hum, right.

TH: And not to look too much, but would you just indicate which step that note would have been on?

PR: Around there (indicating).

TH: You indicated the second step from the floor?

PR: Uh-hum.

TH: And that laid out left to right, pages 1, 2 and 3?

PR: Yeah.

TH: Okay. So as you come down, and we talked about this yesterday ... you get to the what, the third — when do you see it?

PR: Probably on the way down, you know, you know ... I kind of stepped around it and stepped on them and turned around to see what it was.

TH: So you just stepped around it onto the second step or —

PR: Yeah.

TH: Okay.

TD: What do you mean by "stepped around it?"

PR: Well, I am sure if I would have put my foot on a piece of paper on the carpeted steps and for fear of flying, so —

TD: Because it's laid one, two, three, across that step, right?

PR: Right.

TD: So the paper pretty much taking up the whole step or —

PR: I mean, I don't remember leaping from three to one, so I imagine I kind of — kind of got a foothold and went on down past it. I just can't imagine that I would have stepped right on it for fear of flying out from under me.

TH: So somehow you probably stepped on that second step, tiptoed around it?

PR: Right . . . I turned back around to see what it was.

TH: Now, did you normally come down that way in the morning?

PR: Uh huh.

TH: How do you normally go back up?

PR: Same way.

TH: And I think you indicated somewhere before that a lot of times you would leave things —

PR: Right.

TH: — on the steps there?

PR: Yes.

TH: Okay. Like — okay. Remind you, hey, next time you're going up, take this up. Who would know or who would have seen this practice?

PR: Leaving the staircase a lot and leaving things sitting out?

TH: Yes.

PR: Well, the housekeeper, certainly.

TH: Okay. Who else?

PR: My mother, you know, I see her a lot. I mean anybody that was in the house.

TH: So somebody pretty familiar?

PR: Right. Because I wondered that — I wondered, well, why didn't they leave it on the first step, because I very likely would have noticed it?

TH: Okay . . . how would somebody choose to leave it there?

PR: Good question.

TH: But somebody pretty familiar or just lucky?

PR: Maybe.

TH: But if it was — it's somebody who was around your

house regularly?

PR: They would know that this was the staircase we most frequently used.

TH: Okay, that's your habit?

PR: Uh huh.

TD: ... Okay. And could we talk a little bit more about the ransom note here ... If you could spread that out. There was something I was confused about. Let's spread it out one, two, three like it was on the steps. Now, you had made a comment about reading only like the first paragraph or so when you first saw it, right?

PR: Right.

TD: And then there was another time when you had read about, "Don't call
the police," right?

PR: Uh huh.

TD: And I think — can you show me where that was?

PR: Right here.

TD: So that's kind of in the middle there, the second page?

PR: Uh huh.

TD: When did you read that portion?

PR: I think when John had it down on the floor there and in that back hallway. You know, I was kind of glancing at it. Over his shoulder, sort of picked that out.

TD: Okay. When was that in relationship to calling the police?

PR: That was probably just a couple of seconds before.

TD: How did you get to that portion of the note? Did you read the entire thing?

PR: No, no. I couldn't, I just couldn't look at it. I mean I got to this place where my daughter was missing, I went upstairs, she was missing and I remember looking at this, looking, and then I was like, you know, kind of glanced at it.

TD: So it was — how did you get — so tell me how you got to that one portion there about not calling the —

PR: . . . It popped out.

TD: And that was seconds before you called the police?

PR: Uh huh.

TD: Let me see if I have anything else. You would take messages at the kitchen phone. Did you have writing materials?

PR: Yeah, there was lots of pens and . . . you know, a couple of jars with writing things.

The Sharpie pen used to write the ransom note was found in one of those jars.

TH: Trip mentioned this area that said, "Don't call the FBI or the police." And you said you were reading it over John's shoulder at that point and you said —

PR: You know, I was sort of like had the phone, kind of glancing down at it. I saw that and I said, "You know, it says don't call anybody."

TH: Was there any more discussion than that, or you said that, he said that, and you called?

PR: That's about it.

TH: . . . As we go back a little bit, which you brought up this morning, Mrs. Ramsey, about the heart on the hand, I want to make sure that I have got this straight. You said that on the night of the 25th when you put JonBenet down, you didn't recall seeing any drawings or markings, any heart or anything like that.

PR: Right.

TH: Okay. And then, in your words, would you tell me when it is or how it is that you recall something about, something on her hand?

PR: Well, I recently read the autopsy report, part of it, and the heart drawing on her hand. I really don't know which hand, I don't know. I don't know which hand. And I heard some talk about the heart on her hand. But I can't be sure that I actually saw the heart on her hand after we discovered her body. But I have a visual image of the heart on her hand, but I may be drawing that from things I have heard or read. Can't really remember physically seeing the heart on her hand.

TH: . . . One other thing, this morning you mentioned that the doctors in Atlanta, had diagnosed this post-traumatic stress disorder, and I wondered what the symptoms, what symptoms you experience as a result of that?

PR: Well, just very sad and very — crying a lot, fatigue easily.

TH: Okay. Do your symptoms include anything like nightmares?

PR: I had those.

TH: About?

PR: I have flashbacks of seeing my daughter lying dead on the floor in our living room, and I have flashbacks of hearing John scream. I have nightmares where I am, you know, searching, searching, searching trying to find somebody, and trying to find who did this.

TH: Is there something that brings these on?

PR: . . . Well, you know, if I have been doing like what we are doing, concentrating on this, like right now it has been kind of blue.

TH: Things like reading the autopsy, that —

PR: Well, I didn't really — I know she was struck on the head and that there was something tied around the neck, I know. I never really had read anything, all the details.

TH: Okay. Do you have — since then you have?

PR: Well, not read all of them, the medical things, it is kind of hard to read, but, you know, it is difficult.

Patsy was shown a photo of a cabinet above the laundry area outside JonBenet's room.

TH: What is normally kept in there, if you recall?

PR: Tissue.

TH: In the video that the police took walking through, which was taken some time later, there are — there is packages of Pull-Ups.

PR: They would be in there, yeah.

TH: All right. They are partially hanging out in the video?

PR: Yup.

TH: Would those be the Pull-Ups that you would normally put on JonBenet?

PR: Right.

TH: Do you recall the last time you put those on her?

PR: It hadn't been for quite some time, but I remember buying them to take a few with us on the cruise . . . I didn't want her to spoil the mattress. So I bought a new package, and probably had taken some out and put them in the suitcase I was packing. But she hadn't really worn them, you know, very much recently.

TH: Do you recall prior when the last time you put Pull-Ups on her?

PR: No.

TD: You used to have your painting materials in the butler kitchen, right?

TD: You had a paint . . . tray, or I don't know what you call —

The paint tray was found just outside the room where JonBenet's body lay. A brush from that tray had been broken in three pieces. The bristle part was found in the tray. The middle section was used with rope to fashion a handle to the leash-like noose used to strangle JonBenet. A small tip section of the brush was never found. Police found evidence that the tip of the brush may have been used to sexually abuse JonBenet.

PR: It was like a little utility carrier with paint in it and stuff.

TD: Do you remember when you moved those items?

PR: Right. Linda did . . . .

TD: Okay. And do you remember when she did that?

PR: Well, she did it prior to the party on the 23rd because we wanted to hang coats here. I don't know exactly the day she did it, but —

TD: Do you know where she moved them to?

PR: . . . The basement . . . .

TD: Okay.

TH: Well, there is a — I think maybe a quick little look at the tray with some brushes in it in a minute. In that tray of brushes what would you have had in there?

PR: Paint and brushes and probably . . . paint supplies.

TH: . . . Out of the brushes you would have had in there, would you have had any that were broken or damaged or would you —

PR: No, they were all pretty new.

TD: . . . Take a minute, Patsy, and think about the paint tray. Were there any broken paint brushes that you recall?

PR: No, not that I recall. . .

TD: Patsy, I would like to know, the best of your memory, prior to this Christmas, who had gone in that wine cellar?

PR: Well, at Thanksgiving time I asked my cleaning lady, I had kept my big artificial trees in there, and I asked her to come and, you know, put those up while I was gone at Thanksgiving. So I don't know exactly who was with her to help her. She insinuated this is when they were going to also clean some of the windows, she and her husband. I think she also mentioned that her daughter had come to help her . . . .

Okay. You know, it wasn't like a full-blown wine cellar, but we kept boxes of wine in there. And I want to say that — I don't remember whether it was the night of the 23rd, that party or some party we had, I remember somebody saying we are out of red wine. And I said please . . . go to the basement to get some more red wine . . .

TD: Okay. In the months prior to Christmas of 1996, Fleet would have gone in there?

PR: I would say Fleet, the cleaning lady and —

TD: Maybe the husband?

PR: Maybe the husband and maybe the daughter.

TD: How about yourself?

PR: Me. . . .

TD: Would the children go in there?

PR: No. If I had presents in there I would have locked it up.

TH: What else was stored there?

PR: That is what I was trying to think of. I had a little bicycle of Burke's, a little Batman, the first bicycle with little tiny wheels. I couldn't bear to part with that. Part of it was broken, I think.

TD: When and how often, I'm talking about in the months prior to Christmas, when and how often did you go into the wine cellar?

PR: Oh, not very often. I might have a wrapping session, you know, of Christmas things in there, so maybe a couple times before Christmas.

TD: Is that shortly before Christmas or more into November, or what do you think?

PR: No. Probably before Christmas.

TH: There has been talk about hidden keys outside. Did you — did you regularly leave a key hidden somewhere?

PR: I, at one time, used to leave a key under Pierre. Pierre is a little statue guy . . . . You push him back, there was a little key. He sat still on a platform.

TH: He is outside the door by the sun room?

PR: Right. He is on a little platform, and if you lean him back, there was a key under there. But then, you know, you forgot if you used the key, and we were not very diligent about putting it back.

TH: When do you recall the last time the key was under there?

PR: Don't know.

TH: What was your usual method though for coming in?

PR: Garage door opener, go in, and then the inside garage door was unlocked. I had never used the house key ever.

As in her April 1997 interview, Patsy was questioned about the Barbie nightgown found with JonBenet's body. She was shown a picture of it, but the nightgown was in a plastic bag in the photo. Patsy could not get a good look at it.

TH: When would she have worn that last, do you know?

PR: Well, she didn't wear it that night because she had her — she had the long underwear pants and her little white shirt. And the night before on Christmas Eve night she wore the pink little . . . that was under her pillow. And before that I don't remember. But neither of those two nights she wore that.

TH: Does this item have some particular significance?

PR: No. No.

TH: How many nightgowns did she have?

PR: A lot.

TH: Did this one have some particular significance?

PR: No.

TH: Do you remember who gave it to her?

PR: No . . . I'm thinking of a Barbie nightgown that had a big face of Barbie . . . big picture of the head of Barbie on it. So I am not quite sure this is . . . one that she had . . . could have been, I guess.

TH: Do you remember her wearing it on the 23rd?

PR: No.

TH: We've heard at some point this was a particularly favorite nightgown. Did she have such a thing?

PR: Well, her favorite little pajamas were like — was this one piece sort of . . . thing my mother had given her, kind of nylon, a little one piece thing. You stepped into it and put your arms out. Other than that, nothing special.

TD: But would your sister, Pam, call this her travel nightgown for any reason? I could be wrong.

PR: I mean, like pageants did we take one?

TD: Is there a reason she would say that?

PR: I just don't remember making a big deal about taking one special nightgown to the pageants.

TD: Do you know where that was before Christmas?

PR: No.

TH: It would not have been in the wine cellar?

PR: No.

Patsy was shown a photo of the blanket which was wrapped around JonBenet's body in the basement room.

TH: On the 25th when you put JonBenet to bed, do you recall seeing this?

PR: No.

TH: In the bed.

PR: . . . No, I don't. I don't really.

TH: When you put her down, covered her up?

PR: I know I covered her at least with the sheet, but I don't know that. We tend to get real warm, so, you know, you don't do a lot of tucking it in.

TH: Probably not the comforter?

PR: No.

TH: But the cotton blanket, you know, I think those are pretty — it is kind of like the ones in the hospital.

PR: They are not real heavy, right?

TH: So would that —

PR: Yeah. It would not have been unusual to put the sheet and the blanket on her. I truly can't remember.

TD: Patsy, why the long underwear?

PR: Well, I remember I was digging around for something. I was trying to find the pink ones she wore the night before. I couldn't put my hand on them right quick. And so I went to these drawers looking for the pajamas, and she was just laying there, so I didn't want to raise her up and get everything off of her to put a long nightgown, so looking for pajamas bottoms to put on her. I couldn't find any, and the long underwear pants were in their drawer, so I got those.

TH: . . . The last time you were in the wine cellar was Christmas Eve, Christmas Day?

PR: Probably Christmas Eve, bringing packages out.

TH: . . . Where did you do the bulk of your Christmas

shopping, the items you put in there?

PR: Well, all of this stuff right here was from FAO Schwartz in New York. JonBenet got a bicycle that year. I got a bicycle, and she got a twin doll which I mail ordered, and —

TH: Did she get to ride her bike?

PR: She got to ride her bike.

TH: Christmas Day?

PR: Out in the back driveway.

TH: You don't remember the weather that day, was —

PR: Sunny, nice.

TH: So did she get much time on it? Was it training wheel equipped or was she able to ride a two-wheeler by herself?

PR: I don't think it had training wheels. I think it did.

TH: We talked about your painting supplies . . . how about, where would you get household hardware type of items, those kind of things?

PR: . . . I mean light bulbs, that stuff I usually get at the grocery store.

TH: Do you recall purchasing duct tape and cord in the early part of December of '96?

A Ramsey credit card receipt from the McGuckin's hardware store in Boulder showed the purchase of an item that was the same price as a roll of duct tape.

PR: No. I never used this type of stuff. I use — I would buy the multiple rolls of the clear.

TH: Clear tape?

PR: Clear tape.

TH: You don't recall making a purchase of either or both of those things, like I said, back in early December, December 2nd of '96?

PR: No.

TH: Do you ever recall purchasing black duct tape?

PR: No.

TH: Ever have it around the house?

PR: I don't remember seeing any. I have my tape in the little drawer by the refrigerator, but it was usually masking tape and the clear tape for the UPS box.

TH: It seems like you — there can't be a house in the world that doesn't have duct tape because it repairs everything.

PR: Well, I never liked it because it is so gooey. Isn't it gooey?

TH: Yeah.

PR: Most of the stuff I would tape would be stuff for, you know, stuff for the kids. It would be clear. That is what I got.

TH: Okay. How about this cord, that is, nylon utility cord?

PR: No.

TH: You don't recall purchasing anything like that anywhere else?

PR: No.

TH: Do you remember seeing any around the house or attached to anything? Could you have gotten a package tied with such cord?

PR: No. I usually get UPS and they don't use that anymore. I mean, the post office used it, the twine.

TH: Not familiar?

PR: Huh-uh.

Patsy was shown more pictures. She commented on the suitcase that was found on the floor under the broken basement window beneath the outside grate.

PR: Well, that wasn't one of the suitcases that I normally use. We use the roller ones. I think that is one that John Andrew had brought over from his college stuff, you know, like unpacked and brought the suitcase over to our house, but I didn't think it was in there. I thought it was back ... where the hot water heater area was ... Unless Linda moved it over here when she put the paint stuff there, I don't know. That looks out of place.

TH: You are thinking it was last in that area between the wine cellar and the bathroom by the stairs (to the basement)?

PR: Right ....

TH: Do you know what was stored in it, if anything?

PR: I don't know. I have no idea.

TH: Did you ever handle it?

PR: I don't remember. I don't remember.

TH: You might have?

PR: I didn't put it there, let's put it that way. I don't know if I — I mean, I may have moved it out of my way, but I don't remember specifically moving it or putting it somewhere.

TH: Did you ever put anything into it, take anything out of it?

PR: No. I presume it is empty ....

TH: If there was something in it, it would belong to John Andrew then?

PR: Yeah.

TH: Did John Andrew have a Dr. Seuss book?

PR: Did John Andrew have a Dr. Seuss book ... ? I hope not. He is supposed to have college books, not Dr. Seuss books. Why would you ask such a question?

TH: Well, that is because in that suitcase was a Dr. Seuss book.

PR: What book was it? Did it have any kid's name in it?

TD: That I don't know. I think it had John Andrew's name in it.

PR: Oh, it did?

TD: I think. I haven't personally seen it.

PR: I don't know. You got me. I don't know.

TH: Anything else in that photo?

PR: Just that window being open.

TD: What window is that?

PR: This is the basement window which is under that grate that we had the picture of earlier.

TD: Underneath the dining room window.

PR: Right, the breakfast window.

TD: The one that leads to the patio.

PR: Correct.

TD: How many windows are there?

PR: How many are here?

TD: Yeah.

PR: It looks like three . . . one of these windows is the one that John — John got locked out one time, can't remember, at the lake, I think. And he said he broke a window pane and, you know, he reached in and came in through this window right into the house.

TD: What did you do after the window was broken, did you have some involvement with that at all?

PR: Well, yes. When I came back, you know, from the lake, I mean there was glass everywhere all over the floor . . . and I . . . picked up pieces of glass, you know. He never cleaned it up, obviously . . . and I had Linda sweep down there because the kids, the boys would sometimes play in here . . . .

TD: What observations did you make about the window when you cleaned up the glass or about that whole area?

PR: Well, there was one of the panes was broken. I don't remember what it was, but I had asked — that was another one of the odd jobs to have Linda Hoffman and her husband do. He was going to do the odd jobs. I think I asked him to repair that, too, but I don't remember. I don't know whether they did that or not.

TD: So what else do you remember about that area besides the fact there was a hole in the pane and there was glass on the floor?

PR: You mean like when I came back?

TD: Yeah. You were cleaning up down there.

PR: Nothing else, just glass, you know, that I was afraid the kids would get in there.

TD: What about this mark on the wall?

There was a scrape mark running down the wall directly above the suitcase. Some investigators believe an intruder left the mark with his shoe as he stood on the suitcase and climbed up to exit the window below the grate.

PR: Oh, gosh, I don't know if I was in there. I think I would have noticed that because I had all that painted . . . .

TD: Do you remember it not being there when you cleaned up the glass?

PR: No, I don't.

TD: You talked about John Ramsey coming through that window, do you remember any other times that people were in that window?

PR: No.

TD: Did the boys ever play in the window?

PR: No. I mean, because there was a grate on there for that purpose so nobody falls in there. If you were going in the window you had to lift the grate out. It was pretty heavy.

TD: Other than when John Ramsey broke into the house

whenever, was someone in that window, to your knowledge?

PR: Never to my knowledge.

TD: Do you know why the window wasn't fixed?

PR: No, I don't. Was it not fixed?

TD: Well, what do you know about that window, the condition of that window on Christmas of '96, have you —

PR: I just remember a little to-do list that Linda Hoffman had included fixing that pane in that window. Whether (her husband) got to it or not, I don't know because he wasn't able to fix the playroom doors, you know, so he didn't get to everything.

HANEY: We talked earlier about the surgery that you had, a hysterectomy, it is my understanding as a result of that you are not on any hormones, nothing?

PATSY RAMSEY: Nothing.

TH: Prior to or since that surgery, did you discuss with your doctors what kind of — what kind of changes that you would go through as a result of that?

PR: No. I mean, they — just as long as you are alive, that is a good sign.

TH: Well, I'm not obviously up on all of this, but I do know a few years ago my wife was going through some period of time where she was a little short, abrupt or irritable, and as a result, she did have some hormonal medication subsequently and that kind of saw it through.

PR: No. I never had any hormonal stuff.

TH: Has anything come up with mood swings? Did the doctors talk to you about that, the possibility of it or —

PR: No.

TH: Have you experienced any of that?

PR: No, I have not, not prior to this tragedy.

TH: How about since?

PR: Yeah.

TH: You can give me an idea of what might bring something on, the mood swing like that, or how severe it might be.

PR: Well, for a long time, and just like yesterday, we

went into the conference room. I looked out the window and there was a little girl with blond hair and shorts and it looked like JonBenet from the back, and I just get really sad and still crying, you know. I miss her.

TH: Do you get unexplained mood swings or . . . reactions?

PR: You know, if I am sad it is because of that, I lost my precious child, you know. Nothing else.

Patsy was shown a photo of a Bible on John's desk in his third-floor study. The book was found open to Psalms 35 and 36. The first letters of each Psalm are capitalized and stand out on the pages. The first four capitalized letters of Psalm 35 line up as S.B.T.C. in reverse, the mysterious sign-off of the ransom note.

PR: This is on John's desk . . . looks like his Bible.

TH: Do you have any — do you have different Bibles?

PR: Well, we have a lot of Bibles.

TH: Okay.

PR: I don't know if they are different.

TH: You said it is his as opposed to being ours or yours?

PR: I see what you mean. Well, yeah. I think it was his on his desk.

TH: Kept on his desk?

PR: Yeah.

TH: Is that where he normally had it or where it was normally kept?

PR: Yeah. He would read it there.

TH: Okay. Do you know John's habit as far as reading the Bible, was he cover-to-cover or —

PR: No, I don't know. I don't really know his habits.

TH: Could it have been cover-to-cover or at random, depends on —

PR: Right.

TH: Do you know if it would be left open to a particular page for a particular reason?

PR: No.

TH: Now, in the house in addition to several Bibles, you had a ton of books. Let's take a couple of minutes and talk about some of those, some which you may know something about, maybe you don't. How about the book "Mindhunter?"

PR: No.

TH: Do you recall that? Do you recall seeing it around the house?

PR: Huh uh.

TH: You were not reading?

PR: No.

TH: It is a book by John Douglas.

PR: I don't know.

TH: Do you know who he is?

PR: John Douglas, I know.

Early in the case, former FBI profiler John Douglas, the inspiration for the profiler in the Hannibal Lecter books and movies, was asked to question the Ramseys by their attorneys. He believes they are innocent. His book, "Mindhunter," has a section about the way killers stage a crime scene to cast suspicion elsewhere.

TH: Okay. How about everybody in your room, on your bedroom dresser there was a book by David Pilgram, a Danish book?

PR: Not good at remembering authors.

TH: I think this was in Danish. Do you read different languages?

PR: No.

TH: Would John, does he?

PR: No. It was written in Danish?

TH: That is my understanding.

TRIP DEMUTH: Yeah.

TH: How about a book called "Camp Fire Stories?"

PR: "Camp Fire Stories," I think that is one of the kids' books.

TH: Was it?

PR: I think so.

TH: I don't think it is probably a kid book.

PR: All right. Oh . . . ghost story books.

TH: How about "Whirlwind" by Clavell?

PR: I didn't read it.

TH: How about "What Wives Wish Their Husbands Knew About Women?"

PR: My husband's. No.

TH: Okay. How about a book called "Why Johnny Can't Tell Right From Wrong?"

PR: Yeah. That was about — my dad gave me that. That was about education, the school system.

TH: How about "The Sensuous Man?"

PR: I heard of that. I don't remember reading it.

TH: Okay. Do you remember, did you buy it or John buy it?

PR: If I remember right, I didn't buy it. I know I didn't buy it.

TH: How about "The Day After Tomorrow" . . . ?

The mystery book by Allan Folsom centers around a series of beheadings. The ransom note author threatened to behead JonBenet.

PR: Was that a James Bond movie or something? James Bond.

TH: . . . I don't think there is any connection.

PR: No. I don't know. I can't remember that.

TH: What kind of reading did you do? Are you a Tom Clancy, Stephen King?

PR: No.

TH: What kind of books?

PR: To tell you the truth, I don't know that I read all that much. I mean, I read a lot of magazines and that kind of thing.

TH: How about movies, what is the last movie prior to this that you had seen?

PR: Oh, dear.

TH: Maybe we should distinguish, at a theater. Do you go to the movies a lot?

PR: I didn't go to the movies too much. We would usually — well, we didn't rent many movies. The kids watched a lot of movies, the videos in their room, put the big screen up in our room.

TH: You had TVs and recorders, pretty much spread around?

PR: Right. Gosh, I can't remember the last movie. One time it could have been close to Christmas . . . the movie about this guy decorating his house. I mean, it was about Christmas, and he put all the lights on in his house and he turns the light on and the whole town is blacked out. It was hysterical. I don't know the name.

TH: These were more for the kids.

PR: No. For us, too. I don't remember what it was. I just remember that one scene. Anybody know the movie? His whole house was all decorated for Christmas and he was all excited. He plugged it in and turned it on, the whole city dimmed because he had so much, you know . . . I think we saw that around Christmas. I don't know.

TH: So I guess what you are saying is the movies mainly were for the kids?

PR: Yeah.

TH: And can you think of any that you would have rented for yourself?

PR: We saw that one with Mel Gibson. It was like set in Ireland about the Irish war.

TRIP DEMUTH: "Braveheart."

PR: Yeah, "Braveheart."

TH: Scotland.

PR: One of those places over there. That was real good. It was real long, we thought. I remember that one.

TH: Whose choice was that?

PR: John. He and Burke usually go pick them out. I usually fell asleep. He loves like — what is the one, "African Queen," all of the old movies. We get a lot of those.

TD: Like Humphrey Bogart?

PR: Right. I mean, he loved that one.

TD: Who is he?

PR: John. I would fall asleep. He would usually pick the movies and I go to sleep, usually fall asleep . . .

TH: How about things like "Dirty Harry?"

PR: I don't know.

TH: "Speed?"

PR: I think I might have seen that on an airplane. Is that about some bus or something that loses the brakes?

TH: I think so.

PR: I think I watched that on an airplane.

TH: Okay. Now, at our house I am getting the "Dirty Harry," the James Bond, all of those, and my wife wants to watch "Sleepless in Seattle." She gets that and I fall asleep. So do you put John to sleep with some of your choices?

PR: No, because I never — I don't think I picked them very much. He and Burke would get them.

TH: Where did they get them?

PR: Blockbuster.

TH: You know that as far as "Speed" and "Dirty Harry," and I think there is some other movies that even John Andrew had made some mention about the different words, phrases . . . that some of that stuff seems to come into the ransom note.

PR: . . . I have never seen "Dirty Harry," so I don't know.

TD: That surprises me, because I mean, we are the same age, approximately, and I thought everyone at our age group has seen "Dirty Harry."

PR: You must be a lot older than me. I don't know.

TD: Clint Eastwood.

PR: I don't think I have ever seen "Dirty Harry."

TH: . . . How about (Photo) 378?

PR: This is JonBenet's floor, her pants.

TH: Do you recall those particular pants, when she would have worn those last?

PR: Not for sure. Probably recently because they are dropped in the middle of the floor, but I don't remember exactly.

TH: They are kind of inside out.

PR: Right.

TH: 379 is a close up of it. It appears they are stained.

PR: Right.

TH: Is that something that JonBenet had a problem with?

PR: Well she, you know, she was at the age where she was learning to wipe herself and, you know, sometimes she wouldn't do such a great job.

TH: Did she have accidents, if you will, in the course

of the day or the night, as opposed to just bedwetting?

PR: Not usually, no, huh uh. That would probably be more from just not wiping real well.

TH: On Christmas Day were you in that bathroom at all?

PR: Very likely, but I can't say for sure.

TH: Had you been in there that day, would you have done something with them?

PR: Well, I got, you know — that night I got — I know I got the long johns for her out of that bathroom.

TH: Right, out of one of the drawers in there.

PR: Yeah.

TH: Do you recall seeing those on the floor that night when you got the —

PR: No . . . they could have been there. I don't know.

TH: Is it possible that some point during the night she would have gotten up and put those on or thrown them down there or changed in some way, trying to account for those being there?

PR: I just — I can't imagine that. No, because I put those — she was zonked out asleep, so I put her to bed . . . she had worn the black velvet ones to Priscilla's. What she had on earlier that day, I just can't remember. It might have been those. I just can't remember. Could have taken those off, you know, gotten the dress to go to Priscilla's and then left them there.

TH: When she was out riding her bike, do you remember, think back, look back at what she was wearing?

PR: Can't remember.

Patsy was shown a picture of a baseball bat that was found outside the north side of the house near the butler kitchen's door. A fiber from a carpet on the floor of the basement outside the wine cellar had been found on the bat.

<u>PR</u>: That looks like a baseball bat. What is that? It looks like —

<u>TD</u>: . . . That photograph was taken on the north side . . . up by the butler kitchen door.

<u>PR</u>: Oh, really. That is unusual. That is unusual.

<u>TD</u>: Why is that?

<u>PR</u>: It is not unusual for the kids to leave their stuff laying around, but they wouldn't have had it over there. It would have been — remember all of the toys laying under the swing set? It would be that area. So that is — that is very unusual.

<u>TD</u>: They never took their toys on that side of the house?

<u>PR</u>: Nobody hardly went over there.

<u>TH</u>: Okay. The boys —

<u>PR</u>: Run around, I know.

<u>TH</u>: Would they end up playing over there, or do you know, is there any place they wouldn't go outside?

<u>PR</u>: Well, you are right. There is probably no place they wouldn't go, but it would be highly unusual, is what I'm saying, for a baseball bat to be there, because there is not that much space over there. I mean, if they hit a ball and bat, it was usually over where the patio is . . . that area.

<u>TH</u>: How about the bat itself, does that look —

<u>PR</u>: Well, I can't say for sure. Burke would probably know.

<u>TH</u>: Do you know how many bats he might have had? Would he have had more than one?

<u>PR</u>: I don't think so. I mean, I think that looks metal. Metal bats are pretty — I mean, they are not cheap. So I can't imagine — I don't think he had more than one, if he had one.

<u>TH</u>: But he did have one?

<u>PR</u>: It seems like he had one, but I can't say for sure it was that one.

Like I said, he would know. I'm sure he would know. He might know if they ever played over there, but that bat seems weird to me. Yeah, very strange.

In a crucial part of the interrogation, Patsy was shown a crime scene photo of a cereal bowl found on the table of the breakfast room off the kitchen. The bowl contained pineapple chunks and had Patsy's fingerprints on it. Fresh pineapple was found in JonBenet's stomach, and she would have eaten it two to five hours before her death, according to experts consulted by Boulder police.

PR: That little bowl there, it is kind of like a little cereal bowl, but it has this huge spoon sticking out of it, and this doesn't look right . . . this is the breakfast room off the kitchen.

TD: . . . Is that where you make your meals normally?

PR: Yeah.

TD: Which meals would you eat there?

PR: Oh, dinner usually. We usually ate breakfast at the little counter at different times in the kitchen.

TD: Okay. What about lunch?

PR: Lunch would be there.

TD: On the counter in the kitchen, what about snacks?

PR: Counter.

TD: So you only ate dinner in this room then?

PR: Yeah.

TH: . . . When was the last time you recall that table being cleaned off?

PR: After — well, we would have eaten pancakes together at that table on Christmas morning. And then I would have cleaned the table up.

TH: We talked earlier this week about lunch, could you recall what would have been on the menu for lunch?

PR: No.

TH: . . . Would you have eaten there for lunch?

PR: No, because I think we ate a late breakfast, because of — I'm not sure we had lunch that day because we probably, you know, do Christmas, and then we had a big pancake breakfast, and then we were going, you know, 4:00 or 5:00 to the Whites for dinner, so we probably didn't even have lunch.

Somebody else did this, because I would never put a spoon that big in a bowl like that, and I can't tell what that is, whether that is grits or apples or cereal or — I can't tell what that is.

TD: Inside the bowl, you are saying?

PR: Inside the bowl.

TD: Do you recognize the bowl?

PR: Yeah.

TD: Where do you keep them?

PR: In the kitchen.

TD: Where in the kitchen?

PR: Well, in like a cupboard over to — there is kind of big sinks over here. There is an island in the middle and big sinks and above that, the cupboard with dishwear in it.

TD: What would you use these bowls for?

PR: Whatever. Cereal usually. I usually — I think I got those little bowls for like salsa, you know, salsa, chips and salsa.

TH: Those bowls, you described them being on the cabinet or a shelf, and you demonstrated it was higher. Is that something JonBenet could have reached?

PR: No.

TH: Okay. The contents of the bowl, does that appear to be pineapple to you?

PR: Could be. Could be.

TH: That is what has been described as —

PR: Is it? It could be.

TH: Do you eat or does anybody in the family eat a bowl of pineapple?

PR: Well, the kids both ate pineapple, but I would never serve a bowl like that of pineapple. I would think I would put two or three pieces on their plate with the rest of their food or something, because, I mean, it looks weird to set out a bowl like that.

TH: Just still talking about the bowl itself and the pineapple, and there is probably no way to determine from the photograph whether this was fresh or canned. Do you have either or both in stock at the house there, did you?

PR: Usually I would buy those — I bought pineapple, it was fresh pineapple that had been peeled or whatever they do to it, and core it and cut it up a little bit, or some that had been fresh that was sealed there in the produce area.

TH: What store did you buy this from?

PR: Safeway is usually where I buy it from.

TH: It is the fresh pineapple that they do all the work for you?

PR: Correct.

TH: Did you have bags or however it came?

PR: I don't know. It usually went bad pretty quick, so it didn't — you know, I didn't keep it around laying around very long. You know what I mean?

TH: So people ate it fairly regularly or consistently?

PR: Well, I didn't buy it terribly often. But when I did, I usually bought that fresh and serve it out in little portions. This looks weird to me, a bowl with a huge spoon like that with pineapple in it.

TH: Again, JonBenet, you said, couldn't reach the bowl.

If she wanted pineapple, would she get it out herself?

PR: Out of the refrigerator, I don't — no. That wouldn't be something she would really go to.

TH: Did she like pineapple?

PR: She liked it.

TH: Did she eat it as a snack?

PR: Well, we had so many other things that she had for a snack first, you know, before she got pineapple. But she wouldn't do this. She would not have a bowl like this with a big huge spoon like that.

TH: Would you do that?

PR: No . . . that is weird.

TH: Would John do that?

PR: No.

TH: How about Burke?

PR: No. He has a sweet tooth. He doesn't like fruit too much. He likes pineapple a little bit, strawberries a little bit, but he would not pour himself a big bowl of pineapple.

TH: If he got up in the middle of the night would he eat something like that?

PR: No. He would eat something chocolate.

TH: Could he reach the bowl?

PR: He could reach the bowl.

TH: The spoon, where is it kept?

PR: In the silverware drawer in there in the kitchen to the right of the range. But, see, if the kids were making a snack for themselves, even if they were, that is a huge serving spoon. They, you know, they use a little spoon. Now, I don't know if some of those women, you know, Priscilla and them were there that morning, it was early, and I don't know whether they were, you know, fixing things for people to eat, but that doesn't look right to me.

TH: When is the last time that you know of that JonBenet ate pineapple?

PR: I don't know.

TH: There were the remains of pineapple in JonBenet's system.

PR: I had heard that, yeah.

TH: This is not a shock to you?

PR: No, it is not. No.

TH: Okay.

PR: But I did not do this. If she ate that, somebody put that there. I don't know when she would have eaten it. She was sound asleep when we got home.

TH: And you said that earlier you cleaned the table off after the breakfast.

PR: Yes.

TH: That wasn't there.

PR: No, it wasn't.

TH: Is there some way to account for the pineapple in her body?

PR: Not to my knowledge, unless she — you know, I can't remember what was served over at the Whites. Does anybody know? Except there was crab. I remember crab.

TH: That seems to be the only thing you recall that she ate.

PR: Yeah .... Did you fingerprint that?

TH: Yes.

PR: Did it show anything?

TH: Well, what would that tell you, somebody's fingerprints were on it.

PR: Well, if they weren't mine, if they were not John's, maybe somebody fed her pineapple.

TH: What if those fingerprints belonged to one of the two of you?

PR: Well, I don't know.

TH: Well, wait a minute. You started that line.

PR: I didn't put the bowl there, okay? I did not put the bowl there. I would not do this . . . .

TH: Let's go back to your line of reasoning here. If they were not — now talk to me.

PR: Okay.

TH: Look at me. If they are not yours and they are not John's, then they would be somebody else's?

PR: Right.

TH: But now I am telling you they are not somebody else's. Those prints belong to one of the two of you.

PR: They do? You are sure? Well, I don't know. I did not put that there. No.

TH: . . . Wait. Talk to me. Your line of reasoning, and this was your logic a couple sentences ago, they are not yours, they are not John''s, then they are somebody else's, whoever put it there. I'm telling you that it isn't somebody else's.

PR: Well —

TH: You know sometimes the simplest, most obscure little thing could be so significant.

PR: Right. I did not feed JonBenet pineapple, so I don't know how it got in her stomach. I don't know where this bowl of pineapple came from. I can't recall putting that there . . . .

TH: Have you, in the course of the last 18 months, talked to any pathologists or read any reports about pineapple in a body or how long it takes for a body to digest materials?

PR: No. I just have hear . . . somewhere there was pineapple in her stomach.

TH: Right. And, again, I am no scientist or anything, but from what we are told, pineapple goes in at X time, and a certain amount of time later, it is gone. Okay.

It goes through a particular process, and there is a way to estimate times based on that depending on where it is in the body.

PR: When she would have eaten it, so you can tell somewhere in there?

TH: Well, I am really not at liberty to discuss that part of it with you now. Okay.

PR: All right. Do we know this is what she ate?

TH: We are pretty sure it was pineapple.

PR: This pineapple?

TH: Well, I don't think that science has come quite that far that you could say.

PR: I mean, can they tell whether it was fresh or canned?

TH: Well —

PR: Because canned, it is like gooey, you know.

TH: There is some different consistency, but I don't know. But what concerns me is how that bowl with that pineapple, A, got there, and how the pineapple got in JonBenet's system.

PR: I don't know truly . . . was that there since that morning? Did you ask them, somebody asked all those people, the two social workers?

TH: We asked them what they brought. But see —

PR: Was it here earlier that morning?

TH: I don't believe. I don't know when it showed up, okay. But I note there is pineapple in the bowl, pineapple in JonBenet's system. So we are trying to track that down.

PR: Right. Well —

TH: Any ideas, any thoughts?

PR: I don't know. I mean, I don't. I can't explain it.

TH: Had JonBenet and Burke been up in the night, would Burke have maybe fixed that for her knowing she wanted something like that?

PR: I don't know. That is stretching it.

TH: To what?

PR: I mean, I would have heard them. Burke would have gotten up and banged around getting cupboards open and getting stuff in the refrigerator.

TH: Well, if he banged around two floors away, would you have heard that?

PR: I hope I would have.

TH: You wouldn't hear JonBenet's toilet flush one floor away.

PR: Well, that was at the opposite end of the house. The kitchen is down under my —

TH: It is kind of central, is it?

PR: Yeah. I just — he has — I have never known him to fix his sister, in the middle of the night, something to eat. That would be unusual.

TH: Okay.

PR: Okay.

TH: Could it have happened?

PR: Anything could have happened. I mean, we know something strange happened that night, but this looks weird to me. That is all I have. That is all I know. That looks strange to me. And if there was pineapple in her stomach and that pineapple, that is — I would like to know when somebody first saw that there, you know, because there were a lot of people floating around there.

TD: Do I understand you to say that JonBenet would not have fixed herself pineapple?

PR: I very seriously doubt that.

TD: So if she had pineapple in her system, someone had to serve that to her?

PR: That would be my guess.

TD: Okay. And we know that she did have pineapple in her system.

PR: Okay.

TD: Right.

PR: That is why I'm here.

TD: Someone would have had to serve her pineapple.

PR: It seems to me like that.

TD: The Whites have told us that they did not serve her pineapple.

PR: Okay.

TD: We need to figure out when she got pineapple.

PR: Exactly.

TD: Other than the Whites, is there anybody besides yourself that could have served her pineapple?

PR: I don't know. I mean, she was sound asleep when she came home.

TD: Let's back up.

PR: She would not have eaten after that, to my knowledge. So, I mean, we went from the Whites to falling asleep in the car, the Walkers . . . . She was asleep. We put her to bed.

TD: Before you went to the Whites you were the one supervising her that day?

PR: Right. I don't recall her eating pineapple that day.

TD: There was no one else during that day that could have fed her?

PR: There, no. I mean, John was in and out, but, you know, I don't remember pineapple.

TD: So you can understand why it is important for us.

PR: Of course.

TD: Can you also understand that the only people that could have done it is yourself or the Whites?

PR: Or whoever killed JonBenet, right? I mean, there was somebody in our home that night besides my husband, my son and my daughter and myself that killed our daughter, you know. Could they have fed

JonBenet pineapple? That is what I'm saying. This is weird. This is not like something I would set up or that my children would set up.

TD: Okay.

PR: So what, you know, somebody gave her pineapple.

TD: Before we get to that possibility, okay, I want to make sure there is no other possibility, okay, so I need you to think about the day.

PR: Okay.

TD: That is why we asked you, you fed them pancakes in the morning.

PR: Late morning.

TD: Could you have fed them pineapple with the pancakes?

PR: Not that I am aware. Not that I can remember. They don't go together. You wouldn't have pineapple with pancakes.

TD: I wouldn't, but we need to ask.

PR: No.

TD: So no pineapple with the pancakes in the morning, right?

PR: No. I don't remember when I had pineapple in the house.

TD: Want you to move through the day.

PR: I am trying to remember.

TD: Take your time. When you are wrapping presents and what have you, getting things ready, and JonBenet is riding her bike some a little bit.

PR: Well, she rode her bike. We were out there when she was riding her bike.

TD: Okay. There is a time when John goes to the airport, right?

PR: Right.

TD: And the kids were playing with their toys and what

have you, right, and lunch?

PR: I don't remember lunch.

TD: I think you said earlier that you may not have had lunch because there was an —

PR: I had breakfast.

TD: How late was the breakfast?

PR: I don't remember exactly, but probably 10:00, 11:00.

TD: That is what you mean by a late breakfast, okay. How about, you go to the Whites what time, approximately?

PR: Right after, like 4:00, 5:00-ish, so we could have very easily skipped lunch.

TD: Think about that period of time between late breakfast and leaving for the Whites, did you serve them anything during that period of time?

PR: I can't remember. I don't know.

TD: Okay. Priscilla had crab . . . waiting for you when you got to her house, right?

PR: Yeah.

TD: Was JonBenet hungry at the time? Did she eat the cracked crab?

PR: I can't tell you. You know, we got to the house, the kids start running around and we kind of don't —

TD: Okay. But you do remember the cracked crab?

PR: I just remember Priscilla . . . said, "I know your kids like seafood. I will hold this little plate out for JonBenet to make sure she gets some."

TD: You remember that.

PR: I remember that. Well, I thought that is nice to make sure that we don't devour it before the kids get some, but she specifically mentioned JonBenet's name. And at that time it kind of, you know, flew over. But then when you are trying to remember things later, it seems, you know, a little strange.

TD: But you don't remember any other servings between the pancakes and the cracked crab?

PR: No.

TD: What about before breakfast, did you have any — I don't know if you all had snacks while you are opening presents?

PR: No. We had coffee, and the kids don't care about eating. They just want to dig in.

TD: That would be my experience as well. So there was no pineapple served before breakfast?

PR: No.

TD: And you said you would think you would hear Burke if he got up and went down to the kitchen and fixed something. Has he ever gotten up in the night and gone down into the kitchen?

PR: I hear him get up and go to the bathroom. I can hear him urinating in the bathroom.

TD: My question is, does he ever go to the kitchen in the middle of the night and get something to eat?

PR: No. Not that I was aware of, that scenario — sorry — is far-fetched.

TD: We need to explore these things.

PR: I know we do. This is good.

TD: What about JonBenet, did she ever get up in the middle of the night to go down to the kitchen to get something to eat? In your experience has she ever done that before?

PR: No.

TH: Did you over the last couple of nights discuss the bowl of pineapple with John?

PR: I don't recall. I think he mentioned seeing a bowl of pineapple, but we didn't, I didn't discuss it, no.

TH: Okay. So that would have been about the extent of it, he says —

PR: Yes.

TH: Something about, asked about a bowl of pineapple?

PR: Pineapple, right, yeah.

TH: At that time did that jog your recollection at all?

PR: I, I recall that I had heard somewhere or somebody told me that pineapple was in her stomach.

TH: Okay.

PR: I don't know where, somebody told me they saw it on TV or, I don't know, but I know there's been some discussion about pineapple and I, you know, I'm just trying to remember and remember that she had pineapple. I can't remember.

TH: Okay. The next group of photos and these are not numbered — but they show a flashlight.

PR: Uh huh.

TH: A black metal . . . type —

PR: Uh huh.

TH: — flashlight. Do you recognize that?

PR: It looks similar to one that John Andrew gave John for Christmas, birthday or something.

TD: That's similar to the one that John Andrew gave John?

PR: Yeah. . .

TD: And I think last time when you were here on last April . . . you said, "Where that was stored?"

PR: Uh huh.

TD: And I wanted to clarify that a little bit. Do you remember where it was stored?

As she stated during her 1997 interview, Patsy said the flashlight was kept in a drawer in the wet bar sink-cabinet combination on the first floor near the bottom of the spiral staircase.

TD: The drawer that is open?

PR: That's open there, yeah.

TD: And that's the wet bar that's by the spiral staircase, right?

PR: Right.

TD: Okay. Okay. And now looking at photo 380, you don't see a flashlight in (the drawer), right?

PR: Correct. . .where was this flashlight found?

TD: Well, do you remember when you came in on, in April, they showed you a picture of the flashlight? Do you recall that? You may not.

PR: No, not exactly.

TD: Okay. This was on the kitchen counter . . . why would that be out?

PR: I don't know.

TD: Did you guys use this flashlight much?

PR: I didn't, no.

TD: Who did?

PR: John used it.

TD: What did he use it for?

PR: I don't know, looking in the garage and the car or something like that.

TD: Okay. Had you ever seen it on the kitchen counter before?

PR: Not that I recall.

TD: Would it have struck you as unusual, or would that not be outside the realm of possibilities, given the habits of the family?

PR: It seems like it would have been unusual to have made it all the way into the kitchen, because usually if somebody was using the flashlight, they were — John was looking at something in the garage or under the car or something like that.

TD: Okay.

PR: But he might, you know, I'm sure you must have asked him if he . . . ?

TH: And maybe I missed it, do you know when you last saw it in the drawer?

PR: No, I'm not for sure.

TH: Okay. How about, do you recall of using that during say a power outage or to check on the kids at night, anything along those lines?

PR: No, I don't remember that.

Patsy was shown a photo of rope found in John Andrew's bedroom.

PR: I don't recognize it, specifically.

TD: Okay.

TH: Okay. And that, that particular piece of rope, do you ever remember seeing anything like it around? And if you look at photo 115, you notice the . . . ends are unusually secured . . . can you think of any reason to have that kind of rope around?

PR: I've just never seen ends like that, done like that. John had some, you know, boat ropes and things up at the lake, but it seems like when they cut those, they kind of melt the ends of them or something to keep them from fraying or something. I've never seen one done like that.

TH: The kind of ropes you're talking about that John used up there —

PR: For the sailboat or —

TH: Are they colored the same or similar?

PR: Well, some of them have like little blue flecks in them or red, or there's some white ones, you know.

TH: Okay. Do you know what, what those are composed of? Is it a nylon-like that melts?

PR: Yeah, it must, something that melts, yeah. But it seems to me like they somehow torch the ends and kind of keep them from fraying. I can't remember seeing any one looking like that.

TH: You don't remember that being used anywhere in the house or yard or —

PR: No.

TH: Would you think that unusual to be found in the house?

PR: Yeah. I mean, Burke had some ropes that he would play with through something out on the playground, you know, in that, in that picture yesterday the rope around the, the fort, you know, or something.

TH: Right.

PR: Always trying to make a boat or something like that.

TH: This was found inside the house.

PR: Inside the house?

TH: In John Andrew's room?

PR: Oh. Maybe it was a, some rope he used for camping or something, I don't know.

TD: Did he have rope in his room that he would use for camping?

PR: . . . I don't know. I just don't remember seeing this specifically, and I don't remember ever seeing a rope like that.

TD: Do you know John Andrew had rope in that room?

PR: No . . .

Patsy was shown photos taken off a roll of film that John Ramsey turned over to the police in the hours before JonBenet's body was found. The roll was in the camera he used to take pictures that Christmas. To get the film to the end of the roll, John snapped off the lasts few shots. In doing so, he inadvertently photographed the wet bar near the foot of the spiral staircase. The photo showed a black and red scarf left on the sink counter there. Patsy couldn't say whether it was John's scarf or one she had given out as gifts to the men who attended the Ramsey Christmas party on December 23rd.

PR: . . . This (scarf) just looks strange to me . . . .
TH: Well, this photo . . . was on your roll of film in your camera. And on the same roll is the next photo, a Christmas morning photo of the kids.
PR: . . . Oh, God.

It was the first time Patsy had seen the photo. She broke down in tears down at this point. After she regained her composure, the questioning continued.
The photo John Ramsey had taken of the wet bar area, also showed a table near it. On it, were two white lined legal pads. One of them had been used to write the ransom note. It was the same pad that contained Patsy's doodles, other writings and the so-called practice ransom note.

TH: . . . Like I say, this was on your roll of film and it's not exactly the same photograph that was taken by the police.
PR: Uh huh.
TH: And this legal pad that you —
PR: Right.
TH: — identified —
PR: Right.
TH: — do you know when that would have been in that position?
PR: No. So this, this was taken before . . . ?
TH: Before the police photos . . . do you recognize that pad . . . ?

PR: Yeah, but we had a lot of those around . . . I bought
like those at Office Depot's or Office Max or whatever
they are and I usually kept a bunch of them, you know,
kept them over here, right around here in the kitchen.
TD: By the telephone?
PR: Yeah, but, you know, they float all over.
TD: So it wouldn't have been unusual to be where it is?
PR: No. No. Gosh.
TH: Just a second, okay?
PR: Uh huh.
TH: So would this particular note pad be, belong to
somebody in particular or —
PR: No, not necessarily.

*Patsy was shown a photo of her taken at the Whites'
Christmas Day dinner party in the same clothes she was
wearing when police arrived the next day — black velvet
pants, red sweater, and a red and black checkered jacket.
Incredibly, police waited a year before they asked for the
clothing the Ramseys wore to the Whites' party. Forensic
tests showed similarities between fibers from Patsy's jacket
and sweater and fibers found on the duct tape that covered
JonBenet's mouth. Asked about the clothing, Patsy gave
answers that totally confused the issue.*

PR: . . . Priscilla had a jacket like
this. I mean, until I saw this picture, I had thought
that I had worn my Christmas sweater to their house
. . . and then I saw this picture and I said, "Oh, I must
have worn THAT sweater to their house."

But then I thought, well, maybe I had her jacket. I
mean, you know, I don't know.
TD: . . . That you were wearing yours on Christmas and
not hers?

PR: Well, I mean, I could have been in her house in the living room, you know, what I mean, and been cold and she said, "Here put this on." I just can't remember. My point is that we both had jackets similar to that.

TD: Okay.

PR: So I don't know.

TD: And did you buy them at the same time and place?

PR: No, I mean, I don't know, I don't know . . . I really don't remember. FYI, I mean.

TD: So can you tell if that's your jacket you're wearing or —

PR: This one, you mean?

TD: Were they the exact same?

PR: They were pretty close, but I can't, I can't really remember.

TD: Uh huh.

PR: Why I would have hers on. All I'm saying is . . . first time somebody asked me what I had on that day, I think I might have said I had my Christmas sweater on which is . . . little beaded one. And then when I saw this picture, somebody showed me this picture —

TD: Uh huh.

PR: — because they wanted the clothing, I said, "Oh, I must have worn THAT one, so I got that one instead." I think I sent both of them, actually.

TD: You sent both of them?

PR: The . . . beaded one or whatever . . . .

Patsy was shown a non-crime scene photo of a stun gun. Some investigators believe that marks on JonBenet's body were caused by one. She was also asked about a video found in the house that had information about a stun gun on it.

TH: . . . Can you identify what that is?

PR: No. Someone with a flashlight?

TD: Okay. Actually that is a stun gun. I think you and John and various people from the DA's office had some discussion —

PR: Yeah.

TD: — last July about a stun gun?

PR: Right. I don't understand that.

TD: Did you follow up at all following that discussion last July about stun guns or anything about them?

PR: No, just that perhaps one might have been used.

TD: Okay.

PR: And I never have had one or seen one. First time I've seen one. What, what — how — which end is this gun? I mean, it don't look like a gun or anything.

TD: Yeah, it's — and we don't have any side views, these are just kind of from either end.

PR: Okay.

TD: But do you recall inside the house a video from Spy World?

PR: I've heard that, yes.

TD: Okay.

PR: I have never seen the video . . . and I've never viewed the video.

TD: Okay. Do you know how that video came to be in the house?

PR: Best I can remember we were on a business trip or some trip in Florida and went out walking around the hotel and there was a shop that carried like cellular phones and . . . security kind of things and we stopped . . . it was like a, you know, gadget kind of place and went in and John spoke with them . . . .

TD: And where were you at the time?

PR: I was in Florida.

TD: Do you remember where?

PR: I think it was Miami.

TD: Okay. But you never watched it?

PR: No.

TD: And so you don't know that John did —

PR: No.

TD: — or not.

PR: No. I think we just brought it home from the shop or whatever. I didn't even remember it happening until you brought it up.

TD: Did you make any purchases there, when you got this tape?

PR: I don't recall making anything, purchasing anything there.

TH: How often did JonBenet wet the bed? This is something that has come up time and time again.

PR: Not very often.

TH: What is not very often?

PR: Maybe once a week, maybe twice a week, I don't know. Didn't — she was getting — she was much better. I mean she was pretty much out of Pull-Ups largely, she would wear them sometimes. I just didn't see it as a problem.

TH: Okay, I didn't say it was a problem. I was just asking about it, okay?

PR: Okay.

TH: So you say it's getting better?

PR: I mean, better than when she was little.

TH: Right. And when she is little, it's all the time?

PR: Yeah.

TH: So then you start toilet training?

PR: Correct.

TH: And about when do you start that?

PR: Three, two, three.

TH: After you started it, tell me about it, did you

have success?

PR: Yeah. I mean she worked hard for a long time at night . . . .

TH: You say that JonBenet was getting better?

PR: She was going fewer nights wearing Pull-Ups.

TH: And wetting less frequently?

PR: Right.

TH: Did she have a problem occasionally with maybe more than one night, maybe a couple in a row?

PR: Oh, maybe, but it really would depend on if she, you know, had a lot to drink at night late or didn't remember to go to the bathroom . . . .

TH: If she didn't go to the bathroom before she went to bed, was that a pretty good bet that she would wet?

PR: Not necessarily. It would be higher likelihood.

TH: How about say on Christmas night, had been at the Whites for quite a while and then she falls asleep, and she goes right — she is put right to bed?

PR: Right.

TH: Was there a good likelihood that she would have wet that night?

PR: Possibly.

TH: Did anybody take her to the bathroom before putting her to bed?

PR: No, she was sound asleep.

TH: Would she have gotten up herself and gone to the bathroom?

PR: Possibly.

TH: Okay, you said she was getting better at not wetting, so I am assuming she is getting better at taking care of that? Okay. If she got up as a result of that, would she stay up?

PR: Not likely . . . .

TH: Do you recall if she wet the bed on Christmas Eve,

to Christmas morning?

PR: No, no, she did not.

TH: How about going back from then, from Christmas morning, do you recall when the last time she was wet? Because we talked yesterday about the changing of the linen, the sheets, and we couldn't really pin that down.

PR: Right.

TH: Okay. But if there were several stains on there and we figured it was around, if the maximum a week since the linen was changed, would that indicate to you wetting more than once, or —

PR: Well, that got changed once a week, unless she wet the bed and then of course it would be changed, you know.

TH: Did you check the bed on say Christmas Day, morning?

PR: Yeah.

TH: Okay. But you distinctly remember going and checking on that?

PR: Plus she had her pink pajamas on that she had put on the night before. If she had wet, it would have been soaking wet and she wouldn't have had those on in the Christmas picture, so —

TH: Okay. If that's what she, and you say that's what she wore to bed the night before?

PR: Yes.

TH: Okay, all right. Did you ever discuss this with Dr. Beuf, is that her pediatrician?

PR: Not that I remember.

TH: It just wasn't a concern?

PR: No.

TH: Okay. Were the other children her age pretty much potty trained though?

PR: The White children were.

TH: So this was not out of the ordinary, not unusual

for you?

PR: No.

TH: And you say you don't remember if you discussed it with the doctor or —

PR: I really don't remember whether I did or not.

TH: Okay. So if it's in the medical records?

PR: We would have discussed it.

In fact, Patsy had indicated to Dr. Beuf about the bed-wetting, according to records the police had obtained.

TH: Okay. Do you remember anybody suggesting any remedies, any devices . . . anything to help train JonBenet on the bed wetting?

PR: No. I didn't consult a lot of people about it.

TH: Okay?

PR: Yeah.

TH: Did you consult anybody about it?

PR: No, I mean . . . it wasn't a big deal . . . I was not alarmed by it, at all.

TH: So it wasn't something that you might seek some advice about?

PR: No.

TH: Okay. Do you recall like I say discussing it with anybody?

PR: I just, I don't remember discussing it with anybody.

TH: Okay. Do you recall talking to anybody about that as kind of a source of frustration or a little problem, this bedwetting?

PR: You know, it just didn't seem like a problem to me. I have had problems. I had cancer, that's a problem. You know. It didn't seem to be a problem. So I can't really say that I — that it was on my mind to discuss with anybody.

TH: Okay. But it doesn't have to be a problem to discuss something with somebody, right?

PR: I don't remember ever discussing it with anybody, including her doctor.

TH: Okay.

PR: So — you know, if she wet the bed, if she had an accident, I take the sheets off, throw them in the laundry, you know. Que sera, sera.

TH: Okay. You talked, I think, it was yesterday about initially talking to JonBenet about her private areas.

PR: Uh huh.

TH: And you use this swimsuit area, anything that's covered?

PR: Uh huh.

TH: Okay. She went to Dr. Beuf quite — quite a few times?

PR: Uh huh.

TH: What types of exams did Dr. Beuf perform?

PR: Well, he did a yearly physical examination, and then we were there a lot for ear infections, sinus, she had a lot of chronic sinus problems.

TH: Now the ear and sinus problem, was that a continuing thing, recurring?

PR: It was recurring, yeah. She had kind of, you know, a little dark circles you get under your eyes.

TH: Did he recommend any surgery or medication or anything like that?

PR: I mean, we — just amoxicillin and all that kind of stuff. Basic kid stuff, you know.

TH: Was anyone else present during those exams?

PR: The nurse, sometimes.

TH: Okay. Did he ever do any vaginal exam?

PR: Well, I think he, you know, looked in that area, but we didn't do like I would have a vaginal exam, for example.

TH: Okay. And what do you mean, how would you distinguish —

PR: Well, I mean mine would be invasive. Pap smear, et cetera, et cetera. Certainly he did not do that on JonBenet.

TH: Nothing invasive at all?

PR: No.

TH: Did he ever insert anything or use any medical device?

PR: Not that I ever was aware of.

TH: But you were standing there?

PR: Right. So I would say no.

TH: Okay. And did JonBenet have on more than one occasion some vaginitis or infection or —

PR: Well, she would, like we talked about earlier, you know, her wiping habits weren't terrific. And so she had urinated, maybe she wouldn't wipe properly and her panties would get wet, a little damp, which would cause a little irritation, you know, kind of like diaper rash and the same with you know, bowel movements. You know. So I would use — a lot of time I used Desitin or something, she had some redness, you know, so I used Desitin.

TH: Is that something that the doctor prescribed?

PR: No, it's not prescription. Desitin is for diaper rash.

TH: Okay. Did he ever prescribe anything?

PR: No.

TH: ... And you said that you would use this Desitin?

PR: Uh huh.

TH: You know, how often?

PR: You know, I don't know. I just kept the tube in her bathroom drawer there. If she complained that her bottom was hurting I would take a little on a tissue, you know, and put it on there. Not very often.

TH: Okay. Did you ever apply any other ointment or lotion or prescription salve or anything like that?

PR: No.

TD: . . . Do you recall the last time that you had applied the Desitin?

PR: The Desitin? No.

TD: Would it have been days, weeks, months, you know?

PR: Maybe within days. I mean maybe once every couple of weeks she might complain of a little irritation.

TD: Do you remember her complaining, was she a complainer?

PR: No.

TH: Whining every — "Mom, hey Mom, this hurts??

PR: No.

TH: Okay, so did it have to get pretty bad for her to say something or for you to notice it?

PR: Well, usually I would notice it, you know, when she was bathing or something.

TH: How about at bath time? What, is she old enough to take a bath by herself?

PR: No.

TH: So who bathed her?

PR: Me.

TH: Anybody else?

PR: No.

TH: Did JonBenet ever complain about any inappropriate touching by anybody?

PR: No.

TD: Tom, just so I am clear, the Desitin or any ointment or cream you ever did apply was topical?

PR: Topical.

TD: So there was never any internal ointment?

PR: No.

TD: Or cream that you applied on JonBenet?

PR: No.

TH: You made three calls to Dr. Beuf's office on December 7th ... Three in one day. One at 6:28 p.m., one at 6:50 p.m., and one at 6:59 p.m. Do you recall that day?

PR: To the office or his home?

TH: To the office.

PR: No, I don't remember.

TH: Would that have been for something like this, do you remember?

PR: Seems like I would have remembered, you know.

TH: Three times in less than an hour?

PR: Yeah. I just don't —

TH: Seems like you call —

PR: Did I have, is there, you know, a check-up report after that, as to what that was?

TH: Um, sure — well, I would assume that his office made some sort of, at a minimum, a notation?

PR: Yeah.

TH: And or a chart entry, I don't know. I haven't seen that. That's one of the reasons I was asking you.

PR: Yeah.

TH: Okay ... are you aware that there had been prior vaginal intrusion on JonBenet?

PR: No, I am not. Prior to the night she was killed?

TH: Correct.

PR: No, I am not.

TH: Didn't know that?

PR: No, I didn't.

TH: Does that surprise you?

PR: Extremely.

TH: Does that shock you?

PR: It shocks me.

TH: Does it bother you?

PR: Yes, it does.

TH: Who, how could she have been violated like that?

PR: I don't know. This is the absolute first time I ever heard that.

TH: Take a minute, if you would, I mean this seems — you know, you didn't know that before right now, the 25th, at 2:32?

PR: No, I absolutely did not . . . and I would like to see where it says that and who reported that.

TH: Okay.

PR: Do you have that?

TH: Well, I don't have it with us, no. As you can imagine, there is a lot of material, and we surely didn't bring all the photos, but —

PR: Well, can you find that?

TH: Yeah. Because I think it's pretty significant?

PR: I think it's damn significant. You know, I am shocked.

ELLIS ARMISTEAD (Ramsey investigator): To be fair, Tom, that's been a subject of debate in the newspaper . . . I don't want you to alarm my client too much here about whether or not it's absolutely a fact. I just think that should be mentioned to be fair to my client.

TH: And based on the reliable medical information that we have at this point, that is a fact.

PR: Now when you say violated, what are you — what are you telling me here?

TH: That there was some prior vaginal intrusion that something — something was inserted.

PR: Prior to this night that she was assaulted?

TH: That's the —

PR: What report as — I want to see, I want to see what you're talking about here. I am — I am — I don't — I am shocked.

TH: Well, that's one of the things that's been bothering us about the case.

PR: No damn kidding.

TH: What does that tell you?

PR: It doesn't tell me anything. I mean, I knew — I — I —

TH: Okay, for a second —

PR: Did you know about this?

EA: I tried to stay out of the making of the record and inserting myself into the tape-recording of this interview. The newspapers have talked about this. Whether or not —

PR: Well, they talk about a lot of things that are not true.

EA: And there has been a debate among the people who talked about the findings in the autopsy report as to whether there was a prior vaginal intrusion or not. There has been a debate about that. Even in the newspaper.

PR: Well, I do not know of anything and I am very distressed about this.

TH: Who could have done such a thing?

PR: I do not know. I don't have any idea.

TH: What is your best guess?

PR: I couldn't begin to guess. I am shocked. I don't have any idea. I am just — I can't believe, I just can't believe this.

TH: Would that knowledge change your answer to any question that you have been asked?

PR: No, sir. I have answered every question you or anyone else has asked me to the best of my ability.

TH: Would that answer or would that statement, that information, would that lead you in any particular direction? Would you think about a particular person being involved or doing something, with JonBenet?

PR: I don't — I don't — I just am shocked is all I can say. I don't — I don't know what I think. You know, I just want to see where it says that.

TH: And prior to today, had you heard or read or seen anything about —

PR: I had heard that the night she was killed that she may have had — have been sexually assaulted. But not prior to that. Absolutely.

TH: Have you ever suffered any physical abuse?

PR: Absolutely not.

TH: How about anybody in your family ever suffered any physical abuse?

PR: Not to my knowledge.

TH: Your sisters?

PR: Not to my knowledge.

TH: Sexual abuse, have they ever confided in you that —

PR: No. No. What's this got to do with JonBenet?

TH: What it has to do with first of all, is, whether or not you have ever really discussed things like this with people or somebody has confided in you?

PR: No.

TH: A friend. And I mentioned your sisters, you have two, correct? What was your relationship with them growing up?

PR: Very close.

TH: How — what are your ages, how close are you?

PR: I am two and a half years older than my next sister and —

TH: Which is?

PR: Pam.

TH: And —

PR: Seven years older than Paulette.

<u>TH</u>: Okay. But you guys were all raised together?

<u>PR</u>: Yes.

<u>TH</u>: Spend a lot of time together?

<u>PR</u>: Yes.

<u>TH</u>: Were all of you involved in pageants at an early age?

<u>PR</u>: No.

<u>TH</u>: Okay. Were the other two?

<u>PR</u>: Pam was, Miss West Virginia two years after I was, or three. Paulette was not.

<u>TH</u>: Did Paulette have any problem with pageants or object to them or just —

<u>PR</u>: She was a swimmer.

<u>TH</u>: Okay, so that just wasn't her thing?

<u>PR</u>: Right.

<u>TH</u>: In growing up, were all of you treated pretty much the same?

<u>PR</u>: As far as I could tell.

<u>TH</u>: No favorite? Youngest, oldest?

<u>PR</u>: Not from my perspective, no.

Patsy was again questioned about the 911 call she made. An enhanced version of the tape had revealed conversation recorded after Patsy failed to hang up the phone properly. Burke Ramsey's voice is heard on the tape, contradicting the Ramseys' statements that he was asleep.

<u>TH</u>: The morning of the 26th, you pick up the phone, call 911. Do you remember, and we talked before, the conversation?

<u>PR</u>: I am sure you must have it on there.

<u>TH</u>: Absolutely we do. So you know that the telephone calls to the Boulder Police Department are tape-recorded?

PR: I would not have.

TH: . . . In fact, they are recorded from the time that connection is made until it's broken, and that isn't to say if you stop talking that that's the end of it.

PR: Okay.

TH: The morning of the 26th, you called the Boulder Police Department, you talked to a dispatcher?

PR: I guess if that's where it goes, that's where I called.

TH: Correct. And when you stopped talking, there was a time that was tape-recorded for a few seconds where there was some additional conversation, conversation at your house?

PR: By whom?

TH: That's what I am going to ask you.

PR: I mean John Ramsey was down on the floor reading the note. I was frantically calling 911. I have to hear it to know what you're talking about.

TH: Was there any conversation immediately following your last word to the dispatcher?

PR: I don't remember. I was out of my mind, my child was missing. I was trying to convey that to the person on the other end of the line, okay? I don't remember. If you have it on tape and you would like me to hear it, I will listen to it, see if that jogs my memory.

TH: It is on tape.

PR: All right.

TH: When was JonBenet's birthday?

PR: August 6th, 1990.

TH: When is the last time that you visited the gravesite?

PR: About a month ago.

TH: Do you go on a regular basis or —

PR: No.

TH: Frequent?

PR: Not as frequently as I would like.

TH: Did you go on particular days?

PR: No.

TH: Would you go on her birthday or the anniversary of her death or —

PR: Probably not, because there is a bunch of idiots out there waiting for me to show up. It's a very personal time and I don't care to be photographed at my child's gravesite.

TH: We talked yesterday or the day before, too, about, I told you of a personal experience of being a policeman, people tend to lie to me and you told me a few minutes ago that you're telling me everything that you know about.

PR: That's correct.

TH: Okay. And that's all been truthful?

PR: Yes, sir.

TH: And I told you then that I wouldn't lie to you. And I don't have any reason to lie to you.

PR: Great.

TH: And I didn't lie to you about the information, this medical information that I told you about.

PR: Okay, this is very hurtful.

TH: I know that. And if I told you right now that we have in the process of being examined trace evidence that appears to link you to the death of JonBenet, what would you tell me?

PR: That's totally incredible.

TH: How is it impossible?

PR: I did not kill my child. I didn't have a thing to do with it.

TH: And I am not talking, you know, somebody's guess or some rumor or some story.

PR: I don't care what you're talking about.

TH: I am talking about scientific evidence.

PR: I don't give a damn how scientific it is, go back to the damn drawing board. I didn't do it. John Ramsey didn't do it and we didn't have a clue of anybody who did do it. So we all got to be working together from this day forward to try to find out who the hell did it.

I mean, I appreciate being here. I appreciate it, it's very hard to be here. It is a damn sight harder to be sitting at home in Atlanta, Georgia, wondering every second of every day what you guys are doing out here, you know; have you found anything, are we any closer, is the guy out here watching my house?

You know, it's — my life has been hell from that day forward. And I want nothing more than to find out who is responsible for this. Okay. I mean, I want to work with you, not against you. Okay.

This child was the most precious thing in my life, and I can't stand the thought thinking somebody's out there walking on the street, God knows what, molest some other child. Quit screwing around asking me things that are ridiculous and let's find the person, let's end this.

TH: Do you feel any guilt over the death?

PR: I wish I had had a big dog in my house. I wish I had used my security system. All stuff like that.

TH: Are there other things that you think you could have done or might have done to protect JonBenet?

PR: Those are the biggest ones. I mean, you know, it's pretty damn sad that you can't go to sleep at night in your own house. Safely.

TH: What have you personally done to try to find the killer?

PR: I hired all these people. I have, we have a reward out, you know.

<u>TH</u>: How much is the reward?

<u>PR</u>: A hundred thousand dollars.

<u>TH</u>: Do you remember when that was posted?

<u>PR</u>: That was posted very soon afterwards.

<u>TH</u>: Could you tell me why you didn't cooperate with the Boulder police? And I know that there were some problems, but tell me in your own words, what happened, where was the breakdown.

<u>ELLIS ARMISTEAD</u> (Ramsey investigator): You know, I resent the word that she failed to cooperate so much that I want that to appear on whatever transcript is made. I do not feel that Mrs. Ramsey failed to cooperate with the Boulder Police Department and I want that to appear on whatever record is made of this.

<u>TH</u>: Okay.

<u>PR</u>: I don't feel that I failed to cooperate with the police. I mean, I called them the morning that my child was missing. You know, I didn't call the fire department, I didn't call the security company or Ellis Armistead. I called the Boulder Police Department, okay. They were in my home from early morning until days later, I understand. They asked me questions. I told them everything that I could do to help them. I had no idea that we would ever be even remotely accused of being involved in this.

<u>TH</u>: Okay. And maybe that's where we need to clarify this. Was that the source of this friction, that they had accused you or you felt accused?

<u>PR</u>: I, the first — my first knowledge of the fact that I was being considered to be — to have been involved in this was when I was in Atlanta . . . and I remember, saying we have to thank everyone that has sent us these wonderful cards and la-de-da-de-da, and a friend of mine was — I was in the bathroom getting

ready and she said I have to tell you something. She said they are going to ask you if you were involved in JonBenet's death. Because she said there are some people out there that think that you may have did it. And I was just appalled . . . .

TH: Okay, and what didn't you understand? I know that you're not a police officer and not used to dealing with this, but what did — what didn't you understand?

PR: I couldn't imagine that anyone would think that I would or John Ramsey would have anything to do with this. It was just inconceivable to me.

TH: And why is that?

PR: Why would it be? — I mean —

TH: Okay, you read the newspapers?

PR: I do.

TH: Okay?

PR: I did. I don't now.

TH: Okay, prior to this, there was a lady, Susan Smith, back southeast somewhere, drove the car in the lake with her two children. Whom did you suspect right off the bat?

PR: You know, I really hadn't followed that that much, until I mean, I think I mentioned this incident in the CNN interview, because my friend that took me in the bathroom and said, "Hey, guess what?" She said she didn't do it and she did do it, so they immediately are suspecting the parents . . . .

TH: Right, okay. And in fact she did do it?

PR: She did.

TH: Okay. And I think you have been or somebody from the family or the attorneys contacted John Douglas, the guy that wrote the profiler book, former FBI profiler, and he talks about this was somebody who was familiar with the house, close to the family, had been there. You know, a lot of things like that.

PR: Right.

TH: So where does that lead the police? I mean what's the most logical place to start?

PR: I don't know. I mean . . . all I am saying is I took great offense to that, and was devastated to think that anybody would think that about me, me or my husband.

TH: Okay. From a police perspective or an investigative standpoint, you don't start out in left field, you start at home plate.

PR: Okay.

TH: And you go from there.

PR: All right.

TH: Because on the night of the 25th, there were four people in that house?

PR: What?

TH: I am saying when you went to bed there were four people?

PR: We don't know that.

TH: What do you think?

PR: I have always thought that perhaps while we were gone, that the person or persons came into the house and were there when we got back.

TH: What makes you think that?

PR: Because we were gone several hours, and they could have had their way with the house. Have known where flashlights were, where pads of paper were, where Bibles were . . . you know. If we are gone three or four hours. No one knows for sure.

TH: Well, somebody knows?

PR: Somebody knows, you're damn right somebody knows, and I want to find that.

TH: Let's just stay with your theory for a minute here.

This thing that you mentioned, whether it's a theory or not.

PR: Uh huh.

TH: That while you're gone to the Whites somebody comes in?

PR: Uh huh.

TH: When you come home from the Whites, do you notice different lights on, do you notice doors open that weren't open? . . . Okay. Anything out of place then? Would anything have caught your eye?

PR: If it had, by God you would have known it before today. I laid awake nights trying to recall this.

TH: So is there anything in the evidence that you're aware of that gives any credence to that thought?

PR: I haven't seen all the evidence. I mean I appreciate having seen what I have seen for the past two days, if we keep doing that, or three or whatever we have been going. It's hard, it's emotionally hard but I am ready, bring it on, let me see. Maybe there is, maybe Ellis or some of these people could, that we have all been studying this for a year and a half, would turn the light bulb on, you know. But we can't do it if we are going like this.

TH: That's right, we can't do it if we are over here and here?

PR: You're so right, that's why I am here. I said I would come back to Colorado for two reasons, one to do exactly what I am doing so that you guys night and day and night and day and night and day if you want me to help catch this person for a trial. Send the guy up the river that did this . . . .

TH: We have discussed another possible theory, that somebody got in. How about the theory that this was an accident? . . . Somewhere during the night between the time you guys got home, ten-ish, and one, two in the morning, and I am just kind of narrowing it down there because we have a screen, and we have partially digested food, and things like that. Between those times, was, we will say, that JonBenet got up and somebody in that house, legally, lawfully in that house, wasn't the three of you, also happened to be up or get up because she makes a noise, and there is some discussion or something happens, there is an accident, somebody —

PR: You're on the wrong path, buddy.

TH: Somebody accidentally or somebody gets upset over bedwetting, that's one of the things that's been proposed. Okay.

PR: . . . If she got up in the night and ran into somebody, there was somebody there that wasn't supposed to be there. I don't know what transpired after that, whether it was an accident, intentional, premeditated or what not. There was not one of her three family members that were also in that house, period, end of statement . . . .

You know, there has been 101 theories out there . . . and I hope to heaven there is some evidence somewhere, you know, that has more sense to it than what these idiots out there are writing . . . .

TH: And they can write whatever they want?

PR: They sure as hell can, and it doesn't bother me one bit.

TH: Then we can get —

PR: Let's get off it.

TH: That will work.

PR: That will work with me.

TH: Tell me what secrets do you keep from John?
You're hysterical, John is cool, calm, he's the CEO, he's down there studying this note on the floor?

PR: Probably not . . . cool and calm.

TH: Okay. He wasn't emotionally upset like you as far as screaming and hysterical?

PR: He is emotional.

TH: Okay. He was more composed though at least at that point?

PR: I don't know.

TH: Okay. Just seems odd —

PR: He was on the floor, I am on the phone.

TH: Seems odd that he would tell you to call the cops.

PR: Why? Why is that odd?

TH: Well, because, like I said, he seems to be in a little more control.

PR: Yeah, well, at that moment in time, nobody was in any kind of control. When you wake up at the crack of dawn and your child is not in the bed that you put them in the night before, you are not in control. Okay?

TH: Okay.

PR: Now, I don't know who is more or less in or out of control. But you do what you feel like you need to do at the time, and whoever — you know, it's not the time to sit down and write out the script. "I will read, you call." You know. You just do it.

TH: And in the note and at that point you had only read like the first paragraph that says, "We have your daughter . . . small foreign faction," there were instructions in the letter, things like that?

PR: I don't know about that far. I read up to where we have your daughter.

TH: I have got a copy here and I highlighted a bunch of things, some we will talk about and some we won't, okay, but it starts off, "Mr. Ramsey," which I think for a kidnapper is pretty polite. Do you find that at all unusual?

PR: I find this whole thing unusual, okay?

TH: Okay. How about the practice note or this other writing on this other page that starts off, "Mr. and Mrs.?"

PR: I don't know.

TH: It seems a little weird?

PR: It does, the whole thing seems weird.

TH: Okay, the fact that the tablet was one that was there in the house?

PR: Uh huh.

TH: I think we are all in agreement on that?

PR: Okay.

TH: The Sharpie pen was from your house?

PR: Are you sure about that?

TH: Well, I am not completely sure, but I am pretty sure.

PR: Because?

TH: Because of testing, but I couldn't swear to that at this moment. I had not read every bit of laboratory studies.

PR: Every Sharpie pen alike? I mean, I don't know.

TH: No, I mean obviously things, you know, produced at different times are different, but sometimes batches and sometimes individual things. But anyway —

PR: But the tablet was from my house?

TH: . . . We are pretty sure.

PR: Okay.

TH: Now this is a pretty polite kidnapper to write, "Mr." or "Mr. and Mrs." But they are not too well prepared, because they didn't bring — I got here, I forgot my pen. So they find the tablet and write the note.

PR: Uh-hum.

TH: Now, as you're reading through it, "We have your

daughter." Now you said that that kind of set off a . . . .

PR: Right.

TH: "She is safe and unharmed. But follow our instructions to the letter." About that time, you kind of go upstairs . . . so at some later point, you read more of it?

PR: I glanced at it, yeah.

TH: Okay, and I think you said you observed that it said $118,000?

PR: Uh huh.

TH: And what is that to you?

PR: That seemed like a very unusual amount of money. But if it was somebody interested in Access-related, they would have asked for a lot more money than that.

TH: First of all, it's kind of an unusual amount?

PR: It's an unusual amount.

TH: Plus kind of like winning the lottery, who wants to win a little lottery, you want to win the 10 million?

PR: Exactly.

PR: Right, exactly.

TH: What would $118,000 be to you guys, the price of a new sailboat?

PR: . . . No, not — I mean, not a large sum of money, but I mean, I would, you know, it would just seem like especially somebody that made reference to business and all that, you know, they would be knowledgeable that Access had just made a million — billion dollar year something, I mean why would you piddle around with $118,000? You know? So it just seemed unusual to me.

TH: Then in the middle of the next paragraph it says, "Bring an . . . adequate size attache." Again we have a pretty polite kidnapper?

PR: Uh huh.

TH: "The delivery will be exhausting," they are

preparing somebody for all this. And again, unlike any of the other ransom note that I have ever seen.

PR: I have never seen a ransom note.

TH: Well, I have seen a few. Now we start getting, "Immediate execution of your daughter. Denied her remains for proper burial. Two gentlemen will be watching her. Police, FBI, your daughter will be beheaded if she — if she dies, she dies, she dies, 99 percent chance of killing her." You get through all of that?

PR: No, I didn't . . . You know, I caught a few of those words but I just couldn't . . . I couldn't seem to go there.

TH: But still you call the police?

PR: Yes, sir.

TH: Did you and John have any discussion though about all of these admonitions in this letter?

PR: We didn't go over this together, no . . . I mean all this happened so fast. I mean, you know, you're just out of your mind. You know, when you're — I mean I got the lady on the phone, or man, whatever it was, said , "Help, come over here." Why do you think they did say, "Mr. and Mrs. Ramsey" then said, "Mr." only?

TH: Well, I think it's pretty bizarre. That kind of indicates some respect . . . .

PR: Yeah. So why would they have had "Mr. and Mrs." on one and then not use it on —

TH: They seemed to change their focus. Whoever it is, or is this all part of this elaborate cover-up, because if you go to all this trouble to get in and bring maybe some items, you forget others. And the whole goal, I would imagine, with the kidnapping for ransom is, A, to take the collateral with you, so that, B, you can collect your money . . . and they leave the collateral.

PR: Uh huh.

TH: But they leave a note, too?

PR: Uh huh.

TH: Uh-huh. You and John have been totally supportive of each other throughout this whole thing. At least in the interviews that I have seen, we discussed yesterday how there is this perception that you haven't really been at least close . . . .

PR: Perception, yeah.

TH: Well, there is the perception, I think we talked about it at the house that day, when the cops observed that you guys aren't spending time together, he is in one room on the phone, things like that.

PR: It was hardly a social. The man was trying to do everything in his power to get this child back. All right? He was calling to get money, fast. He was working with Linda Arndt and company with getting wires, phone taps, now. I was praying. We were both doing what we do best.

TH: It does seem odd though that in talking with you, that you and John haven't spent an awful lot of time discussing what had happened, like last night you said that, you know, you were tired and so you talked about —

PR: You know, like this morning you say, "Did you talk about this with John," and, you know, I figured you didn't like us to do that too much.

TH: But you had 18 months to do that?

PR: You're right.

TH: And have you talked about it a lot, have you discussed all of these various theories?

PR: Over and over and over.

TH: You say he didn't do it and he says you didn't do it, and didn't have any part in any cover-up, anything like that. Any staging. That only leaves one other person alive in the house at the time, that's Burke.

At the time, investigators were exploring every possibility, but in fact, Burke was never a suspect and has officially been cleared.

PR: And the murderer.

TH: Well, I am saying there is only one other person at that point in time, in the morning, right?

PR: Okay. So?

TH: You, John and Burke?

PR: Correct. That we know of.

TH: So you said it wasn't you and it wasn't John. Could it have been Burke?

PR: No. It wouldn't have been Burke.

TH: Why couldn't it?

PR: ... A 10-year-old, 9-year-old boy ... plus the fact that he loved his sister.

TH: It's not unheard of for a nine or 10-year-old child?

PR: My child it is unheard of.

TH: And why is that? What would make him different from some other nine or 10-year-old?

PR: Because he was not raised in a family of violence. We are a very loving family.

TH: Could it have been an accident?

PR: I — don't know.

TH: Well, you and I don't know because we weren't there?

PR: Right.

TH: So do you think it could have been, he could have pushed her down the stairs —

PR: Burke Ramsey did not do this, okay? He did not do this. Get off it.

<u>TH</u>: How do you know that, though? I mean, have you talked to him about it?

<u>PR</u>: Yes, "We are going to find out who did this to JonBenet." Doctors say that he's handling this the way that a child copes best with the death of — a very close family member. I doubt that a 9- or 10-year-old child could harbor such a thing for a year and a half.

<u>TH</u>: And you say they were very close?

<u>PR</u>: They were very close.

<u>TH</u>: Okay. Did they ever have any little squabbles, did they ever fight?

<u>PR</u>: Maybe she would step on his Legos, he would be unhappy.

<u>TH</u>: But that was it?

<u>PR</u>: Or you know, no violence . . . .

<u>TH</u>: He wouldn't chase after her, "JonBenet, I am going to" —

<u>PR</u>: No way . . . .

*As Patsy was being questioned, so was John Ramsey (JR).
On June 23, 1998, he sat down across a small round table with retired Colorado Springs Detective Lou Smit (LS), a legendary homicide cop, who was brought in to the Ramsey investigation, and Michael Kane, (MK) a former assistant U.S. Attorney and grand jury expert also hired by the Boulder District Attorney's office to move the case forward.*

Also present for the three days of questioning were Ramsey attorney Bryan Morgan (BM) and Ramsey investigator David Williams.

LOU SMIT: I'd like to just start out and ask, first of all, I'm so used to calling you Mr. Ramsey. Is it okay to call you John?

JOHN RAMSEY: Yes.

LS: John, at this particular time, do you have any medical problems at all that you know of?

JR: No.

LS: Okay, are you under, taking any medication?

JR: Taking Prozac.

LS: Okay.

JR: Twenty milligrams in the morning, ten milligrams at night.

LS: Okay . . . when was the last time you took a pill?

JR: This morning.

LS: This morning. About what time?

JR: Probably about 7:30.

LS: And what is the dosage of that?

JR: Twenty milligrams.

LS: And how do you actually feel, medically, right now?

JR: Well, I woke up on Eastern Time, so I feel like I've been up for a while. But I'm fine.

LS: Do you have any problem with this interview continuing?

JR: No.

LS: Is there anything that may be influencing your thoughts or your ability to think clearly at this time?

JR: No.

LS: In the first letter I wrote to you, in passing, when we were first getting involved in this, I did tell you that you and your family would be treated with respect, and we'd do anything in our power to find the killer of your daughter and bring him or her to justice. Do you remember that letter?

JR: Yes, I do.

LS: We still intend to do this. And we need your help. And we do need to work together.

JR: Yes. Well, you folks have always treated us with respect. And I think it's important for you to know from our perspective on this. We've been looking forward to this when you called, and we've been anxious to have an open dialogue with the people that are trying to solve this crime. And, from the beginning, we felt that the, rightly or wrongly, that the Boulder police were not of that frame of mind. That they were, frankly, out to lynch us and that dialogue was never able to be established. So our

intent is to just be open and ongoing, and there's no
higher priority in our lives than to find out who did
this. If we can help do that, we'll spend 24 hours a day,
if we need to. So, that's how Patsy and I look at this.
So, we're here to help.

LS: All right. What I'm going to do — you sent a
letter in April of 1998. And it looked like a personal
letter from you, sent to Bryan Morgan, I believe, and
we got a copy. If you don't mind, what I'd like to do is
read that into the record? Can I do that? Do you have
any problems with that?

JR: No. No problem.

LS: This is — first of all, the letter that we have from
Bryan Morgan, is dated April 15, 1998, and it's a
hand-delivery letter. And it's addressed to (Boulder
District Attorney) Alex Hunter. And Bryan Morgan
writes in his own handwriting, "Dear Alex, as you
know, we proposed last week that the Ramseys meet with
Detective Smit with a Boulder police officer present.
The Ramseys regret that this proposal was not accepted and want to renew their offer to meet with Detective
Smit. I have been instructed to deliver this letter
from John Ramsey to you so that you may know his feelings in his words." And it's signed, "John Ramsey." Mr.
Ramsey, I don't know if I can read your writing very
well, and I would like you to read it, if you will?

JR: "Dear Mr. Hunter, I'm writing this letter because
it seems difficult at times to communicate through
attorneys who are focused on protecting my rights as a
citizen. I want to be very clear on our family's
position. We have no trust or confidence in the
Boulder police. They have tried, from the moment they
walked into our home on December 26, 1996, to convince
others that Patsy or I killed JonBenet. I will hold

them accountable forever for one thing: not accepting help from people who offered it in the beginning and could have brought a wealth of experience to bear on the crime. We, myself and Patsy and Burke, John Andrew and Melinda, will meet any time, anywhere, for as long as you want with investigators from your office.

"If the purpose of a grand jury is to be able to talk to us, that is not necessary. We want to find the killer of our daughter and sister and work with you 24 hours a day to find 'it.'

"I can't refer to this thing as a person, frankly.

"If we are subpoenaed by a grand jury, we will testify regardless of any previous meeting with your investigators. I'm living my life for two purposes now: to find the killer of JonBenet and bring 'it' to the maximum justice our society can impose. While there is a rage within me that says, give me a few minutes alone with this creature and there won't be a need for a trial, I would then have succumbed to the behavior which the killer did.

"Secondly, my living children must not have to live under the legacy that our entertainment industry has given them based on false information and a frenzy created on our family's misery to achieve substantial profits.

"It's time to rise above all this pettiness and politics and get down to the most difficult mission: finding JonBenet's killer. That's all we care about. The police cannot do it. I hope it is not too late to investigate this crime properly at last.

"Finally, I am willing and able to put up a substantial reward, one million dollars, through the help of friends if this will help derive information.

I know this would be used against us by the media
dimwits. But I don't care. Please, let's all do what is
right to get this worst of all killers in our midst.

"Sincerely, John Ramsey."

LS: ... And what prompted you to write that letter?

JR: ... Well, we were, I guess, very frustrated that we
couldn't seem to get off the dime with a serious
investigation with good communication. There seemed
to be just a lot of frivolous motives floating around
that were preventing a serious investigation from
taking place ... and so I sat down and wrote the letter
and I said to Bryan, I said, "Here, you either deliver
this or tear it up, but don't change it." And he called me
about a week later and said, "Well, I just delivered it."

LS: ... Okay. I would like to ask you just a little bit.
It seems to me like the letter indicates that this is a
100 percent commitment on your part?

JR: Uh huh.

LS: What limitations do you have on that? Are there
any limitations that you're putting on this?

JR: None. We want — at long as we are working with an
objective investigation, there are no limitations.

LS: So we can contact you at any time?

JR: Absolutely, as far as I am concerned.

BRYAN MORGAN: Let me say this much. And I, I want to
spare everybody a long speech. But, I take it that at
least you, Detective Smit, understand why we truly do
not believe that we have any confidence in the Boulder
Police Department. When we have given leads to the
Boulder Police Department, those leads have been turned
around and used to poison the well against us ....

It was John who wrote that letter ... and he did it
because of the frustration he felt at not being able to
communicate ... I will put it this way. Let us see how

long we go this week. Let us see and make our own judgment at the end of it . . . . We have a long history of being very skeptical . . . I say let's go through the next several days and we'll see where we are.

JR: Well, you know, we would — the last thing in our mind on December 26th, was that we would be considered suspects. It was hard for us to believe that we were considered suspects. We accepted that and there's been a countless number of instances . . . not only were we suspects, but we were hunted suspects.

I would love not to have attorneys and let's get on with this and figure out who did this . . . and so I'm very encouraged and look at this as a fresh start, I guess. It should have happened 18 months ago.

. . . But our view is that the cruelty that was willfully imposed on us and our family by Boulder police was only exceeded by what the killer did to us. And that's our perspective . . . let's move forward . . . .

LS: You know, gentlemen, I know this is going to be a tough question. But some people say that no matter what, a parent would come in (to be interviewed by police). Even if you were feeling bad. How do you answer that?

JR: We've made lots of offers to come in . . . but I finally just lost confidence in the Boulder police. There's no sense. We started our own investigation last summer because we, we didn't think anybody else was investigating the crime.

As the discussion over the Ramseys' reticence to be interviewed and their criticism of the police ended, Michael Kane observed, "For the record, the investigator (himself) is biting his tongue through all of this."

LS: For the past year and a half, you and Patsy have been in the picture. In fact, you have been THE picture. There's been very little room for anyone else. If you think you were under a—magnifying glass with the police department, you better be aware that you'll be placed under more scrutiny now. You'll be looked at under a microscope by the prosecutors.

John, give us your thoughts and feelings as to what happened to your daughter that night. Personal. Any kind of thoughts?

JR: Well, you hope that she didn't suffer. And if I let myself think beyond that, it's too difficult. But my hope is that she didn't suffer. I think, obviously we know it was an intruder.

We spent some time with John Douglas, who is a profiler for the FBI, and he basically said it's someone that you know. It's somebody that's been in the house and it's somebody that's angry with you or jealous. And you know, we try to put that box around it.

We come up and say that we don't know anybody that evil . . . .

We were getting to be a little more higher profile in the community than I was comfortable with. I thought about security, hadn't done really done anything about it. But there's been an article in the paper a couple weeks before about our company had just passed a billion dollars in sales. And I had this gut feeling when they wanted to do that publicity, that we shouldn't do it . . . .

I don't know if that kind of publicity elevated this in somebody's mind. JonBenet was in a Christmas parade, the December Christmas Parade. In retrospect, after, you know, that was something she shouldn't have done . . . .

So I wonder if those, either of those two events might have elevated us into the crosshairs of this maniac. And if they were angry at me, why didn't they take it out on me? If they were angry at me, why didn't they take it out on my son? Why JonBenet . . . ?

LS: You must have a mental picture of the type of person this is?

JR: My first instinct is, it was a man. Because of some of the similarities apparently, in Patsy's handwriting, I wondered if it was a woman. The ransom note seemed childish, in terms of a young person. I think this person was very sick or trying to be very clever. . .You know, if they really wanted to do this, hurt us and walk away, why did they go to the trouble of leaving a ransom note . . . ?

 . . . think entry was gained through the basement window (the one under the grate that John had broken the previous summer when he'd misplaced his key) . . . because the window was cracked open. There was this large suitcase under it, as if it was used to climb out. That suitcase didn't belong there. I think the person — was in the house, if not when we got home, shortly after. I think she was killed that night, versus in the morning.

LS: What makes you think that?

JR: Well, the note talked about, "I'm going to call you tomorrow." When I found her, she was — her body was cooled. Her arms were stiff . . . .

LS: There's been a lot of speculation by a lot of people that maybe you didn't know anything about the murder, but maybe Patsy did. What do you feel about that?

JR: Monstrous. I mean, Patsy loves both her children dearly. But frankly, she and JonBenet were extremely close and Patsy fought back from Stage IV ovarian cancer which probably . . . would have been fatal in a few months. She fought back to live so she could be with the children . . . and she said that later, she said that she was too young to leave those children. That kept her going and it gave her the will to fight, to beat it. And she beat it.

Plus she's probably the kindest, least mean-spirited person I know. There's not a mean bone in Patsy's body against anyone, let alone her children. So, it's just, I mean it's absolutely out of the question.

LS: So, what do you want to happen to the person who did this?

JR: I thought about that every day. And there's certainly the Christian side of me that says, you know, forgive others' trespasses. But what I've concluded is that, you know, that there is forgiveness, but there is accountability. And this person must be held accountable.

I've gone from, you know, hang him by the neck until dead in the public square, to put a tattoo on his forehead that said, "I killed JonBenet," and let him go through life that way. But that's the rage within me . . . Fundamentally, I would want the harshest, cruelest treatment that our society can put on an individual for doing this . . . My family, my children, this has affected a lot of lives. Plus, JonBenet's life has been lost. She could have been a significant contributor to the world, and that opportunity is gone. And whoever did this needs to suffer.

LS: You know, you mentioned religions before . . . Tell us a little bit about your religious beliefs . . . ?

JR: . . . My spiritual foundation has really grown over the years. I think first, the first blocks were made by my mother who dragged me to church every Sunday. And then I was divorced, I went back to church and that foundation was there. It was helpful. And then we lost

Beth, my oldest daughter, in a car accident; my religious foundations were shaken, big time.

You know, how could that happen . . . this wonderful child . . . where is this God, this caring, loving God? But I did a lot of reading, a lot of thinking and, frankly, my foundations were strengthened ultimately by that. And when we lost JonBenet, I think the foundation was there and helped immensely and was further strengthened for me . . . .

LS: What's in your prayers at night?

JR: I pray that God will bring the killer to the attention of the police. That he will be remorseful and come forward and confess . . . And praying about it helps. But I asked a good friend of mine, who's much further along in the spiritual journey than I am. I said, "Do I need to keep asking God to find this killer or is one request enough?" And he said, "Keep knocking." So I keep knocking . . . .

The discussion about John Ramsey's faith continued for quite a while. Mike Kane remained silent during the exchange, saying he had nothing to add. But he expressed annoyance that the interview seemed to be focusing on other themes, saying, ". . . down the road . . . we'll probably want to get into more specifics . . . ." That began when Lou Smit asked John about an article which appeared in the Boulder Daily Camera just before Christmas.

JR: Well, I remember it talked about (Access Graphics) crossing the billion dollar sales level. I talked to a reporter. I think they had some quotes in the article from me . . . We had a luncheon party . . . for all employees . . . .

LS: Another think that I have written down here is,

on the 21st and 22nd, there was an Amerikids Pageant
. . . Do you remember JonBenet participating in the
pageant just shortly before Christmas?

JR: Yeah, there was one down in Denver that she
participated in . . . I think it's the one she got this
medal at, this All Stars (medal, which JonBenet had
given her father. He wore it at her funeral).

LS: Did you go to that pageant?

JR: I went to the talent part which is always what
I wanted to support JonBenet on . . . Her talent
performance was supposed to be at like 3 o'clock and I got
there at three and it was actually ahead of schedule
because she had already done it and she had won . . . the
whole thing for talent. And I walked in and she took
this (medal) off her neck and put it on my neck . . . .

LS: Okay . . . the next thing I want to cover is the
Christmas party (at the Ramsey home) on the 23rd. If
you could just, in your own words, recall what you
remember about that first.

JR: Well, yeah. We had this Christmas party,
usually a day or two before Christmas primarily for
our family, friends and children. And we invite Santa
Claus to come and we'd have presents for all the kids.
And Santa would give them out and hors d'ouevres, and
we'd start early and usually end early. And . . . that
year of '96, we decided, well, we weren't going to do
that because it was a lot of effort and Patsy just had
her 40th birthday party (a surprise party held
several weeks before her actual birthday of December
29th).

. . . So we decided not to do the Christmas party. I
think we were going to ask a friend or two over . . . .

The Santa Claus which normally came called us
and said he had "got Charles Kuralt here doing a

documentary on me and he's been kind of following me around, and I'd like him to come to your house, you know, for your Christmas party because I think it's a nice one and it's one of my favorites."

And Patsy kind of threw together a Christmas party quickly because she thought that would be fun for the kids. And Patsy is a born publicist, I guess. She enjoys that kind of thing. And so we invited the regular crowd that always came and we put together the Christmas party.

And Santa Claus (retired Colorado University journalism professor Bill McReynolds) came and passed out gifts and it was the standard party that we had every year.

As it turned out, there was no appearance by Charles Kuralt. John Ramsey was skeptical about McReynolds' claim that he was going to star in a documentary about sidewalk Santa Clauses.

JR: . . . I always wondered. . .whether it was really Charles Kuralt.

LS: Who was the person that said that?

JR: Bill McReynolds.

LS: . . . We're going to go into Santa Claus a little bit later . . . in fact, there's even indications that JonBenet may have had a secret Santa Claus . . . that's come up in our reports. . .but what was McReynolds' health about that time?

JR: Well, he claimed to be very frail and the reason that Mrs. Claus came was because he was so frail . . . I think that was the first year she ever came.

LS: Did you ever meet any of his family?

JR: No. Patsy met him in the mall quite frankly. He was

walking down the mall in a Santa Claus outfit a few
years ago. He was passing out candy to the kids . . . I
think he'd done, maybe, three, maybe, parties . . . .

LS: How did JonBenet react?

JR: Oh, she was fascinated with him . . . I'm sure she
thought it was the real Santa Claus . . . .

She apparently, the year before or two years before,
had been given a little bottle of angel dust which was
from Walt Disney as a gift one night when he was there,
and I think it was the summer of '96, he sent us a
saying that he was going in for, I think, it was open
heart surgery . . . and he was taking this little bottle
of angel dust that JonBenet gave to him . . . and we
were touched by that . . . .

LS: Just off the top of your head, do you remember who
was there (at the Christmas party on the 23rd) . . . ?

JR: Yeah. The Fernies, John and Barbara Fernie.
Priscilla and Fleet White. And, of course, their
children, both the Fernies' children, I think, were
there. Priscilla's sister and boyfriend . . . I don't
remember what his name is, from California, was there
. . . Don Paugh, Patsy's father . . . Glen Stine, Susan and
Glen Stine . . . Betty Barnhill, I believe from across the
street. The Barnhills, somebody came looking for the
Barnhills later in the evening, knocked on the door. I
let him in . . . I think we learned later that he was a
tenant they had living in the basement (man's name
deleted) that's the only time I had ever seen him . . . .

LS: Did you go to the Barnhills to pick up a bike?

JR: Yeah, Christmas Eve. We'd given JonBenet a bike, we
got Patsy a bike . . . Anyway (JonBenet's bike) we put in
their basement, and . . . after the kids went to bed,
went to get it to put under the tree. And Joe (Barnhill)
went down to the garage and went down to get it . . . his

garage or his basement.

LS: What happened to the bikes?

JR: . . . JonBenet rode her bike for a moment outside before we went to the Whites, just round the patio . . . JonBenet's bike we gave away . . .

LS: Let's go back then to Christmas Eve . . . Pasta Jay's (restaurant). You went there after what, after church?

JR: After church . . . .

LS: Now you know Pasta Jay (Jay Elowsky) real well?

JR: Yeah.

LS: Because you're business partners with him?

JR: Right . . . I'd go there at least twice a week, probably.

LS: Just as an investigative thought, did Pasta Jay have anybody working for him that may trigger something in your mind . . . ?

JR: I only knew the people that were out in front, the waitresses and so forth. . .(JonBenet) was there all the time. And really, she grew up at Pasta Jay's . . . .

LS: So then Christmas Eve was at Pasta Jay's and then what happened . . . ?

JR: . . . I think we drove up to . . . the star . . . JonBenet was miffed because we wouldn't let her walk up to the star because she had on her church dress . . . she looked beautiful in church. It was a purple dress . . . after we looked at everything, we turned around and came home. The kids went to bed . . . fairly early because they wanted to get up at the crack of dawn . . . As soon as we thought the kids were asleep we got Christmas organized.

LR: And how would you do that . . . ?

JR: Well, we'd . . . haul up the presents and put them under the tree . . . I think (Patsy) kept them in that (wine) cellar room . . . .

LS: Who was in the basement close to the time of Christmas?

JR: Well, certainly we both would have been because Patsy did most of her wrapping down there. And that's where all the present stuff was stored . . . .

LS: So you go to bed and you know the routine . . . .

JR: The kids were up early. I remember both of them running up to our bed early in the morning to get us up to go downstairs.

LS: Do you remember what time?

JR: Oh, I'd be guessing. It could have been 5:30, it could have been 6:30. It was certainly early. Probably before daylight . . . and then I think I had them stay in the bedroom until I went downstairs and turned on the Christmas lights. It's always been kind of fun to make them wait a little bit . . . .

LS: Do you remember kind of what the kids got? What she got?

JR: Well, JonBenet got a bike. . .I think she got a little doll that was one of these look-alike dolls that was supposed to look like her. I remember her looking at it and saying, "This doesn't look like me" . . . holding it up and saying, "This doesn't look like me." And she didn't . . . .

John Ramsey was asked about the trip his family was making the next day to the lake home in Charlevoix, Michigan. He said his pilot friend, Mike Archuleta, was going to fly John's private plane. They were going to stop in Minneapolis by 11 a.m. to pick up John Andrew and Melinda Ramsey, his children from his first marriage and Melinda's fiance, Stewart Long. They were arriving there by commercial jet from Atlanta. The Ramseys were due back in Boulder on December 27th, he said, to get ready to flycommercially on TWA to Orlando, and a scheduled December 28th cruise on the Disney Big Red Boat. John said he brought presents to the private plane on Christmas Day to bring to Charlevoix.

LS: Where were those presents kept?

JR: Well, there were some presents in a little, what we call, the butler's kitchen . . . a lower level kitchen . . . in fact, I think I wrapped some Christmas Day to take to the airplane . . . .

LS: When you wrapped them . . . where would you get the wrapping paper and all the things?

JR: I think . . . down in the basement . . . .

LS: . . . Did you go into the wine cellar at that time in order to get any of these items?

JR: . . . It wouldn't have been out of the question . . . .

LS: . . . Try to think about that a little bit. It's just one of those things that we're trying to determine who all would have gone in there into that room at a specific time. That's why we have to find that out . . . Okay, we're still talking Christmas Day. And what time do you think you left for the airport (to check on the plane)?

JR: It was after breakfast. You know, 11, 12, probably somewhere there . . . probably got home about three-ish, probably . . . .

LS: . . . Now did anybody have anything to eat prior to going to the Whites?

JR: . . . Not to my knowledge. Then again, they're always eating. But we didn't specifically sit down and have any kind of meal or a sandwich or anything before leaving . . . .

LS: Now, when you go up to the Whites, what time do you

think it was that you left your house?

JR: Well, it seemed like it was 4:30, 5:00, somewhere in that range ... It was an early dinner. The kids wanted to play together.

LS: ... Who is that?

JR: With Fleet Jr., Daphne White. And Fleet and Burke were buddies, and Daphne and JonBenet were buddies ... We took Patsy's white Jaguar ....

LS: I would like to just know, perhaps, what you ate (at the Whites) or whether the children ate or if it was different or how things were set up.

JR: Well, all I can specifically remember was the cracked crab. I think they had a turkey dinner ... (Priscilla White) always makes these little hot dogs with barbecue sauce that the kids love. I remember specifically Priscilla coming over with this big plate of cracked crab, making little plates ....

MIKE KANE: ... They're real crab?

JR: Yeah. They're boiled like. They're already broken. They're like just chunks ... somebody has already broken up the legs and I guess it was like King crab that was partially open ... I don't remember if (JonBenet) ate it, but, yeah, she would have liked it.

LS: Do you remember any fruit like apples, oranges or anything like that?

JR: Not specifically. I know we've been asked indirectly a lot about pineapple ... that would have certainly fit in with the dinner, but I don't specifically remember ... but I can tell you there was some finger foods. There were probably carrots and celery and stuff like that ....

LS: What time then did you leave the White's party?

JR: I think we left at about between — 8:30 and 9:00 ... it's always a challenge to get them rounded up and with all her toys and get them detached from what they're doing and haul them away. Getting things out to the car and off we went ... JonBenet sat behind me as the driver. Burke sat next to her on the other side of the back seat. Patsy was in the passenger seat in the front.

LS: Do you remember how JonBenet was dressed?

JR: She had on a little top with a silver star on it and a black pair of pants ....

LS: How about Patsy? How was she dressed?

JR: You know I don't remember other than I've looked at pictures of their party and that's my memory. But I couldn't have told you without looking at the pictures.

LS: And what did the pictures show?

JR: I think in the pictures she had like a red Christmas sweater on.

After leaving the Whites, John said the family stopped twice to drop off gifts at their friends, the Walkers and the Stines.

LS: Now you go home after leaving the Stines. To your knowledge JonBenet is asleep in the back seat and she's directly behind you?

JR: Uh huh.

LS: You pull into the garage ... how do you get into the garage ... ?

JR: We have a garage opener in the car ... I parked on the right side of the garage ... And the kind of routine was that I took JonBenet out and Patsy took care of Burke. But JonBenet was sound asleep. In fact, I was surprised at how she was because I picked her up, or tried to pick her up, and she was really out. Because

I kind of struggled a little bit to get her in my arms
. . . it wasn't graceful getting her out, and yet, she
didn't wake up. . .I had JonBenet in my arms. Her head
was in this arm, and we went in the back door . . . and
up the little spiral staircase.

LS: Does the garage door close automatically?

JR: Well, it doesn't close automatically. There's a
button by the door . . . I don't remember closing the
door myself. I only remember carrying her . . . so
anyway, I took her upstairs, laid her on the bed . . . and
I remember either taking her shoes off or taking her
coat off . . . and then Patsy took over getting her into
bed. I went downstairs . . . I started to get Burke into
bed . . . and he was sitting in the living room working
on a toy, an assembly little toy he got for Christmas
. . . so I sat down and helped him put it together to try
to expedite the process. So we did that together and it
took us 10 or 20 minutes, I guess. And then he went up to
bed . . . I must have gotten him (ready) for bed, but I
don't remember now for sure . . . .

LS: You just go right directly from Burke and came
upstairs . . . ?

JR: Yeah, I believe so . . . I just got ready for bed,
brushed my teeth probably. I did take a Melatonin that
night . . . because I wanted to get to sleep right away,
to sleep well . . . and I might have read for a few
minutes. I think I did. It was probably ten-ish or
something in that range.

LS: Okay. So now did Patsy precede you into bed, or you
did say that she went to bed? Do you remember saying
anything important?

JR: Important? I know that she might have been asleep.
I don't remember saying anything. Patsy is called the
Sleep Queen when she goes to sleep. When she goes to

sleep, she gets in bed and she goes to sleep.

LS: . . . Did either you or Patsy feed JonBenet anything before you went to bed?

JR: No.

LS: And you are positive?

JR: I am positive. She was sound asleep. And I certainly didn't . . . and then Patsy said she did not.

LS: What does Patsy normally do with her clothing when she gets into bed?

JR: Where it lands is where it stays . . . she usually changes in the bathroom so it's usually draped over the tub and off to bed . . . .

LS: Now, let's think throughout the night. I know you probably thought that a hundred times. Did you hear anything throughout the night?

JR: No. Not a thing.

LS: Let's talk about the sounds in your house. Have you ever been wakened by your children before at night?

JR: I don't recall I ever have been . . . .

LS: Would either JonBenet or would Burke ever cry out in their sleep if they had bad dreams?

JR: I remember Burke used to talk in his sleep. But crying out, no . . . .

LS: Could you ever hear Burke talk in his sleep?

JR: I don't remember, no.

LS: . . . How about, in almost every house, especially my house . . . did you ever hear noises associated with . . . home noises?

JR: I really can't . . . I mean we hear noises from — when we hear noises, it was typically from outdoors from students. (Residences for students from Colorado University dotted the Ramsey neighborhood.)

LS: You can hear that from your room?

JR: We always slept with the windows open . . . but it

was winter night so we cracked it (open) probably ...
In the summertime, we would have them open. the only
time (I) remember being awakened is from student
noises or something going on in the street ....

LS: Okay. You wake up the next morning ... what time
do you remember it being?

JR: Well, I think we set the time for 5:30. I remember
waking up before the alarm went off. So it would have
been 5:25 or probably something like that ... we
wanted to take off at 7. It was a three-hour flight to
Minneapolis. That would have gotten us there at 11
(because of different time zones). The kids' flight got
in at eleven-ish ... I didn't want to be late for the
kids' plane ....

LS: What is the first thing upon awaking ...?

JR: I think I went into the bathroom, probably went to
the bathroom, took a shower. Just started to get
dressed ... I remember I was standing at my sink and I
was probably brushing my teeth or combing my hair or
something and I heard Patsy scream ....

LS: You know about what time it was that you heard
her scream?

JR: It would have probably been between 5:30 and
6:00 ....

LS: Did you see your wife get up that morning?

JR: No.

LS: So you had already been in the bathroom when she
got up?

JR: Right.

LS: Describe that scream?

JR: It was just a — she screamed my name and I knew,
I could just tell that something was just terribly
wrong. And I just went charging downstairs ... Patsy
is hysterical. I don't remember exactly what she said.

I believe that it was like, "They have JonBenet," and she gave me this note.

LS: ... You would have been on the second floor then?

JR: Well, I think. But it seems to me that somewhere here on the second floor ....

LS: She had the note in her hand?

JR: As I recall. I remember I spread it out on the (first) floor (hallway), just kind of to absorb everything ... and I just remember just screaming ... Your first impression was that you can't believe it ... the strangest feeling I could ever imagine ....

LS: How were you dressed?

JR: I think I had underwear on ... I don't think I had on my shirt. It was just an underwear thing ... I think I ran upstairs to look at her room. I think Patsy said — I don't know if she checked on Burke ... I remember running around a lot.

LS: ... I notice that you need glasses to read. How was it that you could read that note?

JR: It was fairly large print, as I recall. But I can read, if I have to ....

LS: Was (Patsy) asking you any questions?

JR: "What should we do, what should we do." And if we should call the police. And there was (an instruction in the ransom note) that says not to call the police, so I called the police anyway. But she did, she called 911. And then she also called the Whites and the Fernies.

LS: Why did she do that?

JR: They were close friends. And I remember her just screaming, "Come over, come over."

LS: Did you do anything before the 911 call that you can think of?

JR: I think we both checked JonBenet's room and probably Burke's room before that.

LS: Describe to me how you checked their rooms.

JR: Well, I think I ran upstairs, up the spiral staircase to her room and went in and looked around and she wasn't there.

LS: Describe how you looked around. Did you look under the bed? What did you do?

JR: I don't remember. I tell you I looked more later in the morning . . . she wasn't in her bed.

LS: Patsy was with you at that time when you checked in JonBenet's room? You said "we?"

JR: I don't think she was. I think she checked — I don't think she was with me, as I recall. She might have been right behind me. There was just a lot of running around.

LS: So that's before you called the police, is that right?

JR: I'm pretty sure it was, yeah.

LS: Do you remember either of you going to Burke's room at that time?

JR: I think we did. I think I did. I remember going to his room. I don't remember if it was directly from there to his room or if I went downstairs and back up. But we checked his room pretty shortly thereafter.

LS: Was this before the police were called or after?

JR: I think before or at least — I'm not sure . . . .

LS: When you checked his room what did you see . . . ?

JR: I just looked in and he was in bed and he was asleep. I mean I knew he was there and he was okay . . . .

LS: After that, then what do you do?

JR: Well, sometime in that sequence, I mean, Patsy called 911. I might have looked around the house some more.

LS: You have to describe that just a little bit.

JR: I know I looked in the refrigerator. We have this

walk-in refrigerator. We always worried about the kids getting in there.

LS: Before or after the 911 call?

JR: I think it was after, probably . . . .

LS: Okay. . .Patsy calls the police. Are you there with her when she calls the police?

JR: I'm — yeah.

LS: Where is she at?

JR: She's at the phone in the kitchen. I think I stood kind of right here.

LS: All right. Do you remember what she said on that 911 call?

JR: She was screaming, as I recall. I remember her struggling to make the person understand what the emergency was . . . .

LS: So then what? Then what do you do?

JR: Well, before the first policeman arrived, I went upstairs and put on some pants and a shirt and probably looked through the house some more. You know . . . I started to check some of the areas . . . .

LS: Did you ever check this area, the butler's kitchen?

JR: I don't remember specifically looking there, no. I might have, but I don't remember.

John's answer shed no light on John Fernie's observation that the butler kitchen door to the outside was open when he arrived there that morning.

John said he gave the ransom note to Officer Rick French, the first cop on the scene. It was later sent to police headquarters. Copies were made and returned to the house so, as John put it, "we could figure out." As more police arrived, John said he started wondering if the kidnappers were watching the house, so he went up to Burke's room and looked out of the windows with binoculars he kept in his

*bedroom. He remembered seeing a truck behind the Barnhills'
home across the street and a small white car pass by.*

*John said he had called his pilot, Mike Archuleta, who
said he'd take care of contacting John's older children
when they got to Minneapolis.*

*He also arranged to have his credit card limit boosted,
and John Fernie arranged with a bank to withdraw the
$118,000 demanded in the ransom note.*

*When Detective Linda Arndt arrived, John was instructed
what to say if kidnappers called.*

JR: (She said,) "When this person calls you've got to
insist that you talk to JonBenet and stall for time.
And I said why . . . ? (She said) to tell him it's a hard
job to raise that much money and use the time. But you
must talk to JonBenet . . . ."
LS: . . . Did you ever go down to the basement?
JR: Uh huh. I went . . . I was by myself . . .

*John said he went down to the basement sometime
between 7 a.m. and 9 a.m. looking for a way an intruder
entered his home. He worked his way through the so-called
train room of the basement, where Burke had a model
railroad set up and over to the basement window beneath
the outside grate.*

JR: There's three windows across here . . . the middle
one . . . was broken. There was pane glass broken out of
it, which I attributed to breaking myself . . . it was
open (an inch or so)and there was a suitcase under it
. . . this hard Samsonite suitcase . . . and I closed the
window. I don't know why, but I closed it . . . I latched
it . . . I don't think I looked anywhere else.
LS: . . . Did you tell anybody about that?

JR: I don't really remember . . . I mean part of what is going on, you're in such a state of disbelief this can happen. And the, you know, the window had been broken out. And you say, hah, that's it. But it was a window that I had used to get into the house before. It was cracked and open a little bit. It wasn't terribly unusual for me. Sometimes it would get opened to let cool air in because that basement could get real hot in winter . . . it was still sort of explainable to me that it could have been left open . . . .

. . . The suitcase was unusual. That shouldn't have been there. I took that suitcase downstairs, I remember. But I sure wouldn't have taken it all the way back there and put it against the window . . . I'm 99.9 percent (sure) that I wouldn't have taken it all the way back and set it against that wall.

LS: Any other areas you looked at? You walked into that train room? Did you look in any of the closets or in any other area?

JR: I don't remember doing that . . . .

LS: You didn't go to the wine cellar at that time?

JR: No.

LS: How long would you say you were down there?

JR: Oh, a minute. Thirty seconds to a minute.

MK: When was this?

JR: . . . It was probably some time between seven and nine.

John said he left the house only one time that morning, for 20 seconds, to check a glass-paned door that opened into the garage. It was locked and boxes inside the garage had been piled in front of it. He revealed that John Fernie actually went to the bank to get the ransom money, but police decided to make copies of the bills and he returned without it.

JR: . . . That always struck me as funny. I expected him to come back with a bag of money.

LS: . . . Do you recall the circumstances surrounding Burke leaving?

JR: Vaguely. I went into his room to wake him up. I told him that JonBenet was missing, gone. I remember him crying and just kind of hustling to get up. I remember him delaying to get a toy or Nintendo or something like that before he left to take with him. Fleet took him in his Suburban. They went out the front door . . . I don't even remember that we got him dressed. I remember discussing where should we take him. He needs to get out of here; he needs to be safe.

LS: . . . What I'd like you to (do) is (talk about) the time (sometime shortly after 1 p.m.) that Linda Arndt told you (to check the house).

JR: . . . She said go through every part of the house to see if you see anything that's unusual . . . she wanted me to take someone with me. So Fleet was right there, so he went with me.

LS: What made you decide to go downstairs?

JR: I just wanted to start logically from the bottom up, I guess . . . so I went down to the basement . . . I explained to (Fleet) that this window had been cracked open and I closed it . . . that the window was broken, but I think it was broken by me . . . we got down on our hands and knees looking for some glass just to see.

LS: What did you find?

JR: I think we found a few fragments of glass — not enough to indicate that it was a fresh break . . . we might have put them on the ledge, if I remember. It really wasn't much. We had only found one or two.

John said he came back through the train room.

walked past the boiler and grabbed the handle of the wine cellar room.

JR: . . . The door was latched. I expected it not to be latched. I reached out, flipped the latch and opened the door and immediately looked down. There was a white blanket. And I just knew that I had found her.

One of the controversies in the case centered around John finding the body. Fleet White had been to the basement himself earlier that morning and actually opened the wine cellar door. But it was so dark inside, he couldn't see a thing. And he couldn't find the light switch. So he closed the door and left. Later Fleet would tell police John's scream, indicating he'd found JonBenet, came just moments before he switched the light on.

LS: So now, I just want to get that right because when you opened the door you could see inside the room. Is the light on or off at the time you open the door?
JR: I think it was off. I don't remember it being on. It was off.
LS: Would you be able to see into that room if the light was off?
JR: I saw clearly, instantly. Yeah.
LS: Do you remember turning the light on?
JR: I don't think I did. I remember just this rush that I had found her and there was tape on her mouth. I took the tape off.
LS: Where is Fleet at this time?
JR: I assume he's behind me, but I don't have any recollection.
LS: Okay. What do you actually see now, I mean in this room?

JR: Well, I see a white blanket that's folded across her body neatly ... she was laying on the blanket ... the blanket was caught up around and crossed in front of her as if somebody was tucking her in.

LS: Talk about the tape.

JR: There was a piece of fairly wide black tape (over her mouth), which I immediately took off. Her lips were blue.

LS: ... What did you do with the tape?

JR: I think I took it off with my right hand and just dropped it ....

LS: What else do you remember right at that time?

JR: I just remember just talking and, "Come on baby." And I tried to untie her arms. They were tied up behind her head ....

LS: Were they tied tight?

JR: Yeah, very tight ... her skin was swollen around. And they were not easy to get off. I tried to untie them quickly and I just picked her up, carried her upstairs. I was screaming. In fact, I couldn't even scream.

And then I brought her upstairs into the living room and laid her there, at one point, tried to untie the knot further, and Linda Arndt stopped me from doing it ...

I remember Linda Arndt kneeling down beside her. I was there and Linda said, "She's dead."

... My emotion was that I had found her, which was good. But she was dead, which was horrible. But it was almost better than not knowing. 'Cause not knowing where your child is, is the most horrible feeling, I think, a parent can experience. And that was what had been going through our mind all that morning.

So when I first found her I was like, "Thank God, I found her." I didn't want Patsy to see her that way, and I ran upstairs and got a blanket off one of the chairs.

<u>LS</u>: Upstairs?

<u>JR</u>: Probably up in the TV room. I just ran up these stairs and went back down and put the blanket over her.

<u>LS</u>: At that time, what was Patsy doing?

<u>JR</u>: I don't think she'd come in the room yet. I think, what I remember later, was they wouldn't let her go into that room right then.

Mike Kane had some questions for John, trying to establish the exact time he went down to the basement and found the broken window open. John had said sometime between 7 a.m. and 9 a.m.

<u>MK</u>: . . . And so this was before or do you remember if this was before or after the Whites and Fernies (arrived)?

<u>JR</u>: I think it was after, because they came fairly early.

<u>MK</u>: Was it long after?

<u>JR</u>: I really don't remember specifically. The best I can do, it, it was, I believe, after the police came. Because they had gone through the house . . . It was before ten o'clock . . . probably before nine. So then somewhere between seven and nine.

John was reminded that the ransom note said the kidnappers were going to call between 8 a.m. and 10 a.m.

<u>MK</u>: So it would have been before that?

<u>JR</u>: It would have been before that time period.

<u>MK</u>: But would it have been before the time that you said Linda (Arndt) prepped you? I believe she arrived

later on; she arrived around eight o'clock or so?

JR: No, it was before that.

MK: So after that ten o'clock time period (stated in the ransom note), was there a discussion about, maybe he'll call later or something?

JR: Yeah. I mean first of all the note said, we were going to call you tomorrow. We didn't know if tomorrow was the 26th or the 27th . . . .

MK: . . . So, from ten o'clock on after that time had passed, what do you recall during that time? Were you still waiting for a call?

JR: . . . At some point we sort of figured, okay, maybe we weren't going to get a call.

MK: And what did you do at that point? How did you occupy your time between that and when you went downstairs (and found JonBenet's body)?

JR: I don't think that I did much of anything other than I was just waiting for that call. And the phone rang maybe four, five six times during that period . . . it was always a false alarm.

MK: . . . Was Fleet talking to you at all during that?

JR: Fleet was taking frantic notes, I remember that. I noticed that it was a yellow notepad, and he was just writing, writing, writing, writing.

MK: Do you know what he was writing?

JR: I don't. No. No. I mean it was like every little thing I had to do or should do . . . .

MK: Did you find that odd?

JR: I guess at the time I thought he was just trying to do whatever he could to help, was my impression.

MK: . . . You said that when you went down in the basement that second time with Fleet, and you were back in that room, you were looking for glass on the floor. Why were you?

<u>JR:</u> I was just trying to verify in my own mind that I had in fact broken the window last summer and it was cleaned up, and this wasn't the break I was looking for, if there was a lot of glass there . . . because I wasn't sure that that window — well, I did know it hadn't been fixed.

<u>MK:</u> . . . Now, when you went inside to that room, you described the blanket. And you said it was folded like . . . .

<u>JR:</u> It was like an Indian papoose . . . you know, the blanket was under her completely. It was brought up and folded over . . . at that time I didn't know the extent of the injuries — but it looked like somebody had just put her there comfortably, but tied up with her mouth gagged.

<u>MK:</u> And John, I really understand how difficult this is. Do you remember, was her head exposed? Were her feet exposed?

<u>JR:</u> . . . I mean, yeah, I think her feet were exposed . . . her head was tilted to one side. I was trying to hold her head.

<u>MK:</u> . . . Were her hands tied closely together or were they wide apart?

<u>JR:</u> I remember, yeah, her hands were close together.

<u>MK:</u> . . . And so at that point then, was it then you just took her right upstairs?

<u>JR:</u> I just picked her up and ran screaming upstairs.

<u>MK:</u> . . . You took her out of the blanket and picked her up?

<u>JR:</u> Yeah . . . I got her into the living room . . . and Patsy came in . . . .

<u>MK:</u> . . . This is really important. That blanket — was it like there was care taken? It was neatly folded?

<u>JR:</u> I thought so, yeah.

<u>MK:</u> It wasn't like it was just barely thrown over her?

JR: No, it looked like somebody was trying to make her comfortable, because it was under her, completely under her head and brought up around her, as if you would wrap a . . . .

MK: Papoose?

JR: A papoose.

John admitted he started to make preparations with his pilot friend Mike Archuleta to immediately fly to Atlanta, which he considered his real home, and where Patsy had family. He said Detective Larry Mason told him he needed them to stick around for a couple of days. John was then asked about the reasons why his friendship with Fleet White deteriorated in the days after the murder.

JR: . . . Apparently John Fernie wouldn't let him get on the plane (To JonBenet's funeral in Atlanta) . . . we were told because he was just crazy . . . his biggest issue was that we retained attorneys. And he hated that. I don't know why . . . I remember Priscilla saying, "You don't need attorneys . . . we're not going to get attorneys."

MK: . . . Did you ever feel like you were playing . . . just kind of a Catch 22 . . . if you wanted to dispel suspicions and then you do something that just creates more suspicion, like not talk . . . ?

JR: . . . People that we respected were advising us. And evidence began to grow that they were right . . . We invited . . . Beckner . . . (Mark Beckner, Boulder Police Chief) . . . to come to our home . . . and you know what the police response back we got was? "I'm not going to their home, that would be to their advantage." Well, what does that tell you . . . ?

John was then questioned about pineapple found in JonBenet's system during her autopsy.

LS: Now what have you heard about pineapple?
JR: Well, we were asked if JonBenet had eaten any pineapple, because apparently it was found in her system . . . I don't remember her eating pineapple, I don't remember pineapple . . . at the Whites' house.

Like Patsy, John was shown the crime scene photo showing the bowl of pineapple found on the Ramsey's dining room table. Like Patsy, he commented that the spoon in the bowl was way too large to serve chunks of pineapple.

LS: You say that earlier you had gone in that . . . window (under the grate)?
JR: Well, I can't remember exactly when it was. I've done it maybe — twice, maybe three times during the period of time we owned the house. It was a way I could get in the house if we didn't have a key; that was least expensive to repair. It was one single pane of non-insulated glass, and I think that was done one summer I came back late in the evening. Patsy and the kids were delayed and for some reason I didn't have a key I had come back from a business trip. I think I had a suit on. I think I probably kicked the window with my foot and then reached in and unlatched the window.
LS: . . . And did you ever give keys to the neighbors or anything?
JR: . . . Well, the Barnhills (across the street) had a key . . . I don't know if I remembered that at the time. It was late. I'm sure I wouldn't have gone over anyway.

As questioning began, John was asked about an entrepreneurial magazine found in the house in which he's photographed as one of four award winners.

Three of the faces have the word "NO" written across them. A heart is drawn around John's picture. Ramsey says he has never seen this before.

JOHN RAMSEY: (Whistles.) That's weird. This was a very nice event and a nice award. But it wasn't a big deal for me. But that is bizarre.

LOU SMIT: . . . Could Patsy, or would JonBenet have written that?

JR: No.

LS: . . . Well, the reason it has come to our attention. JonBenet — did you ever read or hear anything about her in the autopsy report? That she had a heart on her hand?

JR: I heard that just recently.

LS: And the heart was in red ink? I don't know what that means. You got any thoughts on that?

JR: . . . She wouldn't have drawn on herself like that.

LS: Have you ever seen her draw on herself?

JR: Oh, they get stuff on their hands. But I don't ever remember her drawing on herself.

LS: . . . You say that you played with her at the Whites . . . do you think you were in close proximity with her where you would have noticed that?

JR: Absolutely ... I do not believe that she would draw a little heart on her hand in the same kind of ink. That has got to be weird.

LS: Well, it's just evidence that was taken right off the bat. It's just that it's out of place and this (magazine) article and the thought (of a) little girl having a heart on her hand ....

People that might have been there that night at the Whites may have seen that heart. Did she say anything about a heart? There was some mention, I think, of a secret Santa Claus. That's why it's good for us to sit down with you, because you know your daughter better than — and so does your wife.

JR: ... The person who did this obviously (left) clues to tantalize us. And that's just another one ....

In a light moment, as John is shown pictures taken inside the Boulder home, John identifies a cigar box found in the wine cellar holding his Cuban cigars.

MIKE KANE: Those cigars I see are to be Cuban, you must have gotten them out of the country?

JR: Yeah.

MK: Where did you get them from?

JR: I used to go to Europe two or three times a year.

MK: So you sneaked them back through customs?

JR: Yeah.

MK: I'm a former Fed.

Like Patsy, John was shown a series of crime scene photographs. One showed a chair blocking the door into the train room in the basement. To get to the broken window in the cellar, someone has to go through that door. Ramsey found the chair blocking the entranceway during his first search of the basement, moved it and then moved it back, he said. The information cast some doubt on the intruder theory.

LS: So you think that the chair would block the door and nobody would have gotten in there without moving it?
JR: Correct.
LS: In other words, let's say that the intruder goes into the train room, gets out, let's say, that window?
JR: Uh huh.
LS: How in effect would he get that chair to block that door, if that is the case, is what I'm saying?
JR: I don't know ... I go down, I say, "Ooh, that door is blocked." I move the chair and went in the room.
LS: So you couldn't have gotten in without moving the chair?
JR: Correct ... I had to move the chair.
LS: The thing I'm trying to figure out in my mind then is, if an intruder went through the door, he'd almost have to pull the chair behind him ... because that would have been his exit ... so that's not very logical as far as ....
JR: I think it is. I mean if this person is that bizarrely clever to have not left any good evidence, but left all these little funny clues around, they ... are clever enough to pull the chair back when they left.

John was next shown a photo of the blanket that was wrapped around his daughter's body.

LS: Where was that blanket on her kept?
JR: ... Patsy said it came off her bed.
LS: Is it something that was on JonBenet's bed?
JR: Well, according to Patsy, yeah. That was the blanket that was on her bed.

MK: . . . I'm going to get into another area here . . . you hired media consultants . . . tell me about that?

JR: As far as I'm concerned . . . it's the biggest mistake we ever made . . . they said we have to be isolated from these piranhas (the press), so we can do our job . . . but keep us from having to deal with these people . . . .

This guy (media consultant Pat Korten) was brought in . . . and it was a total waste of money . . . .

He was a blow bag. He was worthless. What we should have done is . . . hired somebody that knew . . . to be polite . . . I thought he was a total jerk . . . he failed miserably . . . .

John, however, said he doesn't want the story of his daughter's murder to disappear from the news.

JR: There's a perverse (side) of me (that) doesn't want to see it ever go off the front pages, even though it's very harmful to Patsy and I. But I don't want people to forget about it. I want to find this person . . . so I'm helpful even though we're awful tired of people sitting outside our home with binoculars and cameras . . . .

John was again asked to recall the moments after Patsy discovered the ransom note.

MK: What did you do to determine that she was gone?
JR: Patsy and I went to the room, I think I ran up and looked again. That was it.
MK: Did you look anyplace else?
JR: At that time . . . no, I don't think so . . . .
MK: You were pretty adamant about calling the police . . .

was there any discussion about not calling the police?

JR: Yes, for a moment. I mean, Patsy said, "It says not to call the police." I said, "Call them anyway." We called them. I mean, there's no question in my mind that that was the right answer ... we couldn't just sit there. We would have gone mad.

MK: ... (The ransom note) said, "You will withdraw $118,000 dollars from your account." What did you think about when you saw this?

JR: It was just a strange amount. And I was thankful I could do it. Because it wasn't a hundred million. So I could deal with that.

MK: Um-hum.

JR: I thought it was obviously strange ... it seemed amateurish, you know, the whole thing ... It started out, "Dear Mr. Ramsey," and then it went into, "John, John, John." That, to me, is unusual for people to use your name a lot. The only person — at some point — I thought that, gee, that sounds like so and so talking because they use my name a lot ....

Fleet uses your name a lot. John this, John this. And that's unusual. And that was my only impression ... Fleet and Priscilla we thought were our closest friends. So that's a bizarre thought. But it was a thought ....

MK: There are these phrases in (the ransom note) here that seem to have some kind of Hollywood connection? What did you think about that?

JR: ... There was a couple of phrases that came out later, "You must grow a brain" ... and, "other fat cats here," or something like that.

MK: "You're not the only fat cat around."

JR: ... Well, "Grow a brain, fat cats." We'd heard those before.

John recalled a reception given after JonBenet's funeral in Atlanta by his wealthy stockbroker and friend, Rod Westmoreland.

JR: My friends were around me, consoling me and trying to give me advice. And to be a part of that group — it's the Atlanta fat cats.

MK: . . . Have you seen the movie "Dirty Harry?"

JR: Seems like I have. That's an old movie, right . . . it's Clint Eastwood, but I don't remember what it's about . . . .

John said his favorite movies were Harrison Ford movies, movies that have airplanes and boats, old classics like "African Queen." The comedy "Animal House" is one of his favorites, one he's seen five times or more. He was asked if he'd seen the movie "Speed," the flick which has similar dialogue to the "Don't try to grow a brain" line in the ransom note.

JR: I watched "Speed" on . . . an airliner without headphones. And if you ever watch that movie without the sound, it's the stupidest movie you can imagine . . . .

MK: When you looked at this (ransom note) . . . what did you make of it?

JR: I was panicked. Patsy was by the phone and . . . "What should I do, what should I do?" And I don't like to use the phone . . . 'cause if there are reservations to be made or this or that I always get Patsy to do it. That's just the way our family works.

MK: Even under the circumstances?

JR: Even then.

MK: Patsy, how was she acting?

JR: She was hysterical.

MK: Didn't that concern you, that she would make the call being hysterical?

JR: No, no. She said, "What can I do?" and I said, "Call the police." And she was standing by the phone. And it was how it happened . . . I mean, she was hysterical at that time. I was just trying to sort things out and, "Can you call the police . . . ?"

MK: Okay . . . You said something about the possibility of it, (the writer) being a woman? Maybe you could tell me about that a little bit.

JR: Well, there were apparently some similarities of Patsy's handwriting in the notes. All the experts we had looking at it says it's almost at the point of being excluded. But they couldn't quite exclude it because there were just basic things that we all learn to do in handwriting. But I had said (to an expert) if it's a woman, and he said, "No, you can't tell. You can't tell gender by handwriting." That's just my amateur-ish suspicion . . . .

MK: . . . you said you had been thinking about it about . . . the possibility of a woman, and you had thought Priscilla White.

JR: Yeah. We went back to (FBI profiler John) Douglas' analysis that it's somebody you know, it's somebody that's been in the house, it's somebody that's hanging with you who's jealous. And if I put that box around it, and what was subsequently extremely bizarre behavior on both (Fleet and Priscilla's) parts.

MK: What kind of behavior?

JR: A lot of it I didn't see, but just heard about it. But when John Fernie wouldn't let Fleet on the airplane (to Atlanta for JonBenet's funeral) because he thought he was too out of control . . . they went and stayed at my brother's (in Atlanta) and my brother called me and said, "Fleet White just left here and he's on his way over. I think he's extremely dangerous . . . ."

MK: What about Priscilla . . . ?

JR: . . . If I narrowed that box down any further I would pick Priscilla . . . only because it would be very hard for me to believe that Fleet would do such a thing.

MK: You're saying that it wouldn't be hard that Priscilla would, though?

JR: Less hard. And there's a lot of data that flowed in afterwards to us from friends that said, you know, Priscilla was very jealous of Patsy. And they (the Whites) made a comment that they'd rather eat glass than live in a house like Rod Westmoreland's. It was hatred for wealth. It was like strange stuff that was coming out, coming back.

MK: Is Fleet wealthy?

JR: I don't have a clue.

John brought up the name of a former Access Graphics employee, who cooperated with police and was not considered a suspect in the case. The man was fired from the job and later complained about the treatment to Lockheed Martin, the parent company of John's firm.

JR: . . . He became very verbally violent. And he sat in my office and said, "I'm going to bring you to your knees."

John was asked if he saw any similarities between Patsy's handwriting and the ransom note.

MK: . . . You know your wife's handwriting better than anybody. Is there anything in here that you've seen would rule her out?

JR: Well, it's a bizarre note. It's a bizarre thought process. That would rule her out, number one. Patsy just doesn't have that capacity to think that way ... having a mother talk about beheading your child is just nonsense. This is written by a very sick person, in my opinion.

MK: Do you get, in reading that, if the person that wrote it is trying to frame you or frame her?

JR: I don't know. I don't because, frankly, I thought this myself. If somebody really wanted to frame us, they wouldn't have left a note ... that's evidence that I didn't write it, Patsy didn't write it ... it certainly bought some time. I think everybody assumed JonBenet was not in the house ....

Although Patsy said she had read parts of the autopsy report, John said neither of them has viewed the report. He was asked about reports that JonBenet had been molested prior to the day she was killed.

MK: ... Is there anything you can think of that would account for that ... any opportunities she would have had to be alone with somebody or even something innocently that might account for that?

JR: Well, certainly not that we're aware of.

MK: ... Any other family members sit with (JonBenet other) than your mother-in-law?

JR: Yeah. Don Paugh (John's father-in-law and an Access employee) stayed a few times, 'cause he was their grandfather. He had an apartment over on Pearl Street. Not often or for very long. You know, for an hour or two here.

MK: And overnights?

JR: Oh, there might have been one or two.

LS: . . . I know there was a bedwetting problem. And they do have certain kinds of devices for bedwetting to avoid the leak. I don't know what that means. But anything on that ever occurred that you recall?

JR: . . . I don't know if JonBenet had a bedwetting problem, I'm not sure she did. I think all kids wet their beds. I know my older kids certainly did. The kids used to wear these all night Pampers or whatever they were called. I wouldn't classify it as a bedwetting problem that I was aware of.

MK: . . . So there was never any discussions that you had with anybody, with a doctor, with Mrs. Ramsey about it being a problem?

JR: No.

MK: . . . Who usually did the laundry?

JR: Patsy usually does it . . . .

John was asked about his business travel. He said he made several trips to Europe, opening offices in Bristol, England, Paris, and Amsterdam.

MK: . . . People say that they've seen you in the Red Light District in Amsterdam?

JR: I was in the Red Light District once with a group of people, and perhaps even with Patsy, as a tourist. If anything would make you celibate, it would be going to the Red Light District in Amsterdam. It's a nasty place. But we were there as tourists. We were probably there for 30 minutes along with all the other American tourists that were there. That's the only time I was in there, yeah.

John was asked about Patsy's battle against deadly ovarian cancer and how it changed their relationship.

MK: I imagine going through that type of illness, it's very taxing on everybody. How did Patsy handle it?

JR: Patsy was just unbelievable. She was going to beat it. I have never seen her as scared as she was . . . .

MK: How did all this change her?

JR: Patsy very much lived for the moment after that. She enjoyed every day. She tried to maximize her time with the children . . . sometimes I'd complain about something, something at work, and she says, "Well, it's better than cancer." . . . I think she tried to cram as much in every day as she could . . . .

I think we became more close, not that we weren't anyway. I mean, you go through a hardship with someone and you see them more of a person inside than you had before.

MK: Like how do you mean?

JR: . . . You bond in a way that you don't bond if you haven't gone through hardship. That's the best way I can tell you. If it affected our relationship at all, it was constructive.

MK: It made you more close in what sense?

JR: I think you just accept each other more totally for who you are, and respect each other more fully for who they really are.

MK: Can you give me an example of before and after?

JR: No, I can't really. I mean love is an evolving thing. I think you grow more deeply in love as your relationship continues. And it changes from what was probably lust in the beginning to true spiritual love, and that just contributed to that development . . . . After, I think because we were more deeply in love because of this kind of experience together, it was probably more meaningful.

MK: Would you say it was normal?

JR: Oh, yeah, from that standpoint, certainly.

MK: And emotionally?

JR: No issue there at all.

MK: How did it affect her spiritually?

JR: It has affected her a great deal. She became much more spiritual. She believed that she was cured by God . . . .

MK: No lasting effects outside of the neurological?

JR: Perhaps. On her body, she has a big scar up and down her chest. I mean, you couldn't pay her enough to put a bikini on. But other than that, no . . . .

MK: Can you describe, if you could, your wife's range of moods?

JR: She's the most positive person I know. She never was down.

MK: . . . When was she the happiest?

JR: When she was with her family, I guess.

MK: What about today?

JR: Well, she lives for her children, for Burke, quite frankly. And she loves to be with him.

MK: . . . Did you guys ever get in a fight or disagreements?

JR: . . . Not really, no. The only time I got angry was — this was years ago — she had gone to New York with her girlfriend and her mother. They'd gone to shows and they had a great time. And she was on her way home and I got a phone call from this Raul, wanted to know if Patsy got home all right.

And so when she came in, I said, "Who is Raul?" So there was this long story about how they had come out of the show and one of the others said, "Okay, here's a cab, get in." And they jump in and there's this nice cab — it was a Rolls Royce — and there was this guy in the back and it was Raul.

It was a perfectly innocent story, but I was suspicious, I guess. And that's the only time I ever really got angry, I guess, with her.

MK: And how did you resolve it?

JR: I think I kicked the kitchen door, and that was it.

MK: When she got home, did you have this discussion about that?

JR: Oh, yeah. I had to know who Raul was.

MK: Did you believe her?

JR: Oh, yeah, yeah. I mean, she was with her mother, for heaven's sake.

MK: Couldn't her mother have given her an a alibi?

JR: Well, she supported her telling me.

John was asked about weapons he has owned, and revealed he had armed himself with guns in the past year.

MK: . . . Have you got handguns?

JR: We have just in the past year . . . we have three I think. Three, yeah. One in Charlevoix, two in Atlanta . . . 38 caliber specials I guess, one pearl handle 38 . . . .

MK: I think it was John Andrew when he was interviewed said that — he was talking about the beauty pageants and the possibility of this being a work of a, you know, a jealous parent or whatever . . . what did you think as a father seeing your six-year old in make-up?

JR: Oh, I can't say that I liked it. I think — she had fun with it. Every little girl, certainly all my little girls, liked to put on make-up and dress up, and play dress-up and so this was just kind of another level of playing dress-up. But I always kind of did a check — you know, did she really want to do that today?

And I never said, you know, "Hope you win" — "Just

have fun, hope you have fun. Sing good, you know, doesn't matter if you're the prettiest. You're the talent, that's really what counts." It became kind of a thing between us, she always said, "I am there for my talent, Dad" ... I think she drug Patsy to a couple of them that Patsy didn't even want to go to

... These pageants always took a video of the girls, which in retrospect was a huge mistake to allow that.

MK: In what regard?

JR: ... Because it made national news ... these videos that were made, which we shouldn't have allowed, were released to the world. And so it looked like we were putting our daughter on display for the world and in fact, we weren't at all.

MK: Some of the criticism that you have gotten from media and press, public, is that some of these productions with the kids, some of their actions were provocative. What did you feel about that?

JR: It's in the eyes of a beholder. If you look at a little girl in a dress and think something sexual, you got a problem. That's how I look at it.

MK: ... On the 26th, that day, some people ... who were at your house or at the Fernies (where the Ramseys were given lodging) afterwards, have commented that — that you and Patsy didn't spend a lot of time together under this crisis atmosphere. What's your reaction to that?

JR: I don't recall we didn't spend a lot of time together. We were both totally devastated, crushed, ruined. Mentally vegetables. I mean, you know, you just, you don't really care to even be alive after something like that happens.

MK: ... I just wondered why you wouldn't gravitate to each other in that circumstance. You have such a common interest at that point.

JR: I don't know. I mean, I don't recall that we didn't. . .and before we found JonBenet, Patsy kind of stayed in the solarium (sun room) area, and I would go in and check on her periodically and just assure her that we were going to get JonBenet back . . . .

I tried to apply every ounce of energy and mental power I had to figure out what we had to do to get her back.

John was questioned about whether he'd heard of the play "Hey Rube." It was penned by Bill McReynolds' wife, Janet, years earlier and centers around a girl held captive in a basement and tortured to death.

MK: . . . It was based on a book called "The Basement." What have you heard about that?

JR: Oh, just that she had written this play, that it was about a child being murdered or, you know, tortured. I don't know — a very awful play.

MK: Awful in an artistic sense or a dramatic sense?

JR: Dramatic. That it was very sick, and very similar to what happened to JonBenet . . . it just was kind of shocking to us that we had allowed somebody like that to come into our home.

MK: . . . When you say "somebody like that," what do you mean?

JR: Well, that's that perverted and sick. I don't think that way. I don't want to be around anybody that does.

MK: . . . Did you think that Janet McReynolds had something going through her head that made her write that, outside of just a . . . ?

JR: Well, I don't know, but I mean the fact that anybody could apparently write something like that is kind of nauseating.

MK: . . . Do you think or have you thought in the last year and a half that someone was trying to frame you for this?

JR: No. The thought crossed my mind, but I think that's the — I didn't give him credit for being that clever.

MK: Why not?

JR: Because I think they have left too many clues. They left a ransom note . . . .

MK: No, but I mean in the context of someone trying to frame you?

JR: I think it's too much of a stretch. If I were going to do that, I wouldn't have handwritten the note. I would have typed it out . . . I would have done it on a word processor or on a — maybe I wouldn't have left a note at all.

MK: Do you feel like if there were no note, the finger would point more to you or less to you? When I say you, I mean your family.

JR: Well . . . that was Patsy's reaction. She said, "Thank God they left a note." I said, "What do you mean by that?" She said, "Well, they left some evidence" . . . .

So yeah, I mean I think if somebody was really trying to frame us, it could have been a lot more obvious . . . but the fact that, okay, maybe there is a few similarities in (Patsy's) writing, that's about it. I mean if somebody is trying to frame you, that's just too — that's too lucky.

MK: . . . Were you surprised when there were similarities?

JR: Well, the way it was explained to us was that there are certain things that we all learned, when we learned how to write, that are kind of common and that's the kind of things that were there, apparently, in Patsy's samples that they just couldn't say totally exclude it.

MK: ... The SBTC?

JR: I have run numbers and letters. I have tried to figure code. I have looked in the Bible extensively for that reference. Talked to people who know a lot more about the Bible than I do. The only thing I have heard that makes sense are that it's "Star Based Technical Command" — (that) was a term on, I think, "Star Trek," one of those ... "Star Wars," "Star Trek," I think, which kind of fits the movie theme (in the note).

John was asked what he's done personally to solve the murder. It led to revelations about (name deleted), the woman he had an affair with during his first marriage, and the cause for his split with his first wife, Lucinda.

MK: What other things have you done to investigate this? I mean outside of hiring people to do it ... ?

JR: ... Unfortunately I had an affair 20 something years ago and I was trying to figure out where this person was and I looked in the phone book and I found the addresses of — there are several with her name and I wanted it to seem logical. She used to live in the (Atlanta) area, (and I) went to an apartment complex and sat there for a while, to see if I could see her come and go.

MK: When was that?

JR: Oh, I don't know, six months ago, something like that.

LS: Could I interject? You're talking about (name deleted)?

JR: (Nodding slowly.)

LS: ... You had claimed ... that she had kind of

a fatal attraction type personality. How did you attribute that?

JR: Well, just — we hired her as a secretary in a small office, and you know, I was vulnerable, but not — not crossing the line. We were at a Christmas party that this office building had, and she said, "Gee, I left something up in my office, do you have a key?" And so I went up, unlocked the door and as soon as the door was unlocked, she turned around and kissed me. And then I just kind of got sucked in. But it was a — just a very strong physical attraction.

LS: How long did that last for?

JR: Oh, two years, maybe. It was one of the things I got into and I couldn't get out. She was extremely aggressive. Like you know, I tried to, you know . . .

LS: What do you mean, "aggressive?"

JR: I wouldn't answer the phone so she would call 27 times.

LS: At home?

JR: At home. Our marriage probably was not strong or that wouldn't have happened at all, but it certainly ended it. And it was probably the biggest regret I have in my life, but, she was a very . . . volatile person.

LS: Why do you think she hasn't surfaced? I mean your name has been all over the place.

JR: I don't know. And that really surprises me. I am surprised she hasn't come forward and said, "That son-of-a-bitch, you know, I knew him when."

LS: Was it a bad breakup that you had?

JR: Yeah, and I got rid of her finally. You know I just couldn't, I finally got her to stop pursuing me.

LS: But did she make any threats?

JR: No. No. Not — that was 20 years ago, or longer than that maybe.

LS: And you have never heard from her since?

JR: No.

LS: Do you know if she had any children?

JR: She had a son . . . he was probably nine years old or so.

LS: There has been another gal in Tucson?

A woman in Tucson had come forward to publicly claim she had an affair with Ramsey before JonBenet's death.

JR: I have no clue who that woman is. No clue.

LS: I know you said in the last statement that's bullshit?

JR: Total. She called my office several times. We tried with our investigators to get her to ask for money. She never would do. She would call and say, "The newspapers want me to talk, what does John want me to do?" My secretary would come in and say, "Who in the world is this woman?" I didn't know her. I had no clue. I haven't been in Tucson for 20 years, so I turned it over to these guys (his investigators), and they called her back and she said, "I need help, tell me what to do." And so they tried to get her to ask for money.

She never would cross that line to extortion. And we just blew her off. I never talked to her and next thing I know she is (a) celebrity on television.

LS: How would she have gotten Pam's telephone number?

JR: Pam?

LS: Patsy's sister?

JR: I guess I didn't know she talked to Pam . . . .

LS: You're saying that's definitely not true, there is nothing?

JR: There is nothing that happened. I have no clue who

that woman is . . . .

MIKE KANE: Just to follow up on what Lou was
saying about (the woman with whom he had an affair
during his first marriage). You said you finally put a
stop to it. How did you do it?

JR: Well, it was actually Patsy indirectly or
unknowingly helped me with that. I met Patsy, she was
one of the first persons I met that I really cared
about, and I always kind of thought she was kind of a
gift from my (deceased) mother to help me get my life
straightened out . . . .

But Patsy and I were down, we were downstairs in the
apartment (the apartment Patsy stayed in downstairs
from John when they were dating in Atlanta) . . . .

She was . . . cooking hamburgers, and I went upstairs
to get some more wine, and when I got up there, this
(woman) had called and said she was coming over.

I didn't want it to mess up my — what was just
starting to be a relationship with Patsy.

And so I left the apartment, I just left. I didn't want
her to find me anywhere.

And she came over and was apparently knocking on
my door, and Patsy by this time was thinking, where in
the world did I go?

(Patsy) said she came upstairs — she tells the story
later — she came upstairs with these two wine glasses
and here is this woman standing and knocking on my
door and (the woman) said, "Well, where is he? — He's
in with her." And Patsy said, "Her? Her who?"

And (the woman) said "Patsy."

And Patsy, (who is still holding the two wine
glasses) says, "Oh well, I was just bringing these wine
glasses back." (John laughed heartily, joined by his
interrogators.)

She (Patsy) was smooth as a cucumber, and later that evening, I came back, kind of told (Patsy) what had happened. I said I had this girlfriend that was crazy and I just didn't want it to . . . we were just talking and knock, knock, knock on the door, and — actually I think I was going to leave. There was this knock on the door, and I was literally behind the door and Patsy opened the door. It's (the woman), and she said, "I was waiting for John, I want to come in (and) use your phone." And Patsy said, "Oh, our phone is out of order, we just moved in."

And here I was standing behind the door. From that moment on, (the woman) left me alone and I also realized how much . . . what a significant person Patsy was. Because here she was a 23-year-old kid, just standing there. So that was kind of the breaking point.

LS: Have you been able to locate her at all?

JR: Well, I don't know, but I am very surprised that she hasn't surfaced.

LS: That is kind of an unusual thing . . . if I could just . . . I wanted to ask you a question and that's in regards to the pineapple. Did you discuss that at all or try to find out what the reason for the pineapple in the bowl was, last night (with Patsy)?

Patsy by now, has been told during her interrogation session that fingerprints on the bowl match John or hers. In fact, they matched Patsy's.

JR: I think I mentioned that I was puzzled by the bowl, the large bowl of what appeared to be pineapple with a big serving spoon in it. It didn't register with her. She said, "I hope they show you a picture . . . ."

LS: That's a question we have to try to figure out

— what happened there, when that bowl was placed there, and who did that.

JR: Right, (and) where this spoon came from.

LS: And even the pineapple.

JR: Yes, is that what was in the bowl?

LS: Yeah . . . see, that is a question, when did JonBenet eat pineapple?

JR: Well, I don't know. I mean, I will guarantee you it was not after she came home. She was sound asleep. So it had to be at the Whites or prior to that.

LS: . . . Next question is, could someone have gotten her up and fed her pineapple? That is a logical question, and that's the question we have to answer.

JR: I can't imagine that somebody could have gotten her up, fed her pineapple, and she wouldn't have screamed bloody murder.

LS: Why?

JR: What if it was a stranger? . . . Patsy said she didn't give her any — I mean, first of all, if we had said oh, yeah, well, we gave her pineapple, that would have ended the discussion . . . but we didn't.

LS: But the fact though, John, is she has pineapple in her intestines, okay. She has that in there. No one has fed her pineapple that we know of. Could someone have fed her pineapple that night? I mean, if it's in there, it's a positive . . . .

JR: I understand, I understand. I mean, my suspicion when I first heard that was, well, there must have been pineapple at the Whites' house, and I don't remember it but there was all sorts of little finger foods, and the kids were in and out and grabbing this and that. We understand the Whites said no, they didn't serve pineapple . . . but I guess my question would be, well, did the kids go to the refrigerator and get a bite of pineapple at the Whites? If it wasn't there and was it earlier in the day, Patsy would most likely know. She liked pineapple. I guess . . . it would not have been out of the question that she grabbed some out of the refrigerator in the day sometime, but I don't know that she could get the door open. But I mean, it's hard for to me to think that this intruder could have taken her downstairs and fed her pineapple. I just can't buy that.

LS: The pineapple is inside her, so we have to figure out how that pineapple got there. She had to eat it at some point.

JR: Are you sure it was pineapple?

LS: No question. No question. So that's always been the big bugaboo.

JR: What's the — is there a timeline based on where it was in the digestive system?

LS: . . . There is . . . it could be anywhere from two hours to more than that . . . .

JR: Well, my amateur reasoning would be that . . . I believe she was killed that night.

LS: What night?

JR: The 25th . . . Christmas Day night. So if you said midnight, that means there is three hours that I would say there is no way she could have eaten any . . . we didn't feed her any when we got home (at about 9 p.m.) . . . she wouldn't have gotten up, Patsy didn't get up . . . if an intruder drug her down there and tried to feed her something, she would have screamed bloody murder. If she opened her mouth to eat pineapple, she would have screamed bloody murder.

LS: But still it's a fact that it's in there. There is nothing that we can do to change that particular fact.

JR: I understand.

LS: So is there any possibility at all that Patsy could

have done that, have gotten up and gone down there?

JR: No.

LS: Would you have known it if she had?

JR: I wouldn't have known it but she certainly would have said it. I mean, there was no reason she would have denied it. I mean, it would be very easy, if we were trying to hide this, it would be very easy to say, "Oh, yeah, I got up and fed her pineapple, that explains that, then put her back to bed." We didn't.

LS: This is why, you know, people think about those things, and especially detectives.

JR: . . . If we were trying to disguise something, why wouldn't we say, "Oh, yeah, we fed her pineapple before she went to bed, that explains that." We didn't. So I can't — I don't accept that that happened. If it did, I would have said it or Patsy would have said it. Even if we were guilty, I mean, what's the big deal? I mean, you know what I mean, that it didn't happen. I know it didn't happen after she went to bed. So there has to be another answer to that question, (other) than that she got up in the middle of the night and had a big bowl of pineapple and went back to bed, or we got her up . . . .

LS: Did she ever go on her own to go down there and eat pineapple?

JR: I don't recall that she ever did. I don't know. I don't think so. Not that I remember, ever, at night. She was getting to the point where she was — she used to be not afraid of the dark or anything at all, and then she was growing up a little bit and getting afraid of the dark. If the intruder somehow — well, that just doesn't make sense.

I mean JonBenet was a smart, strong little girl. And if she had the opportunity to scream and to kick and fight, she would have done that. No question in my

mind. So I don't buy that, you know, an intruder sat
her down and fed her pineapple.

As questioning began, John Ramsey was shown more photos taken by police inside the Boulder home.

He did not recognize rope found in the guest bedroom that his older son John Andrew occasionally used, although he said it's possible it belonged to the college student.

The flashlight found on the kitchen counter, the suspected murder weapon, looked like the one he owned.

The metal baseball bat found outside and near the butler kitchen's door was something he didn't recognize. A neighbor had reported hearing the clang of metal on concrete sometime after midnight that Christmas night JonBenet was murdered. Some investigators wondered if the bat had been the murder weapon and if the clanging sound had been the intruder dropping the bat as he fled the house.

John also viewed a photo of a plaque he'd gotten during a military tour of duty from 1968 to 1970 at the Subic Bay naval facility in the Philippines. It had been suggested in media accounts that the "SBTC" stood for Subic Bay Training Center, words reportedly printed on the plaque. The accounts were not accurate.

LOU SMIT: ... There has been a lot of things said about Subic Bay Training Center, things of that nature. What does that say on there, by the way?

JOHN RAMSEY: It says Lieutenant J.B. Ramsey, PNBC, Subic, which is where I was stationed ....

LS: Does it say anything about Subic Bay Training

Center, does it have initials on this?

JR: ... PWC ... the public works center ... U.S. Navy Public Works Center, Subic Bay, Philippines ... it says March 1968 to October 1970, CEC, which is Civil Engineer Corps.

John was then shown two photos showing a torn-up letter that was found in the trash can in JonBenet's room.

LS: Have you ever seen a letter like that?

JR: It doesn't look familiar ... it says, "Somebody loves you all. Merry Christmas."

LS: I can tell you that these items were found in the trash can in your daughter's room and it was torn up.

JR: Do you know what the word before "loves" is? "Somebody loves you all."

LS: I am sure that has been looked at very closely. It appears to be a Santa Claus letter.

JR: (trying to read the torn-up letter) ... "Friend, enjoy your holidays, Christmas." Well, it doesn't look like anything I have seen before ... and I don't know what it would be doing, you know, torn up in ....

John then asked if he could talk more about the mysterious bowl of pineapple.

LS: If you would like to, you can talk about it now.

JR: All right. Bryan (Ramsey attorney Bryan Morgan) chastised me a bit on the way home. He said like, "You were very adamant that she wouldn't be eating pineapple. What do you know for sure?" I said, "I know we didn't feed her pineapple. I know I didn't feed her pineapple. I know Patsy didn't feed her pineapple, because she said she didn't."

And I was going on track of there is no way a strange intruder could have gotten her down there without her screaming, kicking and hollering and fed her pineapple. But you asked, I think, if what if it was someone she knew, and that's conceivable. And . . . .

LS: How would you explain it?

JR: . . . There was apparently one of JonBenet's friends or parents that day said JonBenet told them that Santa Claus was going to come visit her that night . . . .

LS: Where did you hear it from?

JR: I think I heard it from our investigators . . . .
If that's true, and if the Santa Claus were somebody she knew, she adored Santa Claus, they had a special relationship. If he was the one, came into her room, as previously promised, she wouldn't have been alarmed, she would have gone downstairs with him, gone wherever he wanted. I don't know why he would have sat down and fed her pineapple, but it's possible.

LS: Do you have any ideas who this could be?

JR: Bill McReynolds (the retired journalism professor who played Santa Claus at the Ramsey Christmas parties) is the only Santa Claus I know. That she knows . . . .

This Bill McReynolds has done it for two or three years . . . if in fact that's who said that to her and in fact was said . . . somebody she knew and was expecting, particularly Santa Claus, she would hop right out of bed, you know, gone to the mall if he wanted to.

LS: You see that, that pineapple is a clue, I mean that's in the case.

JR: . . . Let's have the hypothesis that she ate the pineapple sometime between 9 p.m. when she came home and . . . we found a bowl of pineapple on the kitchen table. I know for a fact that I didn't do it, serve her pineapple. I know for a fact that Patsy didn't because

she said she didn't . . . but if it was somebody she knew
. . . JonBenet liked pineapple, no question about it . . . .

You know, we were suspicious of McReynolds in the
beginning . . . he came to the memorial service (for
JonBenet in Boulder). A good friend of mine who was
there said that you guys need to go back and look at
that video, because when Patsy went up to hug him, he
pushed her away.

And Jim Hudson is the fellow's name that said this.
He said, "My brother's been working with pedophiles
for 35 years." And I described Santa Claus to him, and
he said, "That's the guy." So early on we were saying,
wow, well, Santa Claus, you know, acting so feeble and
how could he have carried her down the stairs, and was
the feebleness an act? Possibly. Was this all part of a
grand play that they put together?

. . . He certainly fits . . . if I am working this
hypothesis through, he fits the box that John Douglas
(the FBI profiler consulted by the Ramseys) drew for
it: somebody we knew, somebody who was in the house,
somebody I think that would have been jealous of
people that had assets . . . I never said a harsh word to
him, but he would have been very jealous, apparently
didn't have two nickels to rub together.

So he and JonBenet had a kind of a special little bond.
She worshipped him as Santa Claus and apparently from
what we understand the guy is, if not a pedophile, he's
a frequent visitor to pornography shops.
LS: Have you investigated that?
JR: We have gotten information to that effect . . . we
have a tape from him . . . it was a tribute to JonBenet
. . . and apparently it starts up and it says, "You left
Santa Claus and went, you know, doing all those fancy
things and you came back to Santa Claus." Our guy said

it was very weird. He (McReynolds) wrote me a letter saying that he carved JonBenet's name in a heart — it had the name of three other little girls that died early.

I mean, I couldn't start saying, "Okay, that's the guy." But that's premature, but that would in my mind explain how, if we said JonBenet ate pineapple between 9 p.m. when she went to bed and when we found her, that is the only way that's plausible to me that she could have eaten. If someone she knew and trusted and said, "Let's go downstairs, there is a surprise." He might have sat there with pineapple . . . .

LS: Those are things that have to be answered.

JR: Yeah . . . last night I thought about it all night.

MIKE KANE: . . . (asking a hypothetical question) . . . Where do you think defense attorneys would go in defending him?

JR: Oh, I think based on the, you know, public crucifixion or persecution that's been made on us, they would probably look at our excuses.

MK: . . . I am going to ask you some questions about you, okay. How would you describe yourself in a paragraph?

JR: Um, um, fairly passive. Sensitive. Not extremely well-spoken. Decent work ethic. Loves his children. Loves his family. Likes free time. And is growing spiritually.

MK: How would others describe you?

JR: Um, quiet, um, that's always how I am described, is quiet. Nice guy. Gentle. Hard to get to know. Doesn't talk a lot.

MK: Was there ever a history of psychiatric problems in your family?

JR: No.

MK: Before JonBenet's death were you ever treated for a psychiatric problem?

JR: No.

MK: Did you ever get counseling through your divorce?

JR: We talked, together talked to a marriage counselor. But after that, no.

MK: What was your, what was your socioeconomic status, growing up, I mean?

JR: We thought we were better off than most, but looking back on . . . we were solidly middle class. My dad worked for the state of Michigan, the state of Nebraska, he was a great man, but didn't make a lot of money. But we thought we had a lot, you know, we felt very — I think most kids tend to feel they are better off than most people. We felt that way, but looking back . . . we felt comfortable.

MK: What was the most traumatic thing as a kid that you can remember, growing up?

JR: I have never really thought about that. I mean I can remember when my mother's brother died. I was just young. I was maybe six or eight years old, um, um, I remember when a friend of ours' son was, who I kind of knew . . . I would have been in grade school . . . was killed. He died in a skiing accident.

When I was in high school, I had a girlfriend who gave me the boot. That was kind of hard. You know, when I got in college, I was president of my fraternity and we had two fraternity brothers that were killed in a car accident, that was very tough. So you know.

MK: Well, I am not suggesting you ever got out-of-hand as a kid, but if you did, how would your father deal with that?

JR: I can specifically remember, and I must have been, could have been seven, eight years old probably, there was a new house being built, and I and a friend of mine went over and threw bricks through the basement

window. That was so much fun, we broke all the
windows in the house. I don't remember feeling like
that was bad, it just was, we did it. We were being
mischievous, and my dad made me rake the yard for
about a month after that.

MK: Was there any corporal discipline?

JR: None that I remember, no.

MK: Has Mrs. Ramsey ever talked about these things
growing up, things that were traumatic to her?

JR: No, she had a nice childhood.

MK: Did she ever talk about how her parents
disciplined her?

JR: All I remember her saying is that her dad is also a
very quiet person. All he had to do was say something
stern you know, and they melted. That was their
discipline, but it was very adequate.

MK: We talked about your, you know, your religious
beliefs now, how about growing up?

JR: Well, we were raised Episcopal. My mother took me
to the Holy Trinity Church, I was an acolyte. When I
got older I went to the church that my friends did,
which as a Methodist church. You know, I think that
for part of my life, you first went to church because
your parents made you, and then you kind of went to
church because you figure it might be a mistake not to.
And your spiritual development, at least for me, has
been a slow process.

MK: And I don't know if I heard you say it or I read it,
(you) went to Michigan State undergrad?

JR: Uh huh.

MK: And did you go to graduate school?

JR: Uh huh.

MK: Where was that?

JR: Michigan State also.

MK: What was that in?

JR: Undergraduate was in electrical engineering, and graduate school was in marketing, business marketing.

MK: Did you get an MBA?

JR: Right.

MK: Okay. What did you like about school?

JR: Um, we had a lot of fun, I mean that was part of it. I mean, we had a lot of laughs. I didn't really settle down, become a good student until my second year of my program. I think as I recall I kind of graduated by the skin of my teeth, in undergraduate school. But I mean we had football games, and parties and campus life.

MK: What are the things you didn't like?

JR: Um, you know, I mean I am sure I didn't like to study. I mean I didn't . . . I was in a hard curriculum. You know. I don't remember anything I didn't like, other than, you know, I wasn't a totally absorbed student. I was a kid that was there kind of having fun and realized he had to stay in school to graduate, and that conflicted a bit with the social part. I made it through.

MK: What year did you go to Michigan State?

JR: I graduated in 1966.

MK: . . . Lou asked you about (the woman John had an affair with during his first marriage) . . . you said your marriage probably wasn't on a solid foundation to begin with. What did you mean by that?

JR: Cindy (John's first wife, Lucinda) is a very wonderful person, she was a wonderful mother for the kids. She was kind, came from a great family. You know, was a perfect wife and we were married for ten and a half years, but we weren't each other's best friend. We were around friends once, and they were — obviously, they were married, and they just laughed at each other's jokes, you could just tell they were buddies. And Cindy was more my mother.

I mean, when I got out of college, I was really looking for a mother replacement. As I analyzed it myself, looking back on it. If I told a joke if it was at all off color, I probably got chewed out. So it was that kind of a mother discipline relationship, that we never really became best friends, and so there was just that element missing in our marriage . . . .

MK: . . . How did you end up in the Navy?

JR: I, my dad was a World War II pilot, said, "If you got to go in the military, go in the Navy, because I used to risk my life flying jelly to the Navy in Burma, silverware." We had plastic forks, whatever . . . .

MK: . . . You stayed (in the Navy) for quite a while?

JR: I stayed in for what I was obligated for, which was three and a half years, approximately and then I stayed in the reserves for a while. Six or eight years.

MK: Have you ever lost consciousness or anything like that?

JR: No.

MK: What kind of medications, were there anything you regularly took?

JR: Well, for my allergies, what finally worked for me was a nasal spray that was cortisone-based, and that kind of came out and I was able to use it, it really helped. And I used that off and on for several years. Other than that, no.

MK: You talked about now taking Prozac and Paxil?

JR: Klonopin.

MK: What attracted you to Patsy?

JR: We met through some friends. She was staying with some friends. . .and Patsy was, I don't know, 22, 23 . . . she had just gotten out of college and I had met her, but ... she didn't really catch my eye or it wasn't an instant affection. I would go down there for dinner and we would play cards or something just as a group, and I really started to admire her wit and just her as a person. And I thought for a 23-year-old she had got a lot on the ball, and then I asked her out and I just felt very, very right and . . . .

MK: And how long did you date before you got engaged?

JR: Oh boy, I don't know. A year, probably, or so . . . I remember that she said I was the only boyfriend she's ever had that (her father) talked to. I was flattered by that.

MK: So you passed that test?

JR: Yeah.

The subject switched from John's personal life back to the crime. He was shown a roll of black duct tape, the kind that was taped over JonBenet's mouth.

LS: Now John, I know we are touching right back on a very delicate spot, but was this tape wrapped around anywhere, was it stuck down?

Police believed the tape could be part of a staged crime scene, loosely put on JonBenet's mouth after her death.

JR: No, it was very firm across her lips.

LS: And you recall that?

JR: Yeah.

LS: And why, did you have to work at it to get this tape off?

JR: No, I mean (it) just came off. It wasn't loose, it was tight enough.

LS: Fine, we won't go into any more of that. But have

you ever seen anything like this before?

<u>JR</u>: . . . Well, if I were to speculate, that's something that Fleet White would have, which . . . .

<u>LS</u>: And why would you say that, have you ever seen anything like that?

<u>JR</u>: Maybe, you know, I can't — I can't remember for sure, but Fleet had, when we got, went up to get our boat ready for this Mackinaw, Mackinaw race was a 300-mile race (from Mackinaw Island in Michigan to Chicago), Fleet had some special tapes, I remember white tape. And possibly I remember black duct tape. The only kind of duct tape I have ever seen (is) gray . . . .

<u>LS</u>: We have to try to find someone that has that. How often have you seen black duct tape?

<u>JR</u>: I don't recall that I ever have . . . .

<u>MK</u>: How about Patsy?

<u>JR</u>: . . . Well, it's possible . . . but the only time I ever remember duct tape was gray duct tape . . .

Although it was now some 18 months after the murder, Boulder police still had not obtained vital records from the Ramseys that would aid the investigation.

Lou Smit asked John if he had any objection to turning over bank records, credit card records, movie rental records "to see if you rented 'Speed' and 'Dirty Harry'," telephone or cell phone records, Access Graphics business records that show purchases, Patsy and John's medical records "to show any type of pathology that you may have in regards to this."

John said it wasn't a problem to turn the items over.

Had the Boulder police failed to ask for these items? Or were Ramsey attorneys stonewalling the investigation?

Ramsey attorney Bryan Morgan stated his clients had always turned over anything requested.

MK: . . . Having been involved in cases over the years myself . . . involving children that have been killed and the parents of the children have been killed, I have seen rock solid marriages end up in divorce because of that, and there is a lot of reasons, obviously there is a lot of tension, there is a lot of guilt that turns into anger and gets directed. Mrs. Ramsey gone through any of that?

JR: No, not really. You know, we talked to someone early on, I don't remember which doctor . . . and we asked that question . . . somebody quoted as well, 70 percent of marriages break up after something like this happens. We said why is that? And I think the reason that in my mind was that because one or the other blames the other for not doing something.

And I think if Patsy and I were both to sit down and blame ourselves for lots of things — not having the alarm on, not checking the doors, not being more security conscious, not letting JonBenet — I mean there's lots of things that in retrospect as a parent, my God, how stupid were we.

But one of the things that my friends kind of reassure me on was you made every effort, we probably sold more burglar alarms and security systems because of this, which is good . . . .

So that's given us some relief from guilt . . . .

MK: . . . What does Mrs. Ramsey feel about the whole pageant business?

JR: Well, she's never really talked about it. I think she saw it as what it was and through her eyes it was just a fun thing for her and JonBenet to do.

MK: I mean in retrospect.

JR: In retrospect, I don't know, I have never asked her that question. It's not a fair question to ask.

MK: I mean has she ever brought it up, when you talked about how you go through these feelings, if I only put the alarm on, if I only did this, has she ever talked about it?
JR: No, because I mean — no, I mean that's because we don't know . . . if it turns out that it's somebody at work that we fired and they took it out on me, that's going to be a heavy burden for me to carry.

John was asked about an impromptu videotaped interview Patsy gave at their home in Atlanta to a producer from Geraldo Rivera's show. Patsy came across as somewhat spaced out. John said Patsy should have told the producer to get lost, but didn't have "a mean bone in her body." The producer apparently returned at a later date and was threatened with arrest if she didn't leave.

MK: (The interview) was pretty schlocky.
JR: Geraldo, he's — we are going to go after him if we can. He is one of the lowest of the low, as far as I am concerned.

Like Patsy, John was asked about books found in his home and his reading habits. He said he liked books by James Clavell and James Michener, that he remembered reading a book about the Lewis and Clark expedition.

In dealing with the death of his daughter, Beth, in a 1992 car accident, John read books on the loss of a child. One in his home was "Goodbye Is Forever." John said he hadn't read it because he didn't like the title. "I don't believe goodbye is forever," he stated.

MK: Okay. What about "Mindhunter," John Douglas' book was there in the house? Had you purchased it?
JR: No. It was there in '96? Interesting.

John admitted reading Stephen King's books "It," a book about the murder of children by a demonic force in the shape of a clown, and "Pet Sematary," a novel about the accidental death of a child, who comes back to haunt his parents.

MK: . . . Have you ever thought about suicide?

JR: Uh huh . . . when I was going through a divorce, suicide's an easy way out. . .and I remember one night thinking about it, but I was at that point, in despair . . . .

I don't remember with Beth (the daughter killed in a 1992 car accident) . . . that was a huge loss for me . . . it took me years to get through that. I couldn't drive home from work without crying for a long time, because I was by myself . . . it took a long time to get me — to get past that where I could think of Beth and smile, and think of happy things . . . .

MK: Have you recently been thinking these thoughts (suicide)?

JR: No, no. Certainly (it's) something you think when you're so far down after something like this, it looks like the only relief, but then — the reason that Patsy and I have come through is because we have Burke, Melinda and John Andrew. If we didn't have other children, we probably would have checked out a long time ago. What's the point?

MK: . . . Do you have any recurrent nightmares about all this?

JR: Oh, I had nightmares for a while. Of course. I can't remember, yeah, I did for a while. But I haven't recently . . . . I can remember one dream where I was holding JonBenet and we were playing and everything was okay, and then I couldn't figure out if I was dreaming or not. You know, it's just — I mean, of course, when you wake up, it's a pretty big downer.

Like Patsy, John was unaware that police had enhanced the tape of her 911 call. She had failed to hang up the phone properly and police say Burke's voice is on the tape, asking "What did you find?" The Ramseys were contending Burke slept through all the commotion that day. John was questioned about the 911 call.

MK: Were you listening, I mean, do you remember hearing her on the phone?

JR: I remember her screaming into the phone, but I don't remember really what she was saying or anything.

MK: And you know these are recorded, 911 calls are always recorded? Have you heard the recording?

JR: No.

MK: All right. Do you know whether she hung up right away, after she stopped talking?

JR: I am sure she did, but I don't — don't remember specifically that.

MK: Do you remember what conversation you had immediately after she stopped talking on the phone?

JR: No.

MK: Could anybody else have been there?

JR: No . . . just Patsy and I.

The idea that a stun gun was used to subdue JonBenet was brought up. John admitted he knew what a stun gun was, and, like Patsy, remembered the visit to Spy World in Florida, where the Ramseys walked out with a promotional videotape that had a mention of stun guns. John said he'd gone into the shop to inquire about devices that tapped phones. The tapping of phones and theft of business dealings had been a concern for his company.

MK: Did you ever hear of Spy World?

JR: Well, that came up, and I couldn't remember for sure the name, but I said, you know, one of the questions that came up was a stun gun thing, and I know fundamentally what they are. I don't know if I could draw one for you, but I know what they are. And I was curious where you buy one, where would somebody buy something like that. Somebody said spy shop.

We were in Coral Gables, and I told these guys, I said — were were in Coral Gables and . . . there was this spy shop that we went into and I was curious about if there was a device that you could buy that you could figure out if your phones were tapped. That had been a big concern about, gee, there is a lot of stuff going on in our business, and gee, what, you know, what if we are naïve and somebody has tapped our phones and, really, that could be very damaging to us in other negotiations and so forth.

So I went in there specifically asking is there a device like that you can buy, and basically the answer I got was no, that's pretty tough to do, but . . . here's all this other stuff you can do, and he showed us how you can put bugs in. It's easy to bug something, pretty difficult to find the bug is kind of what I came out of that. It actually made me more worried about what I was worried about.

But he gave us a video and said here's a catalog of our stuff and we threw it in our suitcase, we never looked at it, threw it in a drawer, sat there for years.

LS: John, who is "we?"

JR: Patsy and I.

LS: Into the store?

JR: Yeah, Patsy and I . . . were just together.

LS: Anybody else with you?

JR: No, I don't think so . . . well, Sun Microsystems was the host, and they had invited us to the Super Bowl game that year, and they put us in a hotel in Coral Gables.

LS: So it was just you and Patsy walking together and you just walked by the store?

JR: I am pretty sure it was just us, yeah, I am sure it was.

LS: Do you know who else you might have been (with) down there . . . or that you visited with, because we may want to talk with these people.

JR: Yes, there's some of the people from Sun Microsystems . . . there was a group of people, probably 60 people . . . but anyway . . . I don't know what was on that tape because we hadn't looked at it. I believe the only reason it didn't (get) tossed into the wastebasket is it made . . . the drawer first . . . .

MK: So you never made any purchases (at Spy World)?

JR: No . . . .

MK: . . . Have you followed up on (whether any of your friends owned stun guns)?

JR: . . . It sounded like something that a woman may have in her purse for personal protection. And the people we knew, Priscilla (White), being from California, and . . . she came from an area where you have security issues and so forth. Might have, you know, if anybody was going to have one, it might be somebody like her. I absolutely don't ever remember her having one . . . .

MK: . . . There was a nightgown that was found down in the wine cellar (the pink Barbie nightgown that was wrapped up in the blanket covering JonBenet).

JR: I have heard about that . . . I had never seen that. I didn't see it when (I) was down (there) . . . sounds very bizarre. I don't know why that would be there . . . .

MK: Could have been brought down in a blanket?

JR: I suppose, I don't know . . . .

LS: . . . We have heard that a Barbie nightgown was one of her favorite nightgowns. What can you tell us about that?

<u>JR</u>: I think she had a Barbie nightgown. Yeah, as I recall. Pink maybe.

<u>LS</u>: The night you put her in bed, do you remember anything about a Barbie nightgown?

<u>JR</u>: ... When I laid her down in the bed she had on what she had worn to the Whites. She had that same shirt on when I found her.

<u>LS</u>: What I am trying to say, John, is where would that Barbie nightgown have been?

<u>JR</u>: It would have either been in her bathroom drawer here, where a lot of them were kept ... by the sink, I believe. It could have been on the floor, or it would have been in the washing machine. That's probably only three places it would have been.

John was shown a crime scene photo of the blanket on the floor of the wine cellar.

<u>LS</u>: ... Tell us what you see.

<u>JR</u>: I see the blanket that looks like the one that was around her. There is a pink something, pink — I think that's the nightgown.

<u>LS</u>: ... It is a nightgown, it is a pink one, it is a Barbie nightgown. ..why do you think, John, that that's down there ...?

<u>JR</u>: Yeah, I don't — it certainly should not be. I don't remember seeing it. But I was pretty focused, I guess, at the time.

<u>LS</u>: Again, you had mentioned the fact that the blanket had been wrapped around her almost like — what did you describe it as?

<u>JR</u>: Well, she looked very, like someone had very carefully placed her on the blanket, wrapped the blanket around her to keep her warm.

LS: And then we have a Barbie or a nightgown . . . and what's your impression?

JR: God, I can only imagine it. That was something very perverted.

MK: . . . All right. Are there any big secrets you kept from Patsy?

JR: No. No. Not that I can think of.

MK: Do you think there was any big secrets she ever kept from you?

JR: No. No. I doubt that very much.

MK: Why? Why is that?

JR: Well, you live with somebody for 18 years, it's pretty hard to keep secrets for one thing, I guess. I don't know what a big secret is but . . . .

MK: How did you keep the (his former mistress) secret from Cindy (Lucinda, John's first wife)?

JR: Well, that was ultimately not possible, obviously . . . I think that affair probably went on for eight months or a year maybe. Before it exploded.

MK: Before she found out about it?

JR: Uh huh.

MK: But you were able to maintain it for that period of time?

JR: (Nodding.)

MK: We talked yesterday about, I think you said (bedwetting) wasn't a problem, that you were aware of, and there has been a lot of publicity about that.

JR: It was total nonsense, but ask the question.

MK: Okay. Did you ever have discussions — you said before it never came up in discussions with Patsy. What about subsequently with all the publicity about it?

JR: Just, I mean, it was one of those ridiculous tabloid pieces of data . . . .

MK: Would it be a big surprise to find out if that was

in fact the case, that you did have a problem with it?

JR: No, I mean all my children wet the bed. It was not a big deal.

MK: But it would be a surprise to you if you found out that in fact it was more of a regular occurrence than what you know right now?

JR: Probably . . . if it was every night, I didn't know that. But. No, just part of raising a child.

MK: I mean but the fact that you didn't know about it — I am not talking about would it be a surprise that she did it. But the fact that say a couple of times a week, she wet the bed, that seems to be a lot more than what you were aware of. Would you be surprised if you found out it was more than what you were aware of?

JR: No.

MK: And why is that?

JR: Because it was a, it's a minor, it's a non-issue. You know, if she was wetting her bed every night when she was 11 years old, I think we have a problem we need to look into medically, but it just wasn't an issue. It wasn't a big deal.

MK: You said that you were aware that there was plastic, her mattress was wrapped in plastic. Did you put that on there?

JR: I don't know. Probably did, but I don't remember.

MK: You said that you thought, I think you said all the kids had that. Did Burke have that on his bed?

JR: Oh, he's had it I am sure, yes. But I don't remember whether he did, you know, then or not. But . . . for us . . . it's so ridiculous. I mean it's just . . . not an issue for us as a family. I mean Melinda wet her bed until she was older than, I don't remember how old, but it was older than — if anybody had a bedwetting problem, you would have said maybe it was Melinda, because it went longer, but it was . . . .

MK: But this is the first one that Patsy had to deal with?

JR: I mean Burke probably did too. No, Burke did. I know he did. You could tell that, you knew if you came downstairs and he was in the other bed, guaranteed what happened. Or he would come upstairs, crawl in bed with us. And have a clean pair of underwear on. So he wet his bed, too.

MK: And I think you have already answered this. You didn't have any discussions with your wife about the urinary tract infections that your daughter had.

JR: No.

MK: What do you know about Mrs. Ramsey having panic attacks?

JR: Um, I don't know what a panic attack is, I guess, for sure. How would you describe it?

MK: Just a feeling that you can't control the moment, overreacting to something maybe more than would be within a normal range. Just feeling, I can't handle the situation.

JR: She is as stable as a rock.

MK: So you have never known her to have those?

JR: (No response.)

MK: Never known her to be treated for those?

JR: No.

MK: Never known her to take any medication for those?

JR: (Shaking his head.)

MK: Would it surprise you to find out that she did?

JR: Yeah. That would.

MK: . . . I got to ask these questions. You have seen other circumstances like the Susan Smith case in North Carolina. Are you aware of that one? Something totally out of it, what any of us could ever imagine, went on.

JR: Yeah.

MK: What do you think of that?

JR: It's horribly tragic. You know, we have lost two children. And would give anything to have them back, anything. I would be out on the street with no possessions to have my children back. And to — it's — we cannot fathom, I cannot fathom how anyone could feel that way about a child.

MK: Yet it has (happened).

JR: I know. And it's, that's horribly tragic.

MK: I know early on when you were describing to Lou, you know, your theories of what might have happened, and one of the suggestions about Mrs. Ramsey being involved in this, you said it was preposterous. What do you base that on?

JR: She lived for the children. Period, pure and simple. She was given a gift to live after facing death and she was there for her children.

MK: Has the thought ever crossed your mind in the last 18 months, or the possibility that this was an accident?

JR: No, no.

MK: Or it started out as an accident?

JR: I mean how could it, how it . . . I mean I saw some dippy FBI guy who said this might have been just the outcome of an accident. The child was strangled, her head was bashed in — that is not an accident. No, absolutely not. I would have given my life for JonBenet in the instant, and I regret that I was unable to. Patsy feels the same way. We know that much about that.

MK: Do you ever give thought to maybe this was the result of a some kind of a demon?

JR: No.

MK: Demonic?

JR: . . . This is a creature that's out there . . . I can tell you this, I can tell you I have suspicion, and I have thought about almost everybody we knew, because you just don't trust people anymore. People that I would never, you think could have been, you know, John Fernie, oh, God, no, but how do you know? I have never, ever had that thought about Patsy. Or Burke.

MK: This is a big, big "if." I mean, if, if it were to come out that there was some pathology Patsy was going through, caused her to do this, would you feel an obligation to protect her rather than find out that that was what killed your daughter?

JR: As a very big "if," if that was what happened, I would not protect her or protect that fact.

MK: Knowing the truth about her?

JR: Knowing the truth. Absolutely not.

MK: . . . Is there anything I have asked or said or done that you feel makes you not want to . . . follow-up . . . ?

JR: . . . No, I mean, you know, we, we are looking forward to being here and I absolutely want to continue an open dialogue . . . we have said to ourselves, look, there is never going to be a victory in this, there is no victory, but if we can find who did this, there could be some closure we can understand, what do we do, if anything, so our — you know, the only thing that's important to us is our existing children. And finding who did this.

MK: And that's what's most important to you. You use the word us — what —

JR: Patsy.

MK: What about you?

JR: Me?

MK: You personally?

JR: Oh, if I had to put those in order . . . I find myself saying this — look, you got three wonderful children, you pick yourself up and get on with it. They need you. So, and that obviously has got to be number one. But number two is, who the hell did this? And number three is, let's make something good come out of this. That's a contribution to society . . . .

LS: . . . Okay. I would like to talk to you about John Andrew's suitcase (the suitcase that was found under the broken window in the basement below the outside grate) . . . and I would like to ask you just some questions. Do you know what a sham is or a duvet?

JR: (Shaking head.)

LS: Two type of things.

JR: Sham is a blanket, right? But duvet, I don't know.

LS: Do you recall any shams or duvets being in your house? I know if you don't know what a duvet it, you probably don't know to say it was in there but . . . .

JR: No, I don't. A sham, I mean, I don't know if I know what a sham was, a small blanket? That's purely a guess, but we had lots of little blankets and stuff like that around.

LS: How about a Dr. Seuss book, do you remember anything in a Dr. Seuss book, either associated with John Andrew or associated with JonBenet or anything that . . . .

JR: Well, we had lots of them kids' books. We had bookshelves full of them. I know that they had — I know I read to them, Dr. Seuss books, so I am sure they were there.

LS: Do you know why there would be a sham and duvet and a Dr. Seuss book in that suitcase?

JR: Could you tell me what a duvet is?

LS: A duvet is also something that fits on like a couch, or almost a little blanket that fits on a couch ... can you think of why there would be a sham or duvet in John Andrew's suitcase along with a Dr. Seuss book?

JR: No. My recollection of where that suitcase came from was he brought some clothes from Atlanta ... and it ended up and it was in his room for a while, then it was in the laundry room outside of his room for a while, and then I carried it downstairs. I presumed it was empty.

LS: ... Okay, we are going to talk a little bit if we can about the wine cellar. Now, did you — what — how often would you go into the wine cellar, let's say before the 26th? We touched on this yesterday ....

JR: Well, throughout the year, hardly at all. I mean the only things that were down there that we would get at, I think we had some wine stored in there, just in boxes at one time. I don't know if there was any — I don't know if there is any left or not. But we would get a case of wine and we would put it down there. Cigars I stuck down there. Um, and of course, you know, Christmas stuff out once a year, put it back. Patsy usually, I think, certainly that year did it or had it done, so I don't remember ever getting in there to get the Christmas stuff out. That's about it. We rarely went in that room.

LS: Have you ever been asked to make up a list of people who you thought could have ever been in that wine cellar?

JR: No.

LS: Is there a way that perhaps you could sit down, it's a little time consuming right now, but at some point write down everybody's name that you may have thought could have possibly been in there, let's say within three months, let's start off with that?

<u>JR</u>: Okay. (Who) went into the room?

<u>LS</u>: Into the room. And that may even be contractors or . . . .

<u>JR</u>: Yes, I will do that.

<u>LS</u>: What have you heard about Hi-Tec shoes?

<u>JR</u>: Just that there was a print found, a Hi-Tec boot, and that's all.

<u>LS</u>: Do you own a Hi-Tec type shoe, or have you ever owned one?

<u>JR</u>: Well, I don't — not that I know of. I mean, I never have been — I never paid much attention to brands of boots I had. I had some — I had some running — not running shoes. Hiking boots. I think I looked at those and they were — they weren't Hi-Tec or anything.

<u>LS</u>: You have already looked at those?

<u>JR</u>: Yeah. I had some kind of dress boots that were more for — but they weren't Hi-Tec boots. So I mean, I don't think we had anything like that. We had — I had some of these felt-lined like duck boots.

<u>LS</u>: If we ever ask you to bring these items in, would you do that to make sure that we got them?

<u>JR</u>: Sure.

<u>LS</u>: And there is a reason for that, of course . . . .

Police were still searching for the source of the Hi-Tec print found in the dust of the wine cellar and the beaver hair found on the duct tape that covered JonBenet's mouth.

<u>LS</u>: I am going to show you a series of photographs . . . they are foot prints or shoe prints, and I would just like to show that to you if I can, and see if you might recognize maybe by looking at shoe prints, sometimes you know what the bottom of a sole looks

like, if you have something similar to that or even maybe one of your friends?

JR: Where was the print found?

LS: In the wine cellar.

JR: In the wine cellar?

LS: Yes. So I would like to show you a series of prints. If you will do that, Mr. Ramsey ... what do you see?

JR: I see "Hi," looks like "Hi-something" you see in a square block with, I can't tell if it's raised or lettering ... I don't know if that's sand or is that mildewy stuff that was in the basement. Looks like there is some — some of the Christmas tree ....

LS: Needles?

JR: ... Needles, yeah, that were laying in there. It almost looks like the wall to me rather than the floor. Is it the floor?

LS: Yes.

JR: Okay.

LS: If that's your impression?

JR: Well, it looks rough. I don't remember the floor being that rough, unless it was back in the corner. Back in the ... corner. There was a lot of moisture that came in there. We had, in fact at one time we had a leak and I extended the drainpipe. The downspout that came in, probably right there, and I extended it out, which stopped the leaking, but the downspout just emptied out in the ground and ended up in this part of the basement, and this kind of looks like that was kind of a nasty end to the wine cellar.

LS: When did you do that?

JR: ... A year or two before (that) Christmas. I did it some time ago.

LS: Did you ever clean or sweep that wine cellar for any reason or know that it had been?

JR: Well, it was absolutely full of junk when we bought the house and lumber and old windows, and we had all this stuff hauled away. It think I had swept it out, yeah.

LS: Do you know when?

JR: Well, it would have been in early — early in the ownership of the house, as we . . . cleaned up the basement.

LS: And that would have been when, what year?

JR: Oh, '92, probably, '93 maybe, '92 most likely. Because the room was just nasty. I had to get all this stuff out and then I discovered a little safe that was down there (cut into the floor). And I cleaned it out. So I think I cleaned it up. I don't know whether I did it after that, but I am sure it was cleaned at one point . . . .

LS: . . . Try to make a list of everyone you can think of that's been in there.

JR: Okay.

LS: Because I know the police have really done some work on collecting shoes. That was a tremendous, tremendous undertaking that they did, because they, you know, all of the contractors and everything, did — a lot of work went into that, just a tremendous amount. But maybe you can think of other people that went in there, or Patsy. And would people normally go in there or would they —

JR: There's no reason to go in there. It was — I don't know if it used to be a coal storage or something that just was a dead-end room. It was, I think there was one light, and it was — that was it. There was no reason to be — the types of people that would have known that we know that was there would have been, say, the painter, because he put his stuff in there. Whoever helped Patsy get the Christmas stuff out, whether it was Linda Hoffman or Rob (a handyman) or Father Rol (the family minister) or whoever it was, but . . . .

LS: . . . Just a couple of questions, and these are just miscellaneous questions that I had. In what area of the house do you think that JonBenet received the injuries to her head? This is just from your own . . . .

JR: Well, I guess my impression is that it was in the basement. But that's just purely an assumption. We didn't hear a thing. I think if she had cried out or — you know, we would have heard that. I didn't know she had any head injury at all. It wasn't — I just didn't see . . . .

LS: You had no knowledge?

JR: I don't know. I just, that's something that's been difficult for me to think about it, is what exactly happened.

LS: And where?

JR: And where.

LS: Do you think that the head injury occurred at the same place as the other injuries, say, with the ligature?

JR: I mean, it's just no reason to — to know that. I mean, I guess — well, like I say, I just — that's very difficult to think about and imagine, but I wondered whether the head injury didn't kill her and after that they strangled her.

LS: All right. This is getting way off of that. Do you know who brought John Andrew to the airport, when he left for Atlanta?

JR: I think it probably was Melinda and Stuart, who were with him. You mean to come to Minneapolis?

LS: No, I am talking about Boulder to Atlanta.

JR: He — oh, leaving for Christmas?

LS: Yes, leaving for Christmas.

JR: I don't. He would either usually take the

Airporter. He usually took the Airporter. But I know he
left his car parked, I think, at friends, driveway kind
of thing.

LS: You don't know the name of the friend?

JR: I don't, but John (Andrew) would, I am sure.

LS: . . . How about your church. Do you have any
suspicion of anybody in your church that may have,
because you went to church all the time when JonBenet
was there, and she would have been visible to somebody
in your church, any suspicions of anybody?

JR: We didn't have any suspicions, of course, while we
were going. It was a congregation of, it was a pretty
mixed congregation, in terms of families, single
people, you know, street people would come in and go to
church. We had this foyer dinner group at our house
prior to Christmas. There was probably 30 or 40 church
people there. Many of whom I had never met before.
There were a couple of odd ducks that were there.

LS: Could you add names?

JR: There was one guy that kind of wears a little cap,
like almost like a Jewish . . . yarmulke . . . but it's a
little bigger than that. Kind of covers his whole head.
Older guy, maybe 55, 60, 65, in that range.

LS: Could you recognize the name?

JR: I don't know if I would recognize the name. I am
sure Father Rol or somebody if I described that, they
would know who it was.

LS: What makes you suspicious of him?

JR: I talked to him for a while and he just — he just
was a little strange. You know, I just, some of the
things he said. Nothing about children or any of that.

LS: Was JonBenet visible at that time in the house?

JR: I am sure she was, yeah. She — but I can't visually
remember her being there, but I am sure she was. Had to be.

LS: Did you see this man in church before?

JR: Yeah, I see him in church. He was, I guess, the one that (I) just sat and talked to for a while and he seemed a little bit of an odd duck. There was a fellow that surfaced later that I am sure you guys are aware of or, because he — he probably said he saw some stuff at our house, and I forget his name, but he was a little bit of a weirdo also. I didn't know him before, but afterwards, we kind of became aware of him. And I guess we had some worries about him, and he would approach me in church and — afterwards, and just you know, be very sympathetic and . . . .

LS: Did he ever tell you that he had seen anything at your house?

JR: I don't know whether he told me directly. We had gotten some information that he was seen in a pickup truck in the alley (behind the Ramsey house) and had washed it or something and the police were watching him at the same time and he was odd . . . . Another thing that happened that night (of the foyer party) was, there was a couple that moved in down the street . . . that had lost a child, and somebody . . . said . . . "Gee, I know these people, they are really nice, I would like to invite them up and have you meet them." They came up that evening.

LS: They lived there?

JR: Yes, I don't remember the names. Arno — yeah, yes, Arnold, unusual name. So this lady or couple, I think it was a couple, invited them up, they came up about 9:30, 10:00, kind of as the church party was winding down, and they stayed in the kitchen, talked for half hour, 45 minutes, and I had never met them before. And —

LS: When was that foyer party?

JR: What was at the foyer party?

<u>LS</u>: When was it?

<u>JR</u>: ... It had been like ... in mid-December.

John was questioned about Randy Simons, the photographer who had taken pageant portfolio pictures of JonBenet. Ramsey investigators had taken a hard look at the shutterbug and considered him a person of interest in the case. John agreed, saying he'd learned Simons had been holed up the mountains somewhere with weapons and bows and arrows. Town residents in Genoa, Colorado, where Simons lived recalled he was accused of shooting a neighbor's dog with a bow and arrow. He also seemed to get very agitated whenever JonBenet's name was brought up, and once ripped a reward poster seeking information about JonBenet's killer from the window of a local diner. Genoa police had to be called when a naked Simons was caught running through the streets of the town. When an officer approached him, he said, "I didn't kill JonBenet." Simons was sent to a psychiatric ward after the incident.

<u>LS</u>: Can you remember talking to anybody real close to Christmas about your trip to Charlevoix ... ?

<u>JR</u>: Yeah. Well, of course, Fleet White and Priscilla White knew our schedule. Of course my secretary did. The people at the lake would have known we were coming, would have had the cleaning lady, the people who did the decorations on the house. Don Paugh, I mean the family would have known we were coming. Seems like there is somebody that Don talked to, I don't know if they asked about our schedule, and this is pulling from deep memory but ... well, Denise probably would have known — my assistant.

<u>LS</u>: Is that your secretary? She got a little upset after this and had to take a vacation and so forth?

JR: Yeah. I didn't know she got real upset. I am sure she got real upset. She had a boyfriend that we kind of wondered about one time that came to us as a kind of a, it was a little strange . . . he hated kids or hated me or something. I shouldn't say, I don't know whether that was true. I remember something about kids and he was dating Denise and if I recall, I met him, you know.

LS: . . . Okay. How about people that occupied offices real close to you, there. I know there was a couple that had offices —

JR: Yes, that was next, Ross Churchill was — no, Don Paugh was on one side and Tom Carson was on the other. Tom was our chief financial officer. He was there when I got there and I kind of took care of him. We had an awkward business relationship, just I never felt comfortable. I didn't trust him, which is absolutely terrible to have a CFO you don't trust. He — I was, he was always a struggle for me to deal with. I just didn't like the guy.

In the April 1997 interview with Patsy, Detective Steve Thomas had said that her mother, Nedra, interpreted the SBTC sign-off in the ransom note as initials for that "son-of-a-bitch, Tom Carson."

LS: Was it a two-way street?

JR: Oh, probably to some degree, I don't think he — Tom might think — at least for a while I think my impression, he always thought he should have had my job instead of me. And some people you're around, in your work environment, that when you're around them it pumps you up and it's a positive thing, and others it's just always a drain. He was just always a drain for me.

LS: Do you think he could have any reason to do this?

I know we are speculating, I know it's hard to say.

JR: Yeah. I mean I thought about it, quite frankly. I mean I thought about everybody. You know, we were looking at, at that time . . . a sale of the business Lockheed (Access Graphics' parent company) had made it kind of known, they — we weren't strategic to them and they were divesting some of their non-strategic businesses, and we were one of those and they were open to offers, and so that was going on. Tom certainly would have been the loser had we been acquired by another company. We were being looked at by a company in Omaha, that was fairly serious or getting fairly serious, and that's how bizarre my thoughts have gotten . . . Tom would have lost in that because clearly they would have put their own CFO in charge of the whole thing and he would have been out, probably.

He was always anxious to get us out from under Lockheed but do it in such a way that he could make a lot of money at it. Tom's agenda was his own agenda, that was one of the problems with the trust issue.

He had two daughters. He was divorced. The only people he dated were people in the office, which was always a problem. My former secretary almost filed a sexual harassment suit on him. He just, he was kind of an awkward, socially, guy. But he came to the memorial, he came to the funeral in Atlanta. It's almost inconceivable to think he could be involved.

LS: Would he have known you were leaving (for Charlevoix)?

JR: Quite possibly. We talked a lot so it wouldn't have been — he probably more than anybody on my staff would have, other than Denise, would have known my schedule . . . .

LS: The lights on in the house. Do you normally leave

certain lights on in the house?

JR: Oh, gosh, we usually left lights on. Sometimes we turned the lights in the, in this laundry area, we would turn them on dim, because there were a bunch of lights in the ceiling, there is a dimmer on them, you turn that down. Sometimes you would leave the light on in the laundry room there. Washer and dryer room. There is a little neon light or frosted light, it was enough to light that area. There was nothing religious about which ones we left on. We tried to leave lights on enough so you could see if you were up at night.

LS: How about in the basement?

JR: Not at all unless it was just accidental.

LS: If you were to go down in that basement at night, would you be able to see your way around down there?

JR: It would be tough. But no lights on, it would be difficult. And there is always a lot of junk around. You know, it was open, the door here, usually the light was on in this (first floor) hall and if you left the door open, it wasn't a very long stairway, it would have provided some illumination . . . .

LS: . . . How about on the first floor?

JR: I think we might have left lights on in the study. Um, we might have left a light on, you know, in front of the window here, sometimes.

LS: The solarium?

JR: In the solarium.

LS: We talked to Mrs. Brumfit next door. She said normally the light was on in the solarium, but that night it was off. Does that sound logical?

JR: Well, it's possible. I mean we came home after dark, we were tired. I wouldn't — Burke and I played in the living room for a little bit. But I can't say for

certain that I turned it on . . . we (at) least had some
lights on normally. We never turned them all off.
I guess I shouldn't say never, but never intentionally
turned them all off. I wasn't comfortable.

LS: Do you know a fellow . . . Chris Wolf?

*Chris Wolf, a sometime journalist, who had been a male
stripper, was brought to the attention of Boulder police by
his ex-girlfriend who reported he was out that Christmas
night and had dirt on him in the morning. She said reports
of JonBenet's murder seemed to upset him. Wolf chalked it
up to a bad relationship and said he had never been out. He
eventually sued the Ramseys for libel, claiming they called
him a suspect in their book, "Death of Innocence."*

JR: Chris Wolf, yeah.

LS: Okay, Robert Christian Wolf, Chris Wolf. Did you
fellows look into it? The reason I am bringing that up
a little bit is I am not positive of this a hundred
percent, but wasn't he a reporter also?

JR: . . . It's possible. I mean he wrote articles for, was
it "Daily Planet," or I forget what we found out, but
apparently he was like a freelance writer, claimed he
wrote about Access Graphics. We found out, but
apparently he was like a freelance writer, claimed he
wrote about Access Graphics.

LS: . . . Have you ever seen the movie "Nick of Time?"

JR: No.

LS: And it's about the kidnap of a 6-year-old and it
just happened to be on cable, according to one of the
. . . things I read, on the 25th.

JR: No, I have never — it doesn't ring a bell at all.
I wasn't aware of that.

LS: . . . One of the things I wanted to ask you is when

you were right close to JonBenet when you were making
these jewelry things (at the Whites' party) on the
— on Christmas evening — first of all, do you think
you would have been close enough to see if there was a
heart on her hand or would you have noticed it?

JR: I think I sure could have. It was on the inside of
the palm? Probably.

LS: But you didn't notice?

JR: I didn't notice anything.

LS: Did you notice any injuries to your daughter, to
her face or neck or anything on your daughter, did she
complain of anything that was hurting?

JR: No.

LS: Not —

JR: Not at all . . . she played upstairs for a good part
of the day or the evening, and she and I and Fleet and
Daphne sat on the floor and made these little jewelry
things in the living room.

LS: So if she had a noticeable mark, would you have
seen that?

JR: Oh, yeah.

LS: Did you ever hear of her being injured in any way
at the Whites or anything that evening?

JR: No. Not that I — I mean . . . no, I mean . . . my
recollection is we, they played and we left and she
fell asleep and obviously had a pretty good time.

LS: A question came up and I just had it in my notes,
there was something that was said, and I don't know if
I heard this on the Internet or heard it over the radio,
various talk shows, people, why did you — how did you
determine JonBenet's date of death to put on her
tombstone? (Her tombstone at the cemetery in Atlanta
gives her date of death as December 25th, 1996).

JR: I didn't know for sure, but the note talked about,

"We are going to call you tomorrow," frankly her body was cool when I found her, the arms were stiff. And I wanted to tell the world that you killed my daughter on Christmas Day. Don't ever forget.

John puzzled over the photo of the stuffed bear dressed in a Santa outfit that was found on the second bed in JonBenet's room. Like Patsy, he didn't know it was a gift given JonBenet and the other children at the Amerikids pageant before Christmas.

LS: And that Santa Claus doll is located where?
JR: In the bed next to JonBenet's.

Another photo of the laundry area outside JonBenet's room also drew puzzled comments from John.

LS: . . . That's a photograph of the upstairs laundry room area?
JR: Uh huh.
LS: There is a knife on the counter. What do you recall about that?
JR: Um, nothing. That looks like a kitchen — a knife that would normally be in the kitchen. It's hard to tell. Looks like it might be a grapefruit knife or something. We normally didn't prepare any food at that counter.
LS: Do you ever recall that knife being there before?
JR: I don't recall, no.

During Patsy's interrogation, she gave confusing responses as to which sweater she was wearing to the Whites' house and the next day when police arrived — a sweater she said she'd thrown over the tub before she went to bed Christmas night.

Patsy said she thought she had worn her so-called Christmas sweater, but said she might have worn a similar one after viewing photos taken at the Whites' dinner party. In the photos of JonBenet's room that John was shown, he is asked to look at one item.

LS: For instance, what is this multicolored . . .

JR: Well, I think it's a sweater of Patsy's but . . .

LS: . . . Is that a sweater that Patsy normally . . .

JR: Well, it looks kind of like one of the sweaters . . . I am pretty sure that's Patsy's sweater . . .

LS: Do you remember when the last time that was that Patsy wore that or anything?

JR: No, I really don't.

LS: . . . You know, we have been here for three days now. We have gone over a lot of things and I think I have gotten to know you pretty good at this time, and you have probably gotten to know us, and, you know, there is a lot of people out there that really do believe that you did this to your daughter, or that your wife did this. And you know that you have said that you didn't do that, and I am going to take you at your word. We know you're a Christian, John, and would you swear to God you didn't do this?

JR: I swear to God I didn't do it. I swear to God.

LS: Do you know anybody else, that your wife could?

JR: No.

LS: You swear to God?

JR: I swear to God. What I told you is the absolute truth. I couldn't be more emphatic, I guess, than that. We love our children. Having lost a child, you just can't — what I heard when we lost Beth was that people came forward and consoled us and I was amazed at how many people carry burdens. There is a business guy came forward and said I lost a child.

I was just, just — happy to — I mean here is a guy that I knew for five years as a business associate, and he was carrying this horrible burden. I thought Beth was the burden I had to carry. And then we have been given the burden of losing JonBenet, who in my mind was a gift to us. She took Beth's place.

At this point John broke down and wept.

JR: . . . More than I can bear . . . people can think that. I just . . . .

The Santa Claus Connection

   Right after their interviews in 1998, John Ramsey (JR) and Patsy Ramsey (PR) were questioned together about Bill McReynolds and his wife Janet, who had played Mr. and Mrs. Santa Claus at their 1996 Christmas party.

   Ramsey investigators and some members of the Boulder District Attorney's office still had suspicions about the retired journalism professor.

   There were coincidences in the McReynoldses' lives that bolstered those suspicions.

   In 1974, on the day after Christmas, a child molester abducted the McReynoldses' 9-year-old daughter, Jill, and a friend. The friend was sexually assaulted. Jill was unharmed.

   Bill's wife, Janet, a former movie critic and writer, had penned a play about a young girl tortured in a basement room.

   For their part, Boulder police, who'd obtained handwriting and blood samples from Bill and Janet, never considered Bill McReynolds, then 67, a strong suspect. He had undergone open heart surgery four months before JonBenet's death and was considered too frail to commit the crime.

   But John and Patsy appeared to be only too willing to cast a spotlight on Santa Claus as they were questioned by Boulder assistant district attorney Mary Keenan (MK) and Broomfield, Colorado, Detective Dan Schuler (DS).

DAN SCHULER: What's the purpose of this whole thing? Okay, the purpose is we want to talk to you to gain additional information about Bill McReynolds, which has kind of piqued our interest a bit. And we want to do everything we can to solve this case for you.

... Mary Keenan has a lot of questions that she has after viewing the interviews, about Bill, and I know you have some concerns yourself about Bill, and we'd like to bring this out in the open so we don't forget what we're doing and what we're focusing on. So we don't forget any minute item. All right. You want to just talk a little bit about Bill to start?

JOHN RAMSEY: Well, we met him on the mall around three years before December '96. He was walking around in a Santa suit passing out candy. We stopped and talked.

PATSY RAMSEY: We were in a ... deli, he came in ... and we talked. I believe he was employed by the downtown Boulder Chamber of Commerce or something to be on the mall and greeting people and whatever.

JR: And, I don't know that it was the same year, I don't know that it was, that we invited him to our house.

PR: Yeah, I think so, '94, for a Christmas party.

JR: And the whole procedure was, he would come in and the kids would all be there ... Patsy had a list of gifts that he'd pass out. He usually had a little saying ... "Oh, you've been really good, you did this, or you've been bad, you did this." I guess we had gifts for the adults sometimes. So he would sit and give out these gifts, and the kids would sit around and he'd read them a story.

PR: He also came to adult parties. We had tons of pictures sitting on Santa's knee, playing that whole role.

DS: Would that be at the same time or at different times?

PR: Well, some Christmases we had three or four different parties and one might be primarily adults, and he would come just to be part of, kind of like a little feature at the party, and all the ladies would sit on his knee and get their picture taken and whatnot.

And then typically closer to Christmas, like Christmas Eve, like in the year of '96, we'd have just a few close friends who had children. And we had Santa come and we'd do the naughty and nice list, and the gifts and all that.

JR: But JonBenet, of course, was fascinated with him because he was Santa Claus. And I remember one year she led him around the house and showed him a bunch of things, I don't know what. But she just took him by the hand and led him around . . . '95, I guess we called him and invited him back for the regular party. In '96, we weren't going to have a party. He called us, I guess you probably heard that, and said that Charles Kuralt was doing a special on him and he wanted to bring him to our party because it was one of his favorites. And will we have it?

PR: I mean, I really hadn't planned on it, but you know, he'd do it for free, and I said I suppose I could. So we decided on the 23rd.

JR: And Mrs. Claus came with him on that visit. That's the only time she's been to our house . . . I remembered thinking that she was really kind of —

PR: Drippy.

JR: — a drip. She really wasn't with it. She was just there, almost acting kind of irritated to be there. Didn't smile much at all . . . He came in and said he was frail and his wife was there to help him.

DS: Was he frail?

JR: Not if he was in New York (to appear on news shows about JonBenet's murder) and off to Europe (a planned vacation to Spain) a few weeks later.

DS: What year was it that JonBenet took him around the house and showed him the house?

PR: Well, it was the preceding year of this, so it would have been probably '95.

MARY KEENAN: What was the story with Charles Kuralt, and did that materialize?

PR: They never came to our house. However, there was an article in the (Boulder Daily) Camera about — 'cause I thought, when he called about that, I thought, that's a little strange. I mean, why did they pick him of all the Santas in the world or whatever? And then, lo and behold, it was in the paper that —

MK: What did you know about his surgery?

PR: Just this letter that said he had open-heart surgery. And then I got this when we got home from the lake that year. And subsequently, a few, I don't know some days later, I stuck my head into the little bakery, you know, down there at Basemar Shopping Center, where his son is a baker. And I said, "How's your dad? How was his surgery?" And he said they'd almost lost him a couple of times. That it was pretty tense.

DS: . . . So, if I'm understanding right, the first time he was in your home was the Christmas season of '94?

PR: Uh huh.

DS: He returned in '95, then again in '96. Now, was he in your home any other times from '94 through '96?

PR: Well, '94, two days after Christmas — I remember this because it was after this was the year we had the big Christmas tour of our house. Okay. And he showed up at the door a couple days after Christmas with a small gingerbread house, which the bakery, his son, had made. And he knew how much we loved Christmas, and he wanted to give this to us. So I invited him in. I said, "How am I going to explain that you're here to the kids?" And he told the children that he was Santa's brother who lived in Nederland and took care of the reindeer throughout the year.

DS: Did JonBenet see him when he brought the gingerbread house at that time?

PR: Uh huh. Yeah.

DS: And what was her reaction to him?

PR: You know, not like — because he wasn't like Santa Claus at that time. He looked sort of, kind of like Santa Claus but. They didn't —

DS: And did you tell her that story?

PR: Yeah. He told Burke and JonBenet.

DS: Did Burke still believe in Santa Claus at that time?

PR: Yeah.

DS: Did you ever run into him outside your house during Christmas season: downtown, in the mall, wherever he might be working?

PR: I saw him at a Christmas parade. He was at a Christmas parade.

DS: Which year?

PR: It would have been '95 probably. It would have been '95.

DS: Was JonBenet in the Christmas parade?

PR: She was in the Christmas parade.

DS: And what was that contact like?

PR: I mean I just saw him on the float; he waved or something.

DS: Did he come over and see you, or did he come over

and see JonBenet?

PR: No.

DS: Did you notice, what you were to think back on now, as any unusual affection that he had towards her?

PR: Well, this '96 Christmas when he was there telling the story about, well, his rendition of Christmas sort of . . . and here in a room full of children, says, "JonBenet, where is Santa?" And I'm not sure if he said, "Where is Santa," or "Where is Christmas kept all year long, JonBenet?" And she said, "In your heart." And he said, "That's right." And I thought: well, how did she know where it was kept? Yeah. I mean, it was kind of like something he had told her before. I mean, it just kind of hit me at that moment. He was like, "JonBenet," and she was like, "In your heart."

DS: . . . The sprinkle gesture. I think that John had referred to it was kind of like the dust that make the reindeer fly, is how he phrased it?

PR: Well, Santa has this glitter in his beard. And I think that prompted JonBenet. She knew that we kept glitter in the craft shelf in the basement there. I think she took him downstairs to give him the bottle of this Disney fairy dust to sprinkle. And we had several bottles of it because I think they used it for some promotion at the office one year . . . we had a couple of them, two or three. And I think she may have given him another one this '96 Christmas.

DS: Could you describe that bottle?

PR: It's just like a little genie bottle, like a little —

DS: Hourglass?

PR: Well, not even like an hourglass, but like a vinegar curette or something, sort of.

DS: Wider at the bottom?

PR: Wider at the bottom, tapers through the top, cork

in the top.

DS: That's what Burke had described to me when we were talking.

PR: Yeah.

DS: Did she give that to him on the 23rd?

PR: I believe she gave him a second bottle then. Because then at the memorial service, Father Rol asked, I think, and I mean I was pretty out of it, but I think he asked if anyone wanted to say anything, or had any fond memories, or something, of JonBenet and up walks . . .

. . . Bill McReynolds at this point. He's not in red and white. And I can't remember what he said.

JR: I don't remember either. We have a video of it . . . giving us back this bottle of fairy dust.

DS: The presents, how would you give the presents to him to pass out to the children?

PR: I left them in a kind of a garbage bag out by the front door hidden. And then he would come fill his bag with them so he had them as he came in the door.

DS: And what about the prearranged notes? Would he rehearse . . . ?

PR: No, I would just float that to him. I mean it was just written out and he'd just read it.

DS: You mean like it was just Santa's list?

PR: Right.

DS: Would he bring like any small items himself to pass out to the children other than what you provided for him?

PR: It seems like he may have brought candy canes, or had asked me to have candy canes to give to them. Seems like I remember candy canes.

DS: If you happen to think of anything like that, let us know, like later on. 'Cause we have an interest in that. What about to any of her pageants that she had?

Would he ever show up to any of those?

PR: No, I never saw him.

DS: When he had the children passing out presents and things like that, would he whisper anything into their ear or anything as he was passing out presents, or would he have them sit on his lap? How would he pass them out?

PR: Well, he usually sat stationary in the chair, and he had this bag and they were gathered kind of at the foot . . . A couple times maybe a couple would come over and sit on his lap.

DS: Would he ever talk to the children softly? Do you recall if he would whisper something in their ear, that you recall?

JR: I don't recall any overt whispering or anything like that. He was very soft spoken.

MK: Did he ever sing?

JR: He sang songs.

MK: You talked about '95 at the Christmas parade. What about '96 Christmas parade?

PR: See, I don't know. 'Cause I wasn't in town. My parents took JonBenet in their car, you know. She rode with several of her small colleagues there. So I don't know if he was there or not.

DS: . . . So JonBenet was in a car?

PR: A convertible, correct.

DS: And what about in '95?

PR: '95 was when we did the sailboat. She was Little Miss Colorado, or something or the other.

DS: Okay.

PR: She sat on the sailboat and sang "Lollipop" . . . .

DS: How good was his Santa suit?

JR: It was marginal, as I recall.

DS: Did it look fairly authentic?

JR: Yeah.

PR: Yeah.

JR: It had been worn; it was a worn Santa suit, to my recollection.

DS: . . . Do you remember his boots at all, off the top of your head?

JR: They weren't — I don't remember them not being consistent with his costume. They weren't big ugly ones or something like that.

DS: Other than his reindeer, do you know what he showed up in?

PR: I think I opened the door prematurely and they were coming out of a little, kind of a little hatchback car. I don't know my cars very well. But small, with the backend sort of lift up.

DS: Like a little compact type of car?

PR: Yeah . . . like a Pinto hatchback or something like that.

John Ramsey recalled seeing a Pinto-like car drive by his home twice at about 7 a.m. on the morning JonBenet's body was found.

MK: . . . Did he ever talk to you about his family at all?

PR: Just that he has a son who is a baker.

JR: He had a daughter or a daughter's friend who was kidnapped on Christmas or near Christmas or something like that.

MK: Did he tell you about that?

JR: No, we heard that later . . . this was the last guy we would have thought about. And these funny things start to happen.

DS: So he's been trying to communicate with you more since JonBenet's death?

PR: Uh huh.

JR: Uh huh.

DS: Do you recall if he ever took any photographs of her? Or let me rephrase it. Not even taking photographs of her, but asking for some photographs of her?

PR: He asked me. I think I took a picture of them one year at the parade, and he said, "Oh, I would love to have a copy of that," or something.

MK: What did JonBenet tell you about the tour she took him on?

PR: Nothing. She just said she gave him fairy dust, you know.

DS: Also it seems in the letter that he made comment that she took him on a guided tour to the house, and he mentions unexpectedly memorable was being taken to the basement. Is that typically where the fairy dust was kept?

PR: Yeah. That was where all the glitter and glue and craft paper.

DS: . . . That was where the window was broken, right?

JR: Yes.

DS: Okay.

MK: Did she also take him upstairs to her room?

PR: I think so.

JR: Yes.

PR: To show him her Christmas trees.

DS: Were you aware she was taking him on the tour?

PR: Yeah. Yeah.

DS: Did you have a sense of how long it took, how long they were off together?

PR: Five or ten minutes. I mean, there were people all over the house. I mean, it wasn't like they were just together.

MK: So when you were talking to JonBenet about

Christmas or reading stories, did she ever comment that Santa Claus does such-and-such?

PR: No.

MK: And did you ever hear about any secret visits from Santa Claus?

PR: No.

JR: The only thing we heard was supposedly the mother of (a friend of JonBenet's) . . . said that . . . JonBenet told . . . her that Santa was going to come visit her . . . after Christmas. So I think the day after Christmas. So the 26th or something like that . . . it's going to be a special visit the next night, or something like that.

DS: Right.

JR: Are you kind of aware of that?

DS: Yes.

MK: Would he know, would you have told him or would JonBenet have told him that you were leaving for Charlevoix in the morning?

JR: It's possible we may have.

PR: It's possible, I guess. But I don't know when. I mean, that night he just came into the chair and sat down and the kids were right there, and he didn't —

JR: Did he ever call on the phone for the kids or anything like that?

PR: Gee, yes. I do remember that he did.

DS: Did he call the children on the phone?

PR: Yeah. He said — My God, I just vaguely remember he called and said — I think it was just when he called me, and I said, "Santa wants to bring over some things."

DS: Did they ever question that?

PR: Well, I said he's coming to our party. I don't think they actually spoke. Then they might have.

JR: I just vaguely seem like I remember them talking to

him on the phone.

PR: Could have been.

DS: Would the children ever answer the phone themselves?

JR: Oh, yeah.

DS: What struck you odd about Bill, now thinking back on everything?

JR: Well, he was very effeminate; he wasn't a jovial Santa Claus. He was kind of a gay Santa Claus; I don't know how else to put it. He always used to "Ho, Ho, Ho," (mimicking).

PR: Not in a deep voice.

JR: It was kind of — this is not Santa Claus.

PR: Give me a ho, ho, ho.

JR: Yeah. So he was a bit strange that way. And he never got out of that act, and I never saw him any different than that. Even when we'd be coming to the door and we'd always be talking to him, as adults.

PR: Yeah. He was always playing the role of the . . . (gesticulating effeminately).

DS: So you saw him several times out of the Santa suit, right?

PR: No.

JR: No. It was always —

PR: He was always circulating the party. He wouldn't say, "Hey, can I have a beer?" He was always (gesticulating effeminately)

JR: . . . Shirley Temple was more of a man than he was.

DS: And Mrs. Claus wasn't very jovial, right?

JR: No.

PR: Mrs. Claus was not, no.

JR: I thought she was not happy to be there.

PR: No. I just presumed she was there to keep him from falling or something. That was the only impression I got.

JR: But she had on Mrs. Santa kind of thing.

DS: White wig and everything?

PR: No ... like a little apron or something.

JR: Yeah.

DS: Would he wear a wig?

PR: No.

JR: No, he had a real beard ... I tell you who you got to talk to is Pam Archuleta (wife of Ramsey pilot Mike Archuleta). She was head of United Way. She said they interviewed him and decided that he was really a weird duck, and they wouldn't use him. She has some very strong opinions about him.

MK: Do you remember what she said about him?

JR: It just supported some of the things that we're hearing. A pedophile, you know.

DS: What would be your best guess about his financial condition?

JR: Well, based on how he was dressed at the memorial service, and what these investigators who visited him said, he didn't have a nickel to his name. In fact, we had heard through our investigators that he had some financial problems at one time.

The things that started concerning us were, he started to fit kind of the profile that (John) Douglas had given us of somebody who's been hanging around us: they kind of like the limelight, he was on the Today show, he was interviewed on television, and then he split. He fits. He's been in the house, could have been jealous of, you know, if we had more money than he did.

... I would also be curious about Mrs. Claus. According to our investigators when they went up to talk to them, they said he was pretty cordial, but she was very controlling and told him to shut up.

MK: I was told ... that a woman called while they were in Spain. She met them, ran into them, and he was talking about JonBenet's death and making inappropriate comments.

<u>DS</u>: Now what those comments were, I don't know.

<u>PR</u>: Wow. That's really (whistle).

<u>JR</u>: 'Cause that was shortly after her death. For a guy who could hardly walk in the door, then he was in the City of New York on the streets (appearing on "Today") a week later and then off to Europe.

<u>PR</u>: Right.

<u>JR</u>: I don't buy it.

EPILOGUE

THE MYSTERY of who killed JonBenet continues.

Was it the monstrous act of seemingly normal parents gone mad? Or did a fiend who still hides in the shadows enter the Ramsey home on a Christmas night and brutally take the life of a 6-year-old child?

The Colorado lawmen assigned the task of winning justice for JonBenet could not answer either question, but instead pointed fingers of guilt at each other.

A little more than a month after the Ramseys' 1998 interviews, Boulder Detective Steve Thomas — who grilled John and Patsy during their April 30, 1997, interview and was convinced they were involved in the murder — quit his job in disgust.

His 8-page resignation letter, dated August 6, 1998 — the day JonBenet would have turned eight — accused Boulder District Attorney Alex Hunter and his office of running scared from the high-powered Ramsey lawyers.

"I believe the district attorney's office is thoroughly compromised," Thomas wrote. He listed a litany of examples that he said tied the hands of the Boulder police.

"During the investigation detectives would discover, collect and bring evidence to the district attorney's office, only to have it summarily dismissed or rationalized as insignificant . . . .

"In a departure from protocol, police reports, physical evidence and investigative information were shared with the Ramseys . . . .

"Innocent people were not 'cleared,' publicly or otherwise, even when it was unmistakably the right thing to do . . . .

"I was told . . . about being unable to 'break' a particular police officer from his resolute accounts of events he had witnessed . . . .

"I was repeatedly reminded by some in the district

attorney's office just how powerful and talented and resourceful particular defense attorneys were . . . .

"While investigative efforts were rebuffed, my search warrant affidavits and attempts to gather evidence in the murder investigation of a 6-year-old child were met with refusals and instead, the suggestion that we 'ask the permission of the Ramseys'."

Thomas went on to write a book about the case, "JonBenet: Inside the Ramsey Murder Investigation."

In it, he accused Patsy of killing her daughter during a bed-wetting rage incident. He later faced John and Patsy Ramsey on CNN's "Larry King Show" and called her a killer to her face.

The Ramseys sued him and won a judgment.

On September 20, 1998, veteran homicide detective Lou Smit, who questioned John Ramsey in the June interviews that year, also quit the case. His feelings were diametrically opposed to Thomas.

"I find that I cannot in good conscience be a part of the persecution of innocent people," Smit wrote in a letter to Alex Hunter. "It would be highly improper and unethical for me to stay when I so strongly believe this."

He added that the Boulder Police Department was "just going in the wrong direction . . . the case tells me that there is substantial, credible evidence of an intruder and lack of evidence that the parents are involved. If this is true, they, too, are tragic victims whose misery has been compounded by a misdirected and flawed investigation, unsubstantiated leaks, rumors and accusations."

Smit believes JonBenet's killer entered the Ramsey home through the window beneath the outside grate, incapacitated the child with a stun gun and murdered her in the basement while her parents slept.

The soft-spoken lawman would continue to investigate the death on his own. He won the right in court to keep all the investigative material he had reviewed for the case.

In a campaign to exonerate the Ramseys, Smit shared

crime scene photos with the media to back up his analysis.

He has gone on national TV time and again to proclaim the Ramseys' innocence: demonstrating at the scene of the crime how an intruder got into the house; demonstrating how the vastness of the home would have prevented the parents from hearing their daughter scream; and demonstrating how the killer exited the home by stepping atop the suitcase found beneath the basement window.

He even took part in stun gun tests on a pig to show that marks on JonBenet's body matched wounds left by the weapon.

Mike Kane, the former federal prosecutor who also questioned John Ramsey in 1998, took centerstage in the murder investigation in September of that year — as the lead prosecutor presenting the case to a grand jury.

Alex Hunter had been under pressure from Colorado Governor Bill Owens — who left no doubt during a press conference that he felt the Ramseys did it. Hunter finally decided to let a panel of eight women and four men decide if there was enough evidence to issue an indictment in the murder.

For 13 months, the grand jury met in secret.

On October 12, 1999, a media horde gathered outside the Boulder County Criminal Justice Center as Alex Hunter strode to a microphone set up outside.

"The Boulder County grand jury has completed its work and will not return. No charges have been filed," Hunter announced as an audible moan went through the press corps. "I must report to you that I and my prosecutorial team believe we do not have sufficient evidence to warrant the filing of charges against anyone who has been investigated at this time."

At that moment, John and Patsy Ramsey were locked in prayer some five miles away and watching Hunter on television in the home of Mike Archuleta, Ramsey's friend and pilot. They had snuck into Boulder from Atlanta undetected by the media and were prepared to testify before the grand jury if called, or be hauled off in handcuffs should an indictment against them be issued.

Neither had happened, and they now went on the offensive.

On March 16, 2000, John and Patsy's book, "The Death of Innocence" was published. It was an emotional account of the Ramseys' life since JonBenet was killed, and included sharp criticism of how the case was mishandled.

The book provided a profile of the murderer as being a male pedophile, between the ages of 25 and 35, who may be an ex-convict and who used techniques he saw in the movie "Ransom," which was playing in Boulder shortly before JonBenet's murder.

The Ramseys speculated that the suspect's original intention may have been to use a stun gun to immobilize JonBenet and kidnap her for the $118,000 demanded in the ransom note.

They offered the theory that the attacker's plan could have failed when JonBenet woke up and recognized her attacker, turning the would-be kidnapper into a killer.

They theorized that the killer entered their home while they were at the Whites' Christmas dinner party, may have known the layout of the house after touring it during a Historic Boulder Homes Tour in Christmas 1994. And they felt the murderer could have become aware of John's business successes through local newspaper stories.

The book heavily criticized the media likening them to "vultures, waiting to find tidbits of flesh to pounce on."

In May 2000, the Ramseys held a press conference in Atlanta with their new attorney, civil litigator L. Lin Wood.

The lawyer had won fame defending Richard Jewell, the security guard wrongly accused in the 1996 bombing at the Olympics. A magazine cover piece on Wood called him the attorney "for the damned."

Wood announced that the Ramseys had taken and passed a lie detector test, which indicated John and Patsy did not "attempt to deceive" when they said they did not know who beat and strangled JonBenet.

"We shouldn't have to prove our innocence . . . but nevertheless we've been forced to," said John Ramsey. "We have not one ounce of trust in the Boulder police."

Patsy Ramsey added: "I really wish we would stop playing games. I wish they would open their minds and their hearts and know that we did not kill our daughter."

The Ramseys stated that the results of the test should persuade police to stop blaming them for their daughter's death. But following their press conference, Boulder Police Chief Mark Beckner issued a statement.

"There is nothing today that is going to change where we are at in the investigation," he said. "If John and Patsy Ramsey really want this investigation to move forward, they should work with us."

Yet another interview, this time with members of the Boulder Police Department invited, took place in late August 2000 in Atlanta.

Before the sitdown, Beckner said questioning would focus on evidence developed in the last two years since the Ramseys' 1998 interrogation session, and the statement the Ramseys made in their book.

Asked if the Ramseys were the focus of the investigation still, Beckner replied, "I don't know if I'd word it that way, but certainly they are under sucpicion."

The day and a half of questioning was a fiasco. Mike Kane exploded in anger at Lin Wood when the Ramsey attorney thought the questioning was bordering on a "fishing expedition."

Kane threatened to walk out of the interview with Patsy Ramsey when the two sides argued over questioning about security precautions for JonBenet's older brother Burke, and about fiber evidence found on the duct tape used to cover her mouth.

Wood said there were "a series of questions that I don't think serve any useful purpose" in finding the killer.

In March 2001, the Ramseys, still pursuing avenues to

proclaim their innocence, sat down with the editors of this book in the Atlanta office of Lin Wood for an interview that was published in the National Enquirer.

"Don Gentile . . . Charlevoix . . . Dairy Queen," Patsy said as she greeted us.

It was a reference to a short interview she granted in the summer of 1997 at the Ramseys' vacation home in Michigan.

At the time she'd stated that the local Dairy Queen made the best hamburgers in town.

In a sort of peace offering, Patsy served up a plate of leftover St. Patrick's Day cookies.

During the two-hour session, the Ramseys, for the first time, admitted their son Burke was awake before police arrived at their home that fateful day.

Had they been caught in a lie?

They said Burke had never brought it up until he was interviewed in 1998, and they were unaware of his statements until much later.

But they said Burke stayed in his bed and pretended to be asleep. They disputed the enhancement of the taped 911 call — first revealed by the "National Enquirer." The tape revealed Burke up and about and asking his parents, "What did you find?"

They had never heard the tape and doubted that Burke's voice is on it. "Well, all I can tell you is that when I made that phone call, Burke Ramsey was nowhere in the vicinity of the telephone."

Could he have been up on the second floor, yelling down? "No, no," said Patsy.

Attorney Lin Wood added: "I haven't heard it but I've been told by someone who had heard it that it sounds like chipmunks.

"If that tape contained Burke's voice, the Boulder Police Department would have leaked it long ago. They would have given it to you.

"That morning, Burke heard his parents at some point screaming. He heard his mom. . .and his description was very vivid of a woman that was in terror. And he feigned sleep."

John chimed in: "We learned that much later. We thought he was asleep but he wasn't."

Patsy spoke about a "mastermind plot" by the Boulder police "to discredit us and to ruin our reputation. We know that without a doubt."

And John added: "The strategy was to bring immense discredit, character assassination, public pressure upon us so that one of us would confess. But they did a great job of convincing the public we were guilty and in fact, it kind of backfired. Because when we didn't confess, because we didn't do it, and they didn't arrest us, the public's now after them to say, "Why don't you arrest them? You've convinced us they're guilty." And they couldn't, 'cause they didn't have a case."

Investigators hired by John and Patsy had come up with the names of significant suspects in their daughter's death, the Ramseys claimed.

But attempts to get the Boulder police to follow up on the information had met a stonewall of non-cooperation.

In early 2002, Patsy's cancer returned.

During a regular checkup at the National Institute of Health in Bethesda, Maryland, doctors found that the disease had begun to attack her liver.

Once again, she underwent weeks of chemotherapy and has reportedly been declared cancer-free.

Burke, their son, is a tall lanky teen who attends high school at the private and pricey Lovett School in Atlanta.

Although the Ramseys' fortune has been depleted, they are not down and out.

The home they bought in the exclusive Vinings section of Atlanta for $680,000 was practically gutted for a massive renovation.

The Ramseys ultimately sold the home for nearly $2 million. Although John told the Enquirer he was unemployable, he ultimately landed a sales job which reportedly nets him $150,000-plus a year in salary.

They had a home built for them in Smyrna, Georgia, where they now reside.

Boulder police say they are still under "an umbrella of suspicion in the case."

In her Enquirer interview, Patsy revealed the last words she spoke to JonBenet as she lay sleeping that Christmas night, the last night of her life.

It was the simple prayer everyone knows:

"Now I lay me down to sleep. I pray the Lord my soul to keep. If I should die before I wake, I pray the Lord my soul to take."

"Patsy wrote that ransom note . . ."

ON FIVE SEPARATE OCCASIONS after the murder, Patsy Ramsey gave samples of her handwriting that analysts from the Colorado Bureau of Investigation then compared to the ransom note.

It was during the fourth session, on April 12, 1997, that the experts sprang a surprise. The right-handed Patsy was told to write out the note with her left hand — and that sample, above all the others, immediately excited intense interest.

The very thought was disturbing. Could JonBenet's mother have written that rambling ransom note dotted with devastating threats to her little daughter like "behead," "execution," "killing" and — over and over again — "she dies?"

Along with the interrogation transcripts on the earlier pages of this book, the National Enquirer obtained Patsy's handwriting samples, held for six years in the secret files of the Boulder police.

And a leading handwriting expert who examined them believes that they prove she wrote the ransom note — with the left-handed exemplar being the most damning.

"You can actually superimpose words from the ransom note over words that Patsy wrote with her left hand and they're a near-perfect match," declared Ted Widmer, who has testified in numerous court cases and taught handwriting identification to police and district attorneys.

"Patsy wrote that ransom note, and she wrote it with her left hand."

That conclusion was echoed by another leading handwriting analyst, Gideon Epstein, who examined the same samples as an expert witness in a lawsuit filed against the Ramseys.

In a recent deposition given under oath, Epstein said, "I am absolutely certain that she wrote the (ransom) note."

As part of the handwriting investigation both Patsy and John were asked to write out a so-called "London Letter"

— an investigative tool that forces the writer to use every letter of the alphabet and numerals from 0 to 9.

They each printed the full ransom note on a white legal pad using a Sharpie pen, just as the author of the note did.

John's samples drew little interest, but Patsy was called back time after time over a five month period.

During one session she was told to write a letter any way she wanted. She chose in one paragraph to use the words "two gentlemen" — exact words from the ransom note.

Then, fifteen weeks after JonBenet's killing, the Colorado Bureau of Investigation analysts asked her to write with her left hand a curiously-altered version of the ransom message.

And a CBI source told the National Enquirer that it was that sample, above all the others, that convinced investigators that "Patsy wrote the note with her opposite hand."

In fact the Enquirer had already learned that Patsy was ambidextrous. One of her high school teachers in Parkersburg, West Virginia — who has never been interviewed by police — clearly remembers that the young Patsy could write with her right and left hand.

And Patsy herself, in an interview with the authors of this book in 2001, conceded that she could write with her left hand. "But not very well," she added hastily.

Ted Widmer, chairman of The Graphological Society of San Francisco and author of the book "Crime and Penmanship," spent days poring over the samples, none of which had ever been previously seen outside the JonBenet murder investigation.

"It is really amazing," he concluded. "If you go through every letter in the ransom note, you can find those matching forms somewhere in the samples Patsy gave to the police."

Widmer echoed the conclusions of former Boulder detective Steve Thomas, a lead investigator in the murder, who revealed that "24 of the alphabet's 26 letters (found in the ransom note) looked as if they had been written by Patsy."

Interestingly, the ransom note copy Patsy was made to

write using her right hand looks nothing like the original, said Widmer. But her left hand sample is very revealing.

"To the untrained eye it may look nothing like the original ransom note, but it is my belief she tried to fake the sample and can probably write much better with her left hand than she is letting you believe.

"She couldn't fake everything, however. There are incredible matches to the real ransom note.

"The word 'carefully' in the first line of the left hand sample is an exact match for the word 'carefully' in the first line of the ransom note. You can practically superimpose one over the other.

"The same is true for the word 'faction' in the fourth line of the sample and the third line of the ransom note; the word 'that' in the third line of the sample and the second line of the ransom note; and the word 'letter' in the 13th line of the sample and the 10th line of the ransom note.

"Also, several times when she writes 'will' in the sample, they show matches to some of the 'will' words in the note.

"Most revealing are the percent signs in both Patsy's left-hand sample and the ransom note. They are perfect little circles that match. You try to do that if you can't write with both hands. You can't do it."

Another compelling clue pointing to Patsy as the author of the ransom note, said Widmer, is found in the sample letter she was asked to compose.

"It's the big spaces she puts between the word 'I' and the word next to that personal pronoun," he declared. "Look at the ransom note. When the pronoun 'I' is written, there are the same big spaces left between it and the next word.

"It was something she didn't think to fake — something that came out naturally."

Was Patsy the author of the ransom note, as some investigators believe?

We present her handwriting samples here so you can judge for yourself.

Mr. Ramsey,

Listen carefully! We are a group of individuals that represent a small foreign faction. We do respect your bussiness but not the country that it serves. At this time we have your daughter in our posession. She is safe and unharmed and if you want her to see 1997, you must follow our instructions to the letter.

You will withdraw $118,000.00 from your account. $100,000 will be in $100 bills and the remaining $18,000 in $20 bills. Make sure that you bring an adequate size attache to the bank. When you get home you will put the money in a brown paper bag. I will call you between 8 and 10 am tomorrow to instruct you on delivery. The delivery will be exhausting so I advise you to be rested. If we monitor you getting the money early, we might call you early to arrange an earlier delivery of the

Original ransom note

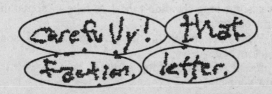

Please take the time to listen (carefully) to
what I have to say. We are one of a group
of individuals (that) represent a small
foreign company We are a (faction) of the
parents group who are located in northern
country. We respect your situation and
would like to serve your needs and desire
Particularly since we will profit too. At
this time we have the instructions from
the business office to bring your sons
and daughters into possession of great
fortunes. We were following the plans for
1997 when we received your (letter)
requesting immediate delivery of an
adequate product. We have exhauste
ourselves in preparing an early delivery
and now we feel rested and assured that
tomorrow will be the day you will be
getting the money. We might call you
tomorrow early in the day to arrange for
an additional pick up providing it isn't
raining cats and dogs. Please remain in
your family home near the Southern coast
of Dublin until we execute the deal. You
are advised to scan not the enforcement
documents while you are waiting.

R 0060   CONFIDENTIAL

Patsy's left-hand sample

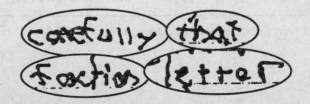

money and hence. I deliver
pick up of your daughter.
Any deviation of my instructions
will result in the immediate
execution of your daughter. You
will also be denied her remains
for proper burial. The two
gentlemen watching over your daughter
do particularly like you so I
advise you not to provoke them.
Speaking to anyone about your
situation, such as police, F.B.I., etc.,
will result in your daughter being
beheaded. If we catch you talking
to a stray dog, she dies. If you
alert bank authorities, she dies.
If the money is in any way
marked or tampered with, she
dies. You will be scanned for
electronic devices and if any are
found, she dies. You can try to
deceive us but be warned that
we are familiar with law enforcement
countermeasures and tactics. You
stand a 99% chance of killing
your daughter if you try to out
smart us. Follow our instructions

Excerpt from original ransom note

Today is May 20, 1997. We are sitting in a lovely office with a large glass topped table. Officer Trujillo is sitting to the left of the table. He has been very quiet throughout the morning. My young attorney (good looking - but he smokes! ☺) is seated across the table from me. He looks bored.

(Two gentlemen) from the C.B.I. are on my right. They have been very professional throughout the morning. I do not envy their job, but I do hope that they will finally be able to dispell the notion that some think (I wrote) the note. I did not.

There is also a gentleman to my immediate left who has been taking copious notes. What a boring job.

The day is lovely outside and I hope that we will soon be finished so that I can go. I miss darling Jonni B. She would have liked this day too.

Love, Mammy

R   0101   CONFIDENTIAL

Patsy's sample letter

The delivery will be exhausting so (I advise) you to be rested. If we monitor you getting the money

Excerpt from original ransom note

Patsey Ramsey

"Our London business is good, but Vienna and Berlin are quite quiet. Mr. D. Lloyd has gone to Switzerland and I hope for good news. He will be there for a week, at 1496 Zermot St., and then goes to Turin and Rome, and will join Col. Parry, and arrive at Athens, Greece, Nov. 27th, or Dec. 2nd. Letters there should be addressed: King James Blvd. 3580. We expect Chas. E. Fuller, Tuesday. Dr. L. L. McQuaid and Robt. Unger, Esq. left on the 'J.X.' Express tonight."

Her 'London letter'

Nearest Relative   865 Brookhaven Drive
                    Atlanta, Georgia 30013

WRITE – DO NOT PRINT – (Capital and Small Letters)

Aa Bb Cc Dd Ee Ff Gg Hh Ii Jj Kk
Ll Mm Nn Oo Pp Qq Rr Ss Tt Uu Vv
Ww Xx Yy Zz aa bb cc dd ee ff
gg hh ii jj kk ll mm nn oo pp qq
rr ss tt uu vv ww xx yy zz
1 2 3 4 5 6 7 8 9 10

Yolanda Ziffman
1234 N. East Ave., SW
5678 S. West Blvd., NW
9012 E. North Pl., SE
3456 W. South St., NE

R 0040

CONFIDENTIAL

The above is a specimen of my handwriting prepared freely and voluntarily.

Date
Witness
Date 2-28-97

Signature

Exemplars Of: (Print)
Ramsey   Patricia   P.
Last Name   First Name   Initial

Sample of her alphabet

and you stand a (100%) chance
of getting her back. Ys u and
your family are under constant
scrutiny as well as the authorities.
Don't try to grow a brain
John. You are not the only
fat cat around so don't think
that killing will be difficult
Don't underestimate us John.
Use that good southern common
sense of yours. It is up to
you now John!

Victory!

S.B.T.C

Original ransom note

100%

100%

You have our 100% guarantee that we are familiar
with our particular product. It is a marked
improvement from previous versions and we are
confident that it will pass your scrutiny. We
have outsmarced the rest of the business world and
have sharpened our interest in preparation of the
account transfer. Follow our instructions and you
will find yourself, your son and your daughter
with the result you desire. With our help you
can draw on the brown paper bag found left-over
files in the executive holder's office.

Patsy's left-hand sample